Interpretation Book Clubs:
Analyzing Themes

Lucy Calkins and Alexandra Marron

Photography by Peter Cunningham

Illustrations by Marjorie Martinelli

HEINEMANN ◆ PORTSMOUTH, NH

This book is dedicated to Kathleen Tolan, our dear friend, whose ideas about reading instruction inspire so much of what we do.—Lucy and Ali

Heinemann
361 Hanover Street
Portsmouth, NH 03801–3912
www.heinemann.com

Offices and agents throughout the world

© 2015 by Lucy Calkins and Alexandra Marron

The authors and publisher wish to thank those who have generously given permission to reprint borrowed material:

Fly Away Home, by Eve Bunting. Clarion Books, Houghton Mifflin, 1991. Used by permission of Houghton Mifflin Harcourt.

Cataloging-in-Publication data is on file with the Library of Congress.

ISBN-13: 978-0-325-07719-2

Series editorial team: Anna Gratz Cockerille, Karen Kawaguchi, Tracy Wells, Felicia O'Brien, Debra Doorack, Jean Lawler, Marielle Palombo, and Sue Paro
Production: Elizabeth Valway, David Stirling, and Abigail Heim
Cover and interior designs: Jenny Jensen Greenleaf
Photography: Peter Cunningham
Illustrations: Marjorie Martinelli
Composition: Publishers' Design and Production Services, Inc.
Manufacturing: Steve Bernier

Printed in the United States of America on acid-free paper
19 18 17 16 15   PAH   1 2 3 4 5

Acknowledgments

THIS BOOK STANDS on the shoulders of the work of the entire Teachers College Reading and Writing Project (TCRWP) community. We could footnote the ideas about interpretation, writing about reading, bands of text complexity, book clubs, touchstone texts, reading like a writer—each of those ideas bears the DNA of so many who have been part of our collaborative thought.

The people whose ideas and hard work have made the biggest difference in this book are those who work side by side with us in the schools that comprise the Teachers College Reading and Writing Project. We're grateful to so many of those colleagues: to Kathleen Tolan whose originality brings sparkle to so many of our methods and to Audra Robb for her brilliant work with literary texts and with writing about reading. Audra's work with *Writing about Reading*, Grade 7, from Units of Study in Argument, Information, and Narrative Writing inspired part of Bend I of this unit, and we are grateful for that. There are so many others, too, whose participation in think tanks, Thursdays, leadership groups, and advanced summer institute sections have fueled this unit. A special thank you to Mary Ehrenworth, Deputy Director of the TCRWP, whose brilliant ideas about interpretation and analytical thinking set this book in motion and helped to inform so many of the choices we made. Your instincts and guidance inspired and supported us every step of the way.

We are grateful, also, to all of the teachers who piloted versions of this unit—and to the hundreds of classrooms where seeds of ideas took hold, flourished, and bloomed. A special thank you to the leaders, teachers, and students at PS/IS 499 in Queens, New York, for their willingness to try new things and share ideas. We get so much of our inspiration from watching you teach. We are grateful to Jennifer Williams, fifth-grade teacher at Arrowhead Elementary in Kenmore, Washington, who not only piloted the unit with her students, but provided us with thoughtful feedback and an incredible wealth of student work along the way. Thank you! We are grateful, also, to Kristin Alvarez, instructional coach at West Woods Upper Elementary School in Farmington, Connecticut, and her fifth-grade teachers: Jill Slayton, Lauren Palermino, and Leah Gilbert. Your dedication and commitment helped us work through kinks, streamline minilessons, and ultimately bring this book to life. We can't thank you enough. A special thank you to Natalie Norris, a dynamic and bright graduate student in the Literacy Specialist program at Teachers College. You seamlessly coordinated the piloting process with hundreds of teachers across the country, ensuring that each teacher had what he or she needed and, in turn, was able to give us the feedback we needed. We'd also like to express our gratitude to our colleagues at Booksource and Hannah Tolan: many thanks for your help in creating booklists to accompany this unit.

There are many colleagues at the Project who have stood by us. Thanks to Julia Mooney, to Laurie Pessah, to Sara Johnson, and above all, to the one person who is indispensable above all others: Mary Ann Mustac.

Our family at Heinemann has been just that—family. Tracy Wells, Felicia O'Brien, and Anna Gratz Cockerille—we cannot thank you enough for your discerning eyes and invaluable input. There are two people who have been the sun, the moon, and the stars to us. First, Karen Kawaguchi, our editor, spent months pouring over every word of this book with the utmost care. Her attention to detail, organization, and follow-through is unmatched, and her humor and light touch made the final stages of writing this book a joy. Abby Heim: We don't know how you balance the work you do with such grace and humanity—you have been manager, coordinator, leader, executor, cheerleader, keeper of the details, and the first go-to person for so many of us. We are eternally grateful for all that you do, and for the love and patience with which you do it.

And finally, we are grateful to each other. It's the fun of writing together, thinking together, yes, even rewriting together, that makes this add up, and we both feel incredibly blessed to have the other in our lives.

—Lucy and Alexandra

Contents

BEND III Thematic Text Sets: Turning Texts Inside Out

An Orientation to the Unit

IN HER MEMOIR, *The Writing Life*, Annie Dillard gives advice that is as important to teachers as it is to writers. She writes:

> "One of the few things I know about writing is this: spend it all. Shoot it, play it, lose it, all, right away, every time. Do not hoard what seems good for a later place in the book, or for another book: give it, give it all, give it now. . . . Something more will arise for later, something better. These things fill from behind, from beneath, like well water."

That is what we have done in writing this book and in planning this unit, and it is what you will do when you teach the unit. Right from the start, you'll teach your fifth-graders the best of what it means to read literature. Prior to the publication of this unit, fifth-graders used to have a long windup before they reached the good stuff: writing about reading, interpretation, and book clubs. You'll see, however, that in this unit we follow Annie Dillard's advice and go for the gold, right from the start—and we suggest you do so as well. Teachers who piloted this book said they'd never seen such extraordinary work from their children, and we are convinced that your children, too, are capable of the same. Clubs begin in Bend II of this unit, and right from the start you rally your students to work in more grown-up ways, taking a new level of ownership for their intellectual engagement in fiction reading.

This unit asks a lot of students and gives a lot to them as well. Take a look at the Narrative Reading Learning Progression, and you will understand why the unit asks as much as it does of fifth-graders. Fifth grade is no time for kids to rest on their laurels! The learning curve between fourth and fifth grade is an especially steep one, and the work that fifth-graders are asked to do is work that many of us didn't do until high school (if then!). Don't let this stress you out, however, because the good news is that sixth-graders revisit much of what is in the fifth-grade learning progression. In fact, many of our

sixth-grade teachers are already planning to launch their year with this book, ensuring their students have access to this new work and a solid foundation for the rest of middle school.

Then, too, you will have a lot to give your students. Fifth grade is the year when all the most extraordinary books become open and available to your children. Now they can read *Bridge to Teribithia*. They can read *Wringer*, *Out of the Dust*, *Esperanza Rising*, *Locomotive*, and so many others. The fact that students will convene in clubs within a week or two of the start of fifth grade is emblematic of the tone and the message that characterize this unit. Many of your students will look ready for middle school already—they will have shot up over the summer—and others will be going through that growth spurt soon. The important thing is that fifth grade is a time for an intellectual as well as a physical growth spurt.

You'll set students up to participate in this growth spurt by telling them that the most important thing they need to learn is to be in charge of their own learning. This needs to be a year for intellectual independence. To launch the year, you suggest to your students that now that they are practically middle schoolers, they need to take seriously the challenge to read thoughtfully and to write well about their reading.

In the second and third bends, you will suggest to students that just as writing makes a person more awake to his or her life, so, too, writing makes a reader more awake to his or her text. Readers who write can see more in a text—they notice more and they make something of what they see. This bend quickly turns to the work of interpretation, teaching students how to read with interpretive lenses. Fifth-graders are at an age when almost everything stands for something else. Nothing is what it seems: sneakers can be a symbol of fitting in or of individuality, an invitation can be a turning point, an overheard comment can be the end of a chapter in life. Things in a fifth-grader's life are weighted with significance, and these meanings shift and change. Asking fifth-graders to take seriously the challenge of reading rich, beautiful books interpretively, and doing this work in the company of friends, is pretty much a perfect way to start fifth grade!

In these bends, you'll start by lifting the level of students' thinking about texts by reminding them of all the interpretation work they have done thus far over the years. You'll remind them about the work they probably did in third and fourth grades to grow ideas about characters. And you'll remind them about the work they did in units like historical fiction, where they probably began the process of developing more nuanced interpretations by studying story elements (like repeated images, setting, and plot) more closely, and discussing interpretations in the company of clubs. You'll then progress to lifting students' images about what it means to read interpretively, using the learning progression and your work with *Home of the Brave* to help students develop images of possibility. You'll provide them with concrete strategies as well.

In Bend III, you'll teach students to read analytically, noticing the way different authors develop the same theme differently. You'll also help them do some important compare-and-contrast work on several texts that develop a similar theme, too.

SUPPORTING SKILL PROGRESSIONS

It will be important for you to skim over the Narrative Reading Progression for fifth grade, filling yourself with an image of the work that you'll be bringing your fifth-graders toward across the year. When your vision is crystal clear, it will be all that much easier to usher children along toward your end goals. At first, the expectations might seem daunting. "The standards expect fifth-graders to do *that*?" you might question. The shifts between fourth and fifth grade are not for the weak of heart! The good news is that much of the work you'll be helping your fifth-graders to do continues to be a goal for them in sixth grade as well—and frankly, these are skills that many of us continue to develop across our lives, well into high school and beyond.

In this section, we will explain some of the major shifts that you'll be supporting between fourth and fifth grade, and we'll detail the ways that work relates to the strands on the Narrative Reading Learning Progression that are addressed in this grade. Some of those strands (and threads) are shown here, although based on your assessments of individual students, you will of course teach toward other strands as well. Some students, for example, will

be working up the ladder of fluency skills or on monitoring for sense. Others may be especially interested in reading like an author or ready to focus more on critical literacy.

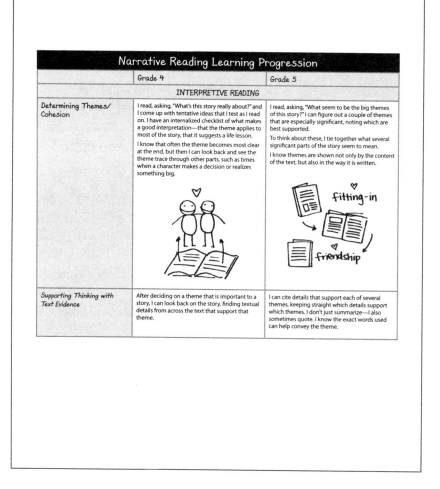

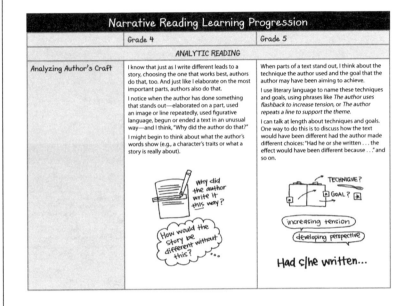

Narrative Reading Learning Progression		
	Grade 4	Grade 5
ANALYTIC READING		
Analyzing Author's Craft	I know that just as I write different leads to a story, choosing the one that works best, authors do that, too. And just like I elaborate on the most important parts, authors also do that. I notice when the author has done something that stands out—elaborated on a part, used an image or line repeatedly, used figurative language, begun or ended a text in an unusual way—and I think, "Why did the author do that?" I might begin to think about what the author's words show (e.g., a character's traits or what a story is really about).	When parts of a text stand out, I think about the technique the author used and the goal that the author may have been aiming to achieve. I use literary language to name these techniques and goals, using phrases like *The author uses flashback to increase tension,* or *The author repeats a line to support the theme.* I can talk at length about techniques and goals. One way to do this is to discuss how the text would have been different had the author made different choices: "Had he or she written . . . the effect would have been different because . . ." and so on.

One thing is certain: the fiction that your students will read during this unit will be more complex. Many of your students will be reading novels that are rich with nuanced characters and multiple subplots, all of which swirl around and connect to multiple themes. The texts they are reading also tend to be more complex structurally. The fact that your students' texts are becoming more difficult has implications for the intellectual work you'll be supporting across this unit. These books offer endless possibilities for insights, interpretations, and rich talk, and they also demand much more from readers. This is why it will be especially important, as discussed below, that students are reading books in a range that is just right for them—replete with opportunities for growth yet able to be read and comprehended independently.

Above all, this is a unit that supports students' work with interpretation and so, not surprisingly "Determining Themes/Cohesion" is an important strand of the learning progression for this unit. You will note the expectation for fifth-graders is that they read, expecting complexity and multiple themes from the start.

Often in a novel, students will jump immediately to name the most important thing the text teaches. The response, "Okay, and what else does it teach?" is an important one, because it nudges students to take up aspects of the text that aren't accounted for by the theme that springs first to mind. And of course the job is not just to think about more than one overarching idea that holds the text together but also to be able to weigh which details from the text best support each of those themes. Selection is important in this work. Which details *best* convey a particular theme? Which themes seem most important in this story? Sorting, categorizing, and ranking details will become a natural part of the interpretive process as students seek to write and talk about the ideas they are developing with text evidence.

It will be an important shift also for your students to learn that when looking for evidence of a theme, they can note not only the content of the story but also the craft of it. Themes are shown not only by the events and interactions in a text but also by the way in which a text is written. This work is captured in the "Analyzing Author's Craft" strand of the progression (and to a lesser extent, by the "Word Work" strand.) By highlighting these strands on the progression, you'll be able to remind students that it is worth paying close attention to techniques that authors have used (including the way they choose to depict characters, events, or settings, their word choice, and in particular, their use of figurative language). You will help your students to note craft techniques in the texts they read, and to name those techniques, talking about them with language that sounds like, "So and so uses (flashback/metaphor/internal dialogue/and so on) to (advance the theme/provide background information/develop the character/build tension/and so on)." It is no easy thing for students to be able to talk and think about authorial techniques,

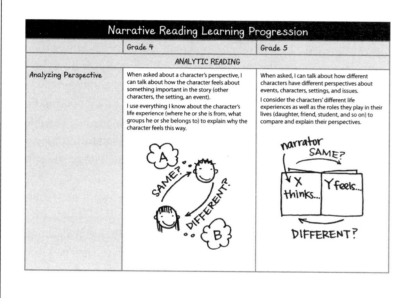

Narrative Reading Learning Progression		
	Grade 4	Grade 5
ANALYTIC READING		
Analyzing Perspective	When asked about a character's perspective, I can talk about how the character feels about something important in the story (other characters, the setting, an event). I use everything I know about the character's life experience (where he or she is from, what groups he or she belongs to) to explain why the character feels this way.	When asked, I can talk about how different characters have different perspectives about events, characters, settings, and issues. I consider the characters' different life experiences as well as the roles they play in their lives (daughter, friend, student, and so on) to compare and explain their perspectives.

and technique cards in Bend III will offer a fun, tactile way for students to begin considering these questions.

The fact that the novels students are reading now (or will be reading soon) are apt to be more complex has important implications for your students' work in the "Orienting" strand. From the start, students will need to expect complexity. The opening of a text may not make sense to them right away, but instead of discarding the text as too hard, they may need to persist a bit longer because it is entirely possible that readers are supposed to read the lead and be confused. The text may be in fragments; there may be more than one point of view. The "Monitoring for Sense" strand reflects changes that students will need to make as they anticipate more complexity from the start. Students will need to be ready to carry questions and postpone closure, expecting that the pieces of a novel will fit together like a puzzle as they read on. Of course, students will continue to work to make sense and to construct a cohesive text, and they will need to work harder at that in some texts, which may or may not be something they are accustomed to. Your fifth-graders will need to draw on their repertoire of fix-up strategies and to be strategic about when and how to use those strategies.

As students approach middle school, expectations for analytic reading increase. Think of analytic reading as the sort of intellectual work that a scholar does, pulling back from a text and surveying it with dispassionate objectivity, hoping to understand how the pieces fit together. This is work that the Common Core State Standards (CCSS) highlight in the Reading: Literature strand (RL 5.5) and that students who write and who read like writers have long done. When students step back from a text and think, "How does this part contribute to the whole text?" or "What is the work this portion of the story does for the whole story?" the payoff is immense, both in reading and students' own writing. The skills in "Analyzing Author's Craft" and "Analyzing Parts of a Story in Relation to the Whole" will not only strengthen students' own writing but also allow students to be probing and, yes, analytic, when they compare texts that advance the same theme but do so differently.

As students progress through this unit, you'll want them to consider the seemingly small scenes, as well as the iconic moments in their texts. When asked, as called for by the standards and progressions, students will learn to talk about how different characters have different perspectives about events, characters, settings, and issues, and how the characters' different life experiences and life roles help explain their perspectives.

but if your students are writers themselves and if you show them how to bring that stance to their reading, they'll quickly become adept at reflecting on the questions, "Why might the author have done this? What might the author have been trying to convey?" Then, too, your introduction of the narrative goal

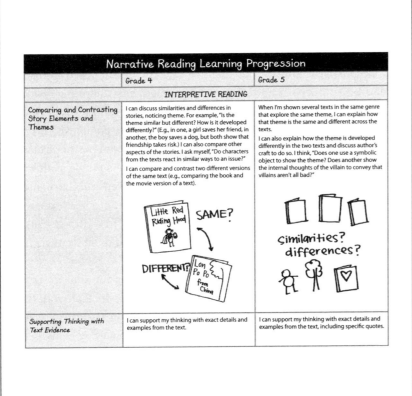

We also want to point out that in fifth grade it becomes increasingly important that your students are analyzing a particular aspect of craft that many children don't even realize exists: "Analyzing Perspective" (see the fourth- and fifth-grade slice of the progression below). The expectations in this area (which relate to CCSS RL 5.6) are a major shift from fourth grade. In fourth grade, students had to identify the point of view of a story (i.e., Is it being told in first person? Third person? If it's being told in first person, which character is telling it? How is that character involved in the story? Is the character a major or minor character?) and the kind of information that it lets the reader know ("Oh, it's told in first person so I know I'll be in only one character's head"). Students also had to be able to discuss how a character is feeling and why. However, the fifth-grade expectations call for more complex work involving perspective. This moves beyond identifying who is telling the story into thinking about how the answer to that question affects how the story is told—and realizing that the perspective is a choice the author made for a reason. The narrator's background, role, membership in a group, and other factors all influence the narrator's perspective on events, people, and interactions, and fifth-graders are asked to think about the relationship between a narrator's point of view, perspective, and the way in which he or she conveys information and understands events.

Then, too, as students do this much more in-depth work on theme and author's craft, that work will also bolster their work in the "Comparing and Contrasting Story Elements and Themes" strand. All that they did to determine themes and analyze how they are shown in one text, they can draw on again as they now study and describe how different texts approach similar themes. This will involve being able to explain how those themes are both similar and different. For instance, while two books might deal with issues and themes surrounding the loss of a friend, students will learn to ask, "How have these two authors approached this issue differently? What is each author saying about loss?" You will also teach students to explain how one text shows a particular theme (the necklace he gave her was more than a necklace because it shows . . .) versus how another text shows this theme (the setting was full of significance in this story because . . .).

As students read more complex texts, they'll need to rely on their foundational skills—how do these parts fit? What does this word mean? The "Word Work" strand does not have dramatically different expectations for fifth-graders, nor does the "Building Vocabulary" thread, but this is work that does not change in importance across the grades. That is, it is *always* important for students to remember and rely on their foundational skills, especially as they begin to reach for more complex texts.

OVERVIEW

As this unit opens, you will help students see that just as they have spent the summer growing too tall for their blue jeans and too big for their old sneakers, so too are they ready to make a growth spurt in reading. You'll challenge them to rise to the occasion of fifth grade by choosing to read novels that are worthy of serious, thoughtful reading and by bringing all they know from their entire school career to the work of reading those novels deeply. Whereas in prior years, the writing about reading that students do early in the year has mostly been confined to Post-its (lest it overwhelm them from getting a volume of reading going), this year, you'll spotlight the importance of writing about reading right from the start.

Bend I: Writing about Reading with Voice and Investment

In this first bend, you'll ask students to become more committed to their readers' notebooks than ever before. As part of that, you'll rally them to regard the writing they do about their reading as every bit as important as the writing they do in the writing workshop. All too often, the writing that students do in their writers' notebooks is full of voice and spirit and thought, while the writing they do about reading seems dull and formulaic. As you start both fifth grade and this unit, you'll invite your children to approach their *reading* notebooks the way they do their *writing* notebooks—with conviction, a sense of purpose, and voice.

In order to give students agency over their growth while also helping them to work toward substantial goals, you may want to provide them with examples of strong notebook entries. Students can study these mentor texts now and return to them throughout the first bend (and unit) to discover new ways in which to lift the level of their own writing. They'll deduce qualities of good writing-to-learn from studying those entries, and you'll pitch in about qualities of good writing about reading as well. One of the important things you'll teach is that reader's notebooks are meant as seedbeds for thought. The writing will not be boxed into tidy five-paragraph essays, but will instead be exploratory. You'll teach students to shift up and down the ladder of abstraction, to switch between writing about big general ideas and using specific concrete details, and to use literary language. In time, you will also teach your students that they can choose to think and write analytically, and you'll equip them to do

this, showing them how to rank, sort, select, combine, and categorize. All the time, you will be training your students to back up their ideas with text evidence.

Of course, during this first bend, you will also be launching the reading workshop for the year, and that will include conducting running records and the performance assessment, as well as inducting students into the routines of a rigorous reading workshop. You will also take a "time out" for a day and channel students to assess their first performance assessment, and as part of that day you will introduce them to learning progressions that will help them to lift the level of their thinking and writing across the unit. We discuss the learning progression skills that are highlighted in the assessment portions of this orientation, though they actually play less of a role in the first bend than in the later bends. Throughout this first bend you will want to set your students up for a year of agency and proactiveness by using language such as, "You used to . . . , but now . . ." and "Years ago . . . , but this year . . . ."

Bend II: Raising the Level of Writing and Talking about Literature

Once students are writing about their reading in ways that matter, they will be ready to move to Bend II. In this bend, you will up the ante by reminding students that as readers sharpen their reading and thinking skills, they are able to see more significance in a text and to trust that they notice things for a reason. Great literature in hand, students will embark on a study of interpretation. At the same time, they'll begin to work in small book clubs that will last for the remainder of the unit. Because members will read and reread copies of the same book (or perhaps two) in sync with each other during this bend, sometimes devoting as much as a week and a half to that book, the choice of text will be especially important. The Getting Ready section of this orientation will elaborate on book choice, and you will find book recommendations in the online resources that accompany this unit.

By studying the skills and strategies of interpretation while reading, writing, and talking about literature, your readers will work together in their clubs to identify the themes that thread through their books. They will learn that the art of interpretation is not about placing a tag on a book with a pre-made cliché on it (such as "Work hard and you will succeed"). Instead, your students will learn that reading interpretively involves linking ideas and building larger theories. You'll teach them to try on the interpretations that others bring to a text, viewing and reviewing the book in light of an idea that may not have been their own. You'll help them to read interpretively—using ideas as lenses, finding and weighing evidence, and finally settling on the most significant themes.

Your students will come to see book clubs as little debate clubs—places where they can try out ideas, be challenged, and ultimately engage in rich book club conversations that hold them accountable for defending their ideas with reasons and evidence. As a part of this, students will study effective book clubs and then reflect on themselves as clubs, setting goals for the ways in which they can strengthen their talk.

During this second bend, you will reinforce an integral idea—that the stories they are reading are about more than one idea, and you'll teach them to keep more than one idea afloat in their minds. You'll teach your readers that multiple themes live in their books, and that these themes can be traced across the expanse of a story. Then, too, they'll come to see that these themes morph and change along with the plotline, allowing for new ideas and new interpretations to emerge.

Bend III: Thematic Text Sets: Turning Texts Inside Out

Once your students are discussing themes actively with their clubs, you'll teach them how to compare and contrast the ways in which themes are developed *across* texts. In the third and final bend, students will study the way in which a theme can be developed differently in different texts. You will give each club a small selection of short texts to read, asking them to choose one that they feel highlights themes that also fit the novel they read. You will teach students techniques for analyzing the different ways in which a single theme might be developed differently in different texts, noticing the roles that characters play in advancing (or pushing back against) a theme. As part of this study, students will come to see that texts are written by authors who make deliberate decisions, not just about what will happen in a story but also about how the story will be told. Students will analyze the ways in which different authors use specific techniques to achieve goals. By studying the ways an author sculpted a particular character, developed a plotline, and described a setting or another element of a story, students will be working to bridge the connection between theme and craft. This is heady, intellectual work, and while all students won't master it just yet, they will be one step closer to understanding the intricate patterns and designs a writer quilts into his or her text. Appropriately, students will end the unit with a literary salon in which they are invited to sip sparkling apple cider (or lemonade or juice!) and discuss literature with friends, classmates, and other attendees.

ASSESSMENT

Because this unit is scheduled to be taught at the very start of the year, it will be important that you are assessing in ways that both allow you to get your readers onto a course of reading and work that will pay off for them and that also helps you begin to know the class of readers you will be teaching this year.

In *Reading Pathways, Grades 3–5: Performance Assessments and Learning Progressions*, you can learn about ways to invite students to help you know them as not just a reading level, but as a complicated reader with passions, tastes, quirks, habits, and history. What have been their best reading experiences? Their worst? What are they passionate about? You'll certainly want to do things like ask your readers to bring in objects or books that as a group create a self-portrait of themselves as readers.

On the other hand, conducting running records of all your students and getting this done within the first week or two of the school year is an important job. *Reading Pathways, Grades 3–5: Performance Assessments and Learning Progressions* provides help doing this efficiently, and presumably you already know how to conduct running records. You can use the texts that are on the Teachers College Reading and Writing Project's website if your district has not equipped you with another system for conducting running records. In a nutshell, to create a running record for an individual student, you start by asking the child to read aloud about 100 words from a leveled book. As the child reads, record with a check mark each word that the youngster reads accurately and record any miscues. Ask a couple of comprehension questions about the text (on our assessments, and most others, these questions are provided for you and are meant to gauge the students' literal *and* inferential comprehension of the text passage). You'll want to consider how well the child can hold on to the key details in the text. You'll also want to ask a few relatively simple, straightforward inferential questions, perhaps about the character's traits or motivations. But be sure that once you've conducted a running record with a text that seems to be at the child's just-right level, you press on and do the same for a text that you expect will be at the child's ceiling, or instructional, level. Sometimes, in fact, the child can also read that level. Additionally, it is only when a child is reading at his or her ceiling that you can actually see enough miscues and misunderstandings to grasp patterns that tell you what work the reader needs to do before he or she can progress up a level. This is vital data you will want to have in hand.

Of course, the data gleaned from a running record reaches beyond matching the child to a level. You'll want to think about the patterns of reading behaviors you notice. For example, does the child lean on the visual information, the print, when solving an unfamiliar word, or does she draw on context clues? Does the child attend to punctuation cues to read in fluent phrases? Does the child monitor for meaning, pausing or rereading to clarify details? Does the child pause to solve new vocabulary? Use this information to prioritize goals for individual students, as well as to form flexible partnerships and small groups to support students in the weeks ahead.

Before the first bend is over, you will want to assess all of your students and to channel students to read books that are within reach for them. Having conducted these assessments will also allow you to group students into book clubs so that they can read alongside other students who are reading at the same (or close to the same) level. You will also want to begin making plans for readers to read such a volume of books at his or her within-reach level that the child will soon be able to progress up a notch. This is especially critical for a youngster who is reading below benchmark and needs to make especially fast progress. It is helpful to make a plan with a child for when you will assess next—and know that oftentimes, we have found that after just two or three weeks of school, summer rust will wear off and a surprising number of students will be ready to progress.

Students who are reading at benchmark will be able to read level S books independently. Readers who are working well below benchmark will likely need guided reading and other supports to help them make gains quickly. You can find more information on strategies for moving students up reading levels in *Reading Pathways, Grades 3–5: Performance Assessments and Learning Progressions* and *A Guide to the Reading Workshop, Intermediate Grades*. For students who struggle to decode or read fluently, you may even want to administer a spelling inventory to let you know their command of spelling patterns, a high-frequency word inventory, and a check on fluency. You can find the assessments mentioned above on our website, www.readingandwritingproject.com,

under Assessments, and then Running Records, Foundational Assessments, and Benchmarks.

Meanwhile, in this unit you'll launch reading logs and talk up the value of a volume of reading. Obviously, your assessments will want to spotlight volume and to attend to these logs. Whenever someone aspires toward a goal, it can help to collect data that provides feedback. People who want to run faster or to lose weight or to develop muscles keep scrupulous data, poring over the data to track their progress. In the same way, you will probably want to induct children into a system for collecting data on their volume of reading. During this first unit of study of the year, you'll probably rally kids to become invested in reading logs in which they record the titles, levels, pages, minutes, and place of their reading. An example of a reading log can be found in the online resources, although if your students have been in a reading workshop before, the concept of recording their reading and checking their volume and rate is probably not new. To ensure the fidelity of these logs, you'll want to make sure that many of your September conferences reference them. You might say, "I notice you've been reading faster. Has it been hard to hold on to the story as you read faster?" If a child's pace has slowed, you might ask, "What's slowing you down? I notice you read less today. What got in the way?" Remember that reading volume matters. It affects reading rate, it affects how quickly children move up levels, and it is a sign of the overall health of your readers.

Before the unit begins, we encourage you to devote a day of your reading workshop to a performance assessment. Chapters 7, 8, and 9 in *Reading Pathways, Grades 3–5: Performance Assessments and Learning Progressions* support this work. As you will see, we've devised one pre-assessment and one post-assessment for every unit. Because this is the first performance assessment of the year that your students will have taken, we suggest you read aloud the text *Stray* and then show children the brief video. The assessment will include four open-ended questions, each focusing on a skill that is important to the unit and to many high-stakes assessments as well. You will find more information on administering and grading these performance assessments in the Unit of Study book itself, and you will be able to access all the materials you need in the online resources.

❧ ONLINE DIGITAL RESOURCES

A variety of resources to accompany this and the other Grade 5 Units of Study for Teaching Reading are available in the Online Resources, including charts and examples of student work shown throughout *Interpretation Book Clubs*, as well as links to other electronic resources. Offering daily support for your teaching, these materials will help you provide a structured learning environment that fosters independence and self-direction.

To access and download all the digital resources for the Grade 5 Units of Study for Teaching Reading:

1. Go to **www.heinemann.com** and click the link in the upper right to log in. (If you do not have an account yet, you will need to create one.)

2. **Enter the following registration code** in the box to register your product: RUOS_Gr5

3. Under **My Online Resources**, click the link for the ***Grade 5 Reading Units of Study***.

4. The digital resources are available in the upper right; click a file name to download. (For any compressed ("ZIP") files, double-click the downloaded file to extract individual files to your hard drive.)

(You may keep copies of these resources on up to six of your own computers or devices. By downloading the files you acknowledge that they are for your individual or classroom use and that neither the resources nor the product code will be distributed or shared.)

HOME OF THE BRAVE PACING GUIDE

We recommend *Home of the Brave* by Katherine Applegate as the demonstration text for this unit of study. It's up to you to make a decision to use this text or another, but if you choose *Home of the Brave*, you'll want to follow the pacing guide that follows to make sure you and your readers are prepared for each session ahead of time. There are times you'll read aloud during a minilesson; however, this will not be when you do the bulk of your reading aloud. To keep minilessons brief and maximize independent reading time, we suggest that you find an additional block of time to set aside for read-aloud. Please note, the page numbers referenced in the Pacing Guide are based on *Home of the Brave* (First Square Fish Edition 2008).

Session	Read Aloud before the Minilesson	Read Aloud during Reading Workshop
BEND I		
Session 1	No specific reading	No specific reading
Session 2	No specific reading	Excerpt from "Snow," pp. 3–5
Session 3	"Old Words, New Words," "Questions," "What the Heck," pp. 6–12	Excerpts from "God with a Wet Nose," pp. 13–14
Session 4	The rest of "God with a Wet Nose," "Welcome to Minnesota," "Family," pp. 14–22	Excerpt from "Old Words, New Words," p. 7 (reread), "Lessons," pp. 23–24
Session 5	No specific reading	No specific reading
Session 6	"Good-Byes," "Father," "Bed," "Brother," pp. 25–38	Students should be able to discuss what they've read so far in *Home of the Brave*.
Session 7	"TV Machine," "Night," "Mama," "Sleep Story," pp. 39–50	Students should be able to discuss what they've read so far in *Home of the Brave*.
BEND II		
Session 8	Make sure you have finished reading aloud Part One of the text (through page 50).	Excerpt from "Paperwork," pp. 53–54
Session 9	The rest of "Paperwork," "Information," "School Clothes," "Once There Was . . . ," "New Desk," "Ready," "Cattle," "Lunch," and "Fries," pp. 54–80	Excerpt from "Night," pp. 43–46
Session 10	"Not Knowing," "Home," "Time," "Helping," "How Not to Wash Dishes," "Not-Smart Boy," "Magic Milk," pp. 81–106	No specific reading
Session 11	"Wet Feet," "Bus," "Lou," "Cows and Cookies," "Night Talk," pp. 107–27	Students should be able to discuss what they've read so far in *Home of the Brave*.
Session 12	"Cowboy," "Working," "Ganwar, Meet Gol," "Idea," "Field Trip," "The Question," "Apple," pp. 129–54	End of "School Clothes," "Once There Was," pp. 62–65

(continues)

Session	Read Aloud before the Minilesson	Read Aloud during Reading Workshop
Session 13	"Grocery Store," "The Story I Tell Hannah on the Way Home," "Library," "Going Up," "Hearts," "White Girl," "Scars," "Bad News," "No More," pp. 155–83	Provide groups of students with copies of pages 20–22 ("Family"), 32–36 ("Bed"), 43–46 ("Night"), 60–62 ("School Clothes), 123–27 ("Night Talk"), 138–45 ("Ganwar, Meet Gol" and "An Idea"), and 178–83 ("Bad News" and "No More").
Session 14	"Last Day," "Summer," "More Bad News," "Sleep Story," pp. 184–200	No specific reading
BEND III		
Session 15	*Fly Away Home*	Excerpts from *Fly Away Home*
Session 16	"Confession," "Running Away," "Bus," "Treed," pp. 201–12	Students should be able to discuss what they've read so far in *Home of the Brave*.
Session 17	"Ganwar," "Talk," "Changes," pp. 213–24	Students should be able to discuss what they've read so far in *Home of the Brave*.
Session 18	"Herding," "Traffic Jam," pp. 225–32	"Snow" (p. 3)
Session 19	"Cops," "Zoo," "Homecoming," pp. 233–49. "Reader's Guide," including "Background" and "Historical Context," pp. 259–63	Excerpt from "More Bad News" (p. 196)

Dear Teacher,

In a moment, you will turn to Session 1 of this unit and this yearlong curriculum. We imagine you, like those kids in the Narnia series, pushing through the wardrobe and into a new world. The heroine of that story—interestingly, named Lucy—found herself standing in a wintery forest. A snowy bough brushed against her; ahead, a lantern shone. Soon there was the sound of sleigh bells, and Lucy was off on an effort to bring goodness into the world.

Our fantasy is that you'll find that this book draws you into an adventure that is equally important—and that it does this for your children, too. We say that not because our writing is so magical, but because, after all, if these units do their job, they bring your students through that wardrobe into a land of rich literacy.

Before you turn the page, we want to make a plea for you to take the time to give your children a performance assessment that will allow them—and you—to see, glowing in front of you, not a lantern, but a set of goals. Alongside our colleagues, we have worked harder than you could ever imagine to design performance assessments for this unit and all of our units—pre-assessments and post-assessments. And we want to be sure that in these units, assessments are not part of the Dark Side, but instead take their rightful place as tools that help to guide next steps for you and your students.

Those of you familiar with our writing units of study know that we recommend on-demand writing assessments in the genre of the unit, as both pre- and post-assessments. Here in reading workshop, we propose assessments aligned to the major reading work of the unit. You'll be asking your students to read a short story (or to listen to it, for those who find it too hard to read) and to answer a few key questions that map onto key skills that you will teach during the unit.

The assessments and the directions for giving and scoring them are included in the Online Resources for this unit.

You may wonder why they aren't here—why you need to bother tracking them down. The reason is this. Within a few months from the day we write this letter, thousands of fifth-graders will take the first assessment. We are absolutely sure to learn from the experience. Using our Online Resources as a means of providing assessments to you allows us to engage in a cycle of continuous improvement that will benefit you and your children. We will continue to update the content to reflect our newest and best thinking.

So reserve a day for the assessments, arrange for printing and copying the materials, and begin now to talk with your colleagues about whether you will score the assessments yourselves, or if you will want the children to self-assess. It's so important that this is a shared decision across your team and school. Our general thought is that if your fifth-graders have grown up with the Reading Units of Study or have used the writing checklists to study their work, they have enough experience with these assessments to score the assessment themselves. See the Online Resources for Session 3 of this unit for a more detailed vision of how this could go. The crucial step will be in getting the work back to students quickly, with instruction and tools to help them see the reading goals they might be working on immediately. Only then can the assessment truly serve as one of many guiding lights you'll offer through the path of the unit.

Please know we are eager to learn from what you learn/notice/suggest. Write to readingassessments@readingandwritingproject.com with your observations and recommendations.

Happy assessing,

Lucy and Ali

Taking Charge of Your Reading Life

IN THIS SESSION, you'll teach students that they can have a growth spurt as readers if they work with resolve toward ambitious, specific goals to become stronger readers.

GETTING READY

✔ Study the "Setting Up Your Classroom" section in the Welcome to the Unit for management and room arrangement information that is crucial to plan and begin your reading workshop.

✔ Provide a reading notebook for each student (see Active Engagement and Share).

✔ Provide bins of books for students to select and read in class (see Conferring and Small-Group Work, Mid-Workshop Teaching).

✔ Prepare a sheet of paper on a clipboard with the heading, "Suggestions for Making This Year's Reading Workshop as Powerful as Possible" so you can jot ideas from students (see Share and Homework).

I F YOU THINK ABOUT TIMES when a teacher has come into your life and taught you in ways that have made a profound difference, you'll probably realize that the teacher didn't just teach you content. That teacher probably rallied you to imagine big things for yourself, to see yourself as capable of more than you'd ever imagined. In his book, *Visible Learning* (Routledge, 2008) John Hattie cites research showing that just a few things make a profound difference in accelerating learners' growth. One of those things is your relationship with learners. It matters that you see enormous potential in your students and help them believe in that potential.

Although the work of helping learners believe in their own potential is most easily accomplished one-to-one, preaching has a place in whole-class teaching. This lesson helps you say to your fifth-graders, "I see your potential, I see your promise. I just know this year is going to be a life-changing one." Right from the start, you'll be treating your fifth-graders as readers on the cusp of becoming extraordinary. You'll want to become accustomed to using phrases such as, "You used to . . . but now . . ." and "From this day forth . . ." and "I can tell, this year, you're going to . . ."

This will be especially important in Bend I of this unit, as a great deal of the work focuses on agency. Rather than waiting for you to explicitly guide them through new reading strategies, your students will be diving right into raising the level of their reading by setting themselves tasks.

In many schools, fifth-graders are the elders of the school, and this unit builds on that, rallying your students to work in grown-up ways. Right from the start, you want your students to know that yes indeed, people can work at their reading, aiming to get better at it, and you'll rally them to aim to do just that. Today and across the first bend of the unit, you'll inspire students to ratchet up their reading lives by working with agency and resolve toward goals they select. Although this bend will focus especially on the contribution that writing can make to reading, today your teaching will mostly rally students to author reading lives for themselves with intentionality. Some readers will resolve to read more, others to read a greater variety of texts, yet others to tackle more complex texts or new genres.

Either way, today you help your students set themselves up to work at their reading—taking charge of their reading lives. Ultimately, your kids will not throw themselves heart and soul into the work of the year unless you can help them know that they are behind the steering wheel.

"You'll inspire students to ratchet up their reading lives by working with agency and resolve toward goals they select."

Taking Charge of Your Reading Life

CONNECTION

Welcome students by noting that they've grown bigger and by anticipating the growth spurts they'll have this year. Suggest this can be a growth spurt year for their reading, too.

"Fifth-graders, you can barely fit into our meeting area this year, you've grown so much! And the truth is that this year and next, you'll go through even more dramatic growth spurts. You'll outgrow shirts and shoes, rules and roles.

"I've been thinking about this because, as your teacher, I want to do everything possible to make sure that this year you also have a growth spurt as a reader. I've been thinking, 'What can *I* do to make this the best year ever for each of you as a reader?'

"Here's the thing: I've come to the conclusion that the best thing I can do to make this an amazing year for you and your reading lives is to make it so that *you're* in charge of your reading."

Name the teaching point.

"Readers, today I want to teach you that in this upcoming year, you can go through a growth spurt as a reader, you can sprout up as a reader. But that will only happen if you work on your reading, if you take on the goal of getting better at reading, and if you work with deliberateness toward the specific goals you set."

TEACHING

Rally students to take stock of themselves as readers and to set ambitious goals.

"You might be thinking that I'm nuts. You might be thinking, 'Actually, I don't need to *work on my reading*, I can already read just fine.' You might be thinking, 'In fact, I learned to read in first grade and I haven't had any trouble since.' But just as there's a big difference between the kind of writing you do as a first-grader and the kind you do as a fifth-grader, so, too, there's a big difference in the kind of reading you do.

◆ COACHING

It is almost always the case that the first mini-lessons in a bend or especially in a unit are apt to be broad ones. You need to rally readers to the direction of the unit.

You'll find that using direct quotes livens not only a narrative but also a minilesson. When you teach this minilesson, have some fun with this part. "You might be thinking that I'm nuts." "Actually, I don't need to work on my reading." Those lines are meant to work when said aloud.

"If you start this year saying, 'My reading is fine. I'm all done growing as a reader,' then that will be the way the year is for you—and that would be a shame. But if you start this year, studying yourself as a reader and making ambitious and important goals for yourself, you stand a good chance of growing dramatically as a reader this year (and that is true even if you start as a strong reader).

"For that to happen, though, you need to identify areas where your reading isn't perfect, and set goals for yourself. You see, researchers are clear that to get stronger at anything—at skating, at playing the trumpet, at reading—you need to take on projects that are a stretch for you, to set high goals, to work deliberately to improve, and to give yourself feedback.

"So here we are at the start of a new year. I'm going to ask each of you to take study yourself as a reader, to take stock. It will take me weeks to know each one of you and the kind of reader you are—but *you* already know yourself. So think hard about this: what's the most important way you can get better as a reader? Right now, think about your own reading life. In what ways is your reading life strong? In what ways could your reading life get stronger?"

Demonstrate by setting a goal for yourself, then debrief in ways that rally kids to think seriously about their aspirations.

"I'm going to be doing similar thinking." I lifted my eyes skyward, and thought about my own reading life. "I'm thinking about the *amount* of reading I do. Lately, I've always had a book going, a book I carry with me and I've been reading a lot, so I think I'm okay on the sheer amount of reading I do. I'm thinking about the books that I choose to read. I don't tend to commit to a reading project and to stick with it. I might read one mystery, then one political biography. I don't usually stick with a series of books that go together, and I think it would be good if I did because then I'd be able to think across them, you know?

"The other thing is that sometimes my books get confusing. A character will show up halfway through the book, and I have a vague sense that I know that character from earlier in the book, but I tend to just keep reading, hoping I'll figure out who the character is as I go on. I know that when someone walks on stage in the middle of a book, I should pause to figure out the story that is behind that character, but I don't usually do that."

Then I paused, as if taking a half step backward to name what I'd just done. "Fifth-graders, do you see how I thought seriously about how my reading life is going and how I zoomed in on a few important things that aren't the best habits? You can do this too—now, and whenever you want to ratchet up the level of your reading."

ACTIVE ENGAGEMENT

Engage students in making serious plans for a more thoughtful and mature reading life.

"What goals could make a real difference in your reading life this year?" I asked. "Might you want to tackle more difficult books? Is your #1 goal to read more—after all, nothing could matter more than the amount of reading you do? Or might you take on a new genre—push yourself to read new kinds of books?

Obviously you will want to choose goals that actually would be important for your reading life. Mention volume, however, even if only in passing since that will probably be the goal that most of your students select as a starting point.

"Right here, right now, think about your goals. You are fifth-graders now, so I am hoping you can bring your most mature self to this. When you have an idea for a goal, jot it down in your notebook. Then underneath that goal, jot some practical steps you might follow."

As kids thought and jotted, I voiced over. "I can see you're admitting to some stuff that is honest—like the fact that you need to turn the television off, or to not have long gaps between one book and the next. This is important thinking. There's a saying, 'Two heads are better than one.' Form a little group with kids sitting near you, and talk about the big work you want to tackle as a reader this year, and about practical steps you will take." As kids talked, I voiced over, "I can see you are getting ideas from each other. Add to your goals if you do!"

Listen in to children's plans, so that you can refer to them either in conferences or when you talk to the class. Listen especially to be sure kids are not doing "rote work." You want them to be thinking hard, truly trying to outgrow themselves. When you hear the latter, voice over, "I can hear that you are determined to outgrow yourself . . . you must be a particularly determined person. I really admire that."

LINK

Stir kids up by praising their initiative, hint at the role of accountability, and send them off to read.

"Readers, the seriousness with which you took on this work bodes well for you. If you can take charge of your reading life, you'll get more reading done, read harder books, and develop habits that help you succeed in school and in life.

"You've jotted an initial plan in your reading notebook. Think about what you can do today to meet your goals—or in general, to make yourself into a more mature and ambitious reader than you were last year. Time to read. Take even this little act—of getting to a reading spot and getting into your book, as a chance to work on your reading. Off you go."

 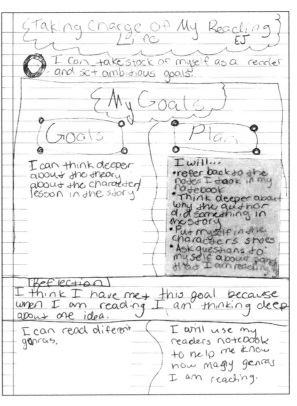

FIG. 1–1   Students set goals for themselves as readers and create action plans.

Shoring Up the Essentials

STARTING TOMORROW, you'll need to devote most of the reading workshop to assessing your readers. So today, you will probably want to circulate, getting to know students' identities as readers and rallying them to work with great enthusiasm. You'll also need to check in on a few essentials.

Build students' identities as readers.

Even as students select books, you can begin helping them to take their reading seriously. You see a youngster pick up a book and glance at the back cover. "I'm totally impressed," you say, "at the way you look over a book before diving into it. Are you thinking, 'What family of books does this belong to? Is it more like such and such or more like . . . ?'" The youngster is apt to nod, whether or not he was actually doing that work, so you can follow up by asking, "What *are* you noticing about this book?"

As students choose books, you can also celebrate their emerging identities: "So you are a total science fiction buff, are you? I'll need you to help others get excited about science fiction, too." Or, "You're like me—you go straight to historical fiction. It's such a complicated genre, isn't it—with history *and* a plot unfolding? It's impressive that you don't flinch from tackling those challenges." Or, "I can see you testing that book out to make sure you can not just read it, but that you can *really* understand it and think deeply about it. It shows a lot of wisdom that you are starting the year off reading books that you'll be able to think deeply about."

This sort of responsiveness can continue throughout the workshop, but meanwhile, you'll also want to check in on essentials.

Check in on essentials, taking informal assessments.

Once readers have chosen books, notice whether it seems easy for them to get involved in those books. Do they immediately get their noses into books, turning pages at an appropriate rate? If you see readers who aren't engaged even beyond those early

moments—look for restlessness, squirming, very slow progress through the pages, requests for the bathroom pass—give these readers your immediate attention.

The first thing to check is whether these readers are matched to their books. You'll give a formal assessment in a few days, but for now, just scan the back of the book to gather information about the storyline and character. Then ask the child to read you half a page, and to tell you how that passage fits with what's happened so far. See if the reader can talk about the text using the names of characters, and if her rendition of the story makes sense. Ask a few questions tailored to the section the child just read, quickly flipping through the book to compare what the child has said with the text. If

(continues)

MID-WORKSHOP TEACHING

Reminding Readers to Work with Resolve

Standing in the middle of the room, I said, "Readers, researchers have found that people do not get better simply by doing something a lot. Instead, people get better by goal-driven, deliberate work. I know many of you don't think of reading as *work*, and don't 'deliberately work on' your reading. But right now, think, 'What could I do for the next twenty minutes to lift the level of my thinking, my reading?' Some of you might find that you need to add to your goal sheet already."

I left some silence for thinking, then said, "For you to outgrow yourself this year, you need to take the first step. Taking that first step means that today's reading is not business as usual. What's that saying—'A one-thousand-mile march begins with one step?' For you to outgrow yourself this year, you need to take that first step. Do that work between now and the end of today's workshop."

---

you feel unsure about a child's statement (for instance, a statement about a character's personality or a theory the child is developing), ask her to turn to the part of the story that made her think that. "Where in the story did that take place?" you might ask. "What evidence are you finding to support this theory? Can you show me a few specific places?" This will give you a glimpse into the validity of the child's thinking, and meanwhile, when she cites specific passages, you'll have a chance to listen to the child reading aloud.

If you sense that the reader is confused, you may want to word your awareness like this: "Is this book pretty confusing?" Readers are more apt to jump on that—yes, yes, this *book* is confusing—rather than to rush to admit that a book is too hard. And once the reader has agreed the book is confusing, you can essentially regard that as a youngster's indication that yes, the book is a bit beyond reach. "When books are confusing, that often means they are hard for you. Most readers find it helpful to start the year off reading a ton of easier books—that's a good way to rub off the summer rust. In a few weeks, you can ramp up the difficulty level of your books."

You could say it differently: "I'm going to recommend that you tackle this book in a little bit, once you've gotten some quick and easier books under your belt." Then bringing out some more accessible books, you can ask, "Which of these looks appealing to you?" Be absolutely sure that you don't take the youngster down one or two notches when what that student actually needs is to be moved to books that are three or four levels easier, because the only thing that will pay off is getting the reader into books that are comprehensible to him or to her. You might make a note to yourself, indicating that this child should be one of the first you assess when you start running records. This will ensure he gets into a just-right book as quickly as possible.

Checking in on Goal-Setting

Channel readers to reflect on today's goal-driven work.

"Readers, just for today, will you come together for our share? Sit where you sat during the minilesson." Once children had gathered, I said, "It's been helpful for me to begin to know you as readers. Just watching you work today, I noticed the way you chose books—so many of you came to the bookshelves with favorite authors or a favorite genre in mind and with a sense of what sorts of books are within reach for you. I was impressed!

"Will you get back into a conversation with the kids you talked with this morning, and tell each other about the new work you tried to do today? Compare notes on ways you worked with resolve toward your goals."

As students talked, I chimed in with prompts: "Be specific! Say, 'For example, I might . . .'" "Listeners: contribute. What *else* might the reader do another time to achieve his or her goal?"

Rally the class to invent ways to make this year's reading workshop the best it can be. As the kids talk, listen, record, and create a list that you read aloud.

"This class is only going to be the best reading workshop in the world if each of you helps make it that way. What ideas do you have? What has worked in other years? Do you want book buzzes on Friday? A shelf of 'Readers' Choice' books? A shared online document full of book recommendations? Continue to talk in small clusters, but this time talk about ideas you have for how we can make this class into the best reading workshop it can be."

The room erupted in conversations. I listened and jotted like crazy. After a bit, I reconvened the class. "I'm getting great ideas," I said, and read from my clipboard.

Suggestions for Making This Year's Reading Workshop as Powerful as Possible
- Put books on topics of special interest into labeled bins or shelves.
- Hold "Hot Topic" discussions on topics like making a movie of the book or possible sequels.
- Create a collection of video trailers on great books.
- Get more books in languages other than English.
- When you find or write great stuff related to a book, file it inside the back cover.
- Make a collection of great, easy books for when your mind needs a break.

FIG. 1–2 One teacher's class chart, listing out some of the class's resolutions

"We need to stop but when you think of other ideas, would you tell me those ideas, or add them to our list? I'll copy these onto chart paper and leave it up here so we can begin working on these ideas. Meanwhile—start thinking if you can help make any of these ideas into realities."

THINK AND DO MORE: READING WORKSHOP, READING GOALS, EVIDENCE OF YOUR WORK AS A READER

Readers, for homework tonight, will you do three things?

First, take time to think more about your ideas for how our class can work together to make this year the best possible year for reading. Think back over the reading workshops you have been in during other years and remember things that have worked for you. What rituals do you think we should put into place? What could really help? If you have more ideas, be ready to add them to our list tomorrow.

Here is the list that we made today in class—by all means, jot down more ideas!

Suggestions for Making This Year's Reading Workshop as Powerful as Possible
- Put books on topics of special interest into labeled bins or shelves.
- Hold "Hot Topic" discussions on topics like making a movie of the book or possible sequels.
- Create a collection of video trailers on great books.
- Get more books in languages other than English.
- When you find or write great stuff related to a book, file it inside the back cover.
- Make a collection of great, easy books for when your mind needs a break.

Secondly, continue to work with resolve toward goals that are important to you. How will your reading tonight be different than just any ol' reading because you are working to make this a breakthrough year for you and reading?

And here is my new request. Will you think about how you can create evidence of the new work you are doing as a reader? Start collecting that evidence. As part of this, be ready to record the reading you do in a new reading log, which you'll be given tomorrow. Tonight, just note on a Post-it the time you start reading and the time you finish reading and the number of pages read.

Writing Well about Reading

T HE FIRST SESSIONS OF THIS UNIT carry special loads of responsibility because you are establishing the norms of the new community. You are helping students step into the roles they'll play this year, ramping up expectations for the year ahead—and all the while, launching a new unit and a new bend in the road of a unit.

Nothing matters more than the fact that your kids need to read up a storm this year, reading books that are just within reach. And so today and often in this first bend, you'll continue to rally students to do just that. If need be, add another minilesson that addresses the importance of students engaging in a volume of reading, and selecting books that draw them in. Never underestimate the importance of the time you spend talking up particular books, reading snippets aloud, suggesting new books that are similar to class favorites, and sharing your own enthusiasm for reading.

This session will recruit students to invest themselves not only in reading but also in writing about reading. Your message for this first bend will be that as fifth-graders, your students need to read more complex novels and to think in more complex ways. Learning to write well about reading is the single most important thing they can do to ratchet up the level of this thinking work. In the online resources that accompany this unit, you will find a comprehensive list of books that lend themselves particularly well to an interpretation unit, and you'll want to steer children to these kinds of books from the outset.

Chances are fairly good that by fourth grade, teachers in your school will tell you that writing about reading met with mixed results last year—that a fair proportion of youngsters cranked out a lot of lifeless Post-its and notebook entries. If that is the case, it will be important for you to demolish old images of reading notebooks, replacing those old images with something entirely new and jazzy. With this in mind, you'll send your students off during this session to participate in a gallery walk.

We've included possible entries for this gallery in this unit's online resources and you are welcome to select from that collection, printing the entries you select in color. The goal is to recruit your students' commitment to their reader's notebook. Although ideally, your students will be invigorated by entries that are especially probing and original, the

IN THIS SESSION, you'll guide students through an inquiry to explore and establish what it means to write well about reading.

GETTING READY

✔ Provide a pocket folder with blank reading logs for each student. Either you or the child will also want to stash a pen, Post-its, and a reader's notebook in this folder. Your students will use this folder regularly throughout this unit, so be sure they have it with them whenever they read (see Connection).

✔ Prepare a chart listing reading partnerships for Partner 1 and Partner 2 (see Connection).

✔ If using *Home of the Brave* as your demonstration text, be prepared to read aloud an excerpt from "Snow," pages 3–5 (see Teaching and Active Engagement).

✔ Before class, set up a gallery of effective fifth-grade writing-about-reading, with each piece of writing attached to a larger piece of chart paper and markers in display areas (see Teaching and Active Engagement).

✔ For this and all upcoming sessions, ensure that students have their own within-reach, independent reading books to read and write about (see Link, Conferring and Small-Group Work, Mid-Workshop Teaching, and Share).

✔ For homework, provide copies of writing exemplars from gallery walk, plus Session 1 chart, "Suggestions for Making This Year's Reading Workshop as Powerful as Possible" (see Homework).

truth is that for now, entries that include colorful drawings and graphics in imaginative ways will probably make the biggest impression. Your end goal is not for your students to make their reading notebooks more artistic. What *is* a big deal is to inspire them to believe that the reading notebooks can be *theirs*—and to believe in the importance of writing well about reading. The sequence of minilessons in this bend will channel students to do some of that very important writing work.

"Nothing matters more than the fact that your kids need to read up a storm this year."

The teaching methods for this minilesson are not the usual—you don't demonstrate or coach, but instead, you invite children into an inquiry. And you don't even harvest the insights the children develop through that inquiry. Instead, you ask students to show what they have learned by doing some writing about reading that reflects that learning. This bend in the unit ends with a second gallery—this time with students sharing some of their own best work with partners.

Writing Well about Reading

CONNECTION

Channel readers to fill in logs and discuss with partners, using that moment to give them ballpark figures about volume of reading expectations.

"When you arrive in the meeting area, find your new logs and enter the reading you did last night," I said. I'd already placed new pocket folders (complete with blank logs) into a seating chart of sorts, so students sat where those folders directed them, beside their first reading partner. A chart listed the partnerships, giving some the role of Partner 1, and others, Partner 2. As students worked, I voiced over, saying, "Now that you are fifth-graders, you'll probably work at least forty minutes a night on your reading, though there will be lots of times when you can't stop so you read into the night! Now talk to your reading partner about your plans to get a lot of reading done this year."

As readers talked, I circulated, reminding many of them that generally, readers can read two-thirds of a page a minute, so they would probably read at least twenty pages an evening. Then I asked for their attention.

"Earlier I pointed out that you'll be 'working on your reading' for at least forty minutes a night. I didn't say, 'You'll be *reading* for forty minutes,' I said. 'You'll be *working* on your reading . . .'"

You will not yet have assessed readers enough to place them in matched partnerships, but because this bend in the unit highlights writing about reading, it will be important for readers to have partners from the start so they have an audience for that writing. Use data from previous years to make matched partnerships to the best of your ability (despite the fact that they will be reading different books), but mostly, plan to alter these partnerships in Bend II.

Shift from emphasizing volume of reading to quality of thinking. This will set up the emphasis on writing/thinking about reading that will be the focus for the day and for the new bend.

"Now that you are in fifth grade, the thinking you do as you read becomes all-important. There's no prize for reading a ton of pages or reading extra hard books if you read in a way that later, when asked, 'What did you think about while reading your book?' you say, 'Umm . . . ah . . . Actually, I can't remember what I read. But I read it, honest!' Just putting your eyes over the pages won't matter one bit. Instead, the one thing that matters now that you are in fifth grade is the thinking that you do as you read.

"You *already know* that for you to have a growth spurt as a reader, you need to work with deliberateness toward specific goals. Here's the *new* thing. Because the thinking you do as you read is the most crucial thing, and because writing is the best way to improve that thinking, it is important for you to have goals that help you write well about your reading."

		Student Reading Log						
Name:								
Date	Title of Book		Level	Home or School	Page Started	Page Ended	Minutes Read	Genre

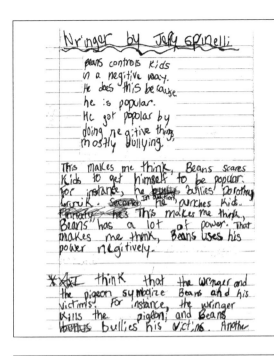
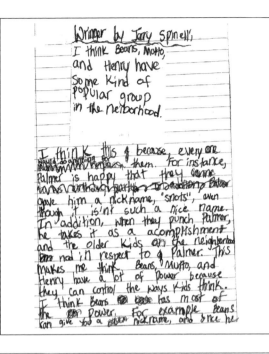

Wringer by Jerry Spinelli

Beans controls kids in a negitive way. He does this because he is popular. He got popular by doing negitive things, mostly bullying.

This makes me think, Beans scares kids to get himself to be popular. For instance, he bullies Dorothy, Gurik. Second, he punches kids. Finaly, This makes me think, Beans has a lot of power. That makes me think, Beans uses his power negitively.

**I think that the Wringer and the pigeon symbolize Beans and his victims. For instance, the wringer kills the pigeon, and Beans bullies bullies his victims. Another

Wringer by Jerry Spinelli,

I think Beans, Mutto, and Henry have some kind of popular group in the neiborhood.

I think this because everyone ... them. For instance, Palmer is happy that they ... gave him a nickname, "snots", even though it isn't such a nice name. In addition, when they punch Palmer, he takes it as a acomplishment and the older kids ... the neighborhood ... nod in respect to Palmer. This makes me think, Beans, Mutto, and Henry have a lot of power because they can control the ways kids think. I think Beans has most of the power. For example Beans can give you a nickname, and once he

example is, the pigeon gets killed, and Beans victims gets bullyed. Maybe Beans and the people around him will reflect off of the pigeons and wringers. If this is true, Beans probably doesn't relize the other side of the encounter. He doesn't know what its like to be on the victims side, just like the wringers belive that killing the pigeons is "putting out of their misery". A theme I can pull from that is before you do something think about that action from the other perspective. Maybe Beans the people around him will reflect off of the wringers and pigeons because Palmer doesn't want to be a wringer and kill the pigeons, so maybe he will try to be mean, and fail. All of this illustrates in books. When one thing symbolizes the other, they can be switched and the other can symbolize the first. This relates to the central theme that you should think about things from the other perspective.

does it, that is your permanent ... and everyone has to call you that. Another example is, Palmer says that Beans is the head of the group. Beans can control the way kids think. An event in the story that proves this is, Palmer has always wanted to be part of Beans group and it was like his life goal. All of this shows, Mutto, Henry, and especially Beans have a lot of power over kids in their neighborhood. They really change kids lifes. I think that they use their power negitiry. One reason is, they have ... power so whatever they do, kids will have to love it, so they punch kids on their birthday, and the kid reciving the punches loves it. They treat the event with respect, and ... littler kids treat it with amazment.

FIG. 2–1 Story examples of writing about *Wringer*. A strong entry begins with a short, clear, question that you will then give students the opportunity to explore and answer. Inquiry questions generally don't have "yes" or "no" answers, but instead open up a variety of possibilities to be explored.

✤ **Name the question that will guide the inquiry.**

"So our work for today is to answer this question: 'What are some qualities of strong writing about reading?'"

TEACHING AND ACTIVE ENGAGEMENT

To launch an inquiry into what it means to write well about reading, read the start of the unit's demonstration text, channeling students to dictate to each other a less-than-great and a great entry.

"Let's get started on figuring out how exactly you can write well about reading. I'm going to read aloud from the book that will thread through this unit. *Home of the Brave* is a short, intense book. It's about a boy named Kek who comes to Minnesota from Africa after many people in his village—including his father and brother—are killed. I'll just read a page and a half, and the pages are sparse. Listen closely so that when I stop reading, you and your partner can write-in-the-air, dictating to each other what a typical, not-great fifth-grade notebook entry about this would sound like. *Then*, the harder job, write-in-the-air the best, most mature and thoughtful entry you could imagine. Let me give you a heads-up that the start is a bit confusing—it will take some intellectual work to figure out what's going on. The book starts like this":

Snow

When the flying boat

returns to earth at last,

I open my eyes

and gaze out the round window.

What is all the white? I whisper.

Where is all the world?

The helping man greets me

and there are many lines and questions

and pieces of paper.

[. . .]

I shake my head.

I say, This America is hard work.

His laughter makes little clouds.

Prepare for a minilesson that departs from the norm. It's unusual to read aloud new text within the reading minilesson. Granted, you will often reread a snippet of the read-aloud text or talk about that text, but it isn't common to actually read the text aloud within part of the minilesson. Because the start of Home of the Brave *is confusing and important, we embed a tiny read-aloud into this minilesson.*

At the end of the chapter, I closed the book and reminded the students to first, write-in-the-air what a *not* great entry might sound like, then to do the same for a great entry. As children talked, I quickly distributed some pieces of really effective fifth-grade writing-about-reading to spots throughout the classroom, with each piece of writing attached to a larger piece of chart paper.

Ask students to extrapolate the qualities of good writing about reading, using this to suggest they aren't clear about this and to drumroll the upcoming work.

After a few minutes, I said, "Partners, I know you aren't finished, but will you talk above all about the differences between not-so-great writing about reading and *great* writing about reading? The bigger question I am asking is this: what does *great* writing about reading look like? For example, how could any of us write *really, really* well about those first pages of *Home of the Brave*?"

As children talked, I listened, fascinated.

After a bit I said, "Readers, I need your attention—urgently. I'm noticing that many of you aren't sure what constitutes strong writing about reading. You have some ideas, but they seem a bit shaky."

Channel the class to participate in a gallery walk. Send students off to move among displays you will have set up, studying and annotating effective writing about reading.

"Remember that for anyone to have a growth spurt, it helps to have crystal clear goals. Let's work over the next few days to get clarity about what good writing about reading is like. You know that song from an old-fashioned movie named *South Pacific*: 'If you don't have a dream, how are you gonna have a dream come true?'

"To help you develop images of strong writing about reading, I've set up a gallery of writing about reading that has been done by other fifth-graders. This gallery shows writing that I think is powerful, though you may or may not agree." The children were intrigued. "Partners in Row 1, you'll go to display #1—see where I've laid out that display? Row 2, go to display #2, and so on. You'll see marker pens at the display areas. Annotate the text by underlining key parts, labeling what you see, filling the chart paper with graffiti that captures whatever you notice and think. Do this with lips sealed, absolutely quietly. Any conversations can happen on the chart paper. Writing back and forth to each other: 'Notice this . . . I agree . . . why do you think that's so great?' Get started."

As children work, you will notice many things. You could easily launch into a huge whole-class conversation right now, and that conversation would be worthwhile. The class could compile a chart of the do's and don'ts of effective writing about reading. You'll notice we don't actually channel you to do that. This is because our intention is to start today, informing students' images of good writing. So we devote less time to documenting and more time to altering those images.

Reinforce the idea that students must read the exemplar pieces absolutely quietly. This ban on talk channels them to have more to write and to use the colored pens and chart paper in out-of-the-box ways that are actually similar to what you hope they'll do in their reader's notebooks. Signal, lips sealed, to ask students what they notice, or write on the chart paper, "What do you notice?"

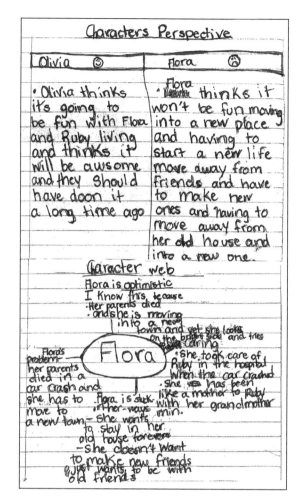

Characters Perspective

Olivia	Flora
• Olivia thinks it's going to be fun with Flora and Ruby living and thinks it will be awsome and they should have doon it a long time ago	• Flora thinks it won't be fun moving into a new place and having to start a new life move away from friends and have to make new ones and having to move away from her old house and into a new one.

Character web

Flora is optimistic I know this because • Her parents died • and she is moving into a new town and yet she looks on the bright side and tries being caring

Flora's problem: her parents died in a car crash and she has to move to a new town

Flora is stuck in other ways

• She took care of Ruby in the hospital when the car crashed
• she has been like a mother to Ruby

— She wants to stay in her old house forever
— She doesn't want to make new friends she just wants to be with old friends

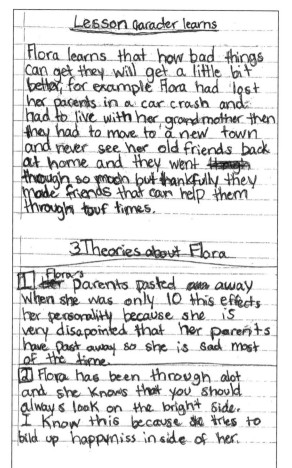

Lesson Character learns

Flora learns that how bad things can get they will get a little bit better, for example Flora had lost her parents in a car crash and had to live with her grandmother then they had to move to a new town and never see her old friends back at home and they went ~~though~~ through so much but thankfully they made friends that can help them through touf times.

3 Theories about Flora

① Flora's parents pasted away when she was only 10 this effects her personality because she is very disapointed that her parents have past away so she is sad most of the time.

② Flora has been through alot and she knows that you should always look on the bright side. I know this because she tries to bild up happyniss inside of her.

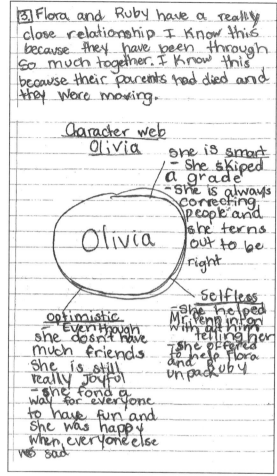

③ Flora and Ruby have a reallly close relationship I know this because they have been through so much together. I know this because their parents had died and they were moving.

Character web
Olivia

she is smart
- She skiped a grade
- she is always correcting people and she terns out to be right

optimistic
— Even though she dosn't have much friends she is still really joyful
— she fond a way for everyone to have fun and she was happy when everyone else was sad

selfless
— she helped Mr. Penn in on telling her to help Flora and unpack Ruby

FIG. 2–2 Flora and Olivia's entries exemplify a variety of skill work for students to study.

After a few minutes at one display, I signaled for groups to rotate clockwise, with each group traveling to a second display. This work spilled beyond the normal boundaries of the reading minilesson, usurping some of the actual reading time—but I felt sure it was worth it.

Channel students to point to parts in the text, and then to underline or star those parts and to respond in the margins. Once a student has done so, write back or voice over, "Why do you say that? Do you see other examples?"

LINK

Send kids off to read, explaining that instead of partner conversations, they'll be writing about their independent reading books, making entries that could form their own gallery.

"Readers, our minilesson was longer than usual, so although I'd love for us to talk about whatever you noticed, it is past time to read. Once you have read, you'll have time to show what you learned by doing your own writing about reading, this time making that writing about reading really great. So read, aware that you'll write about that reading later."

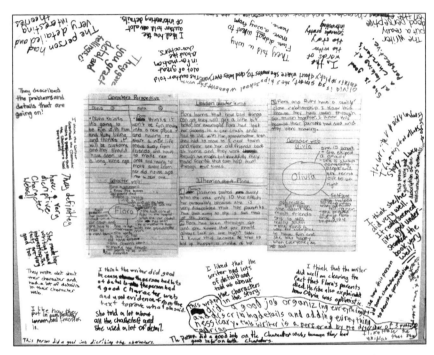

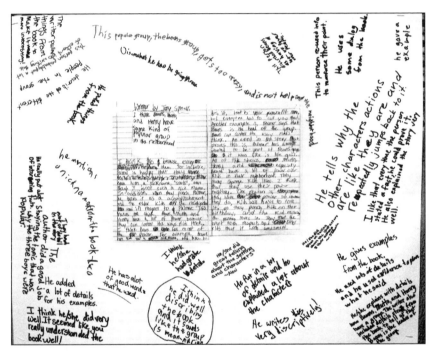

FIG. 2–3   Students engage in a close study of mentor writing about reading.

Starting to Assess Readers
Conducting Running Records

TODAY AND FOR UPCOMING DAYS until the job is completed, you'll need to conduct running records to ascertain the highest level of text difficulty that each student can read with accuracy, fluency, and comprehension. This unit expects that within a week and a half, you will have conducted running records for each student. At that point, you will be able to put students into books that represent their within-reach level (the highest level the student can read while still grasping the text). To move through your class with that efficiency, you'll need to cut some corners and do everything possible to maximize progress. In this conferring section, then, we'll focus on helping you conduct running records.

First, encourage students to work with matched books from the start. Use reports of last year's levels of text difficulty and scores on last year's high-stakes test to double-check that students' self-assessments seem roughly right. For example, expect that children who scored a 1 on the high-stakes test will probably be reading books that are level L/M or below. If a youngster received a 1 on the state test and is reading close to benchmark level (T) for fifth grade, something is wrong with that picture! Work first with those students, and start by assessing them at dramatically lower levels. Nothing is worse than having to inch lower and lower as the child struggles with each level!

Reading Pathways contains lots of hints for conducting running records efficiently. It suggests that you gather a small group—say, four readers—and orient them to the assessment en masse, keeping them all with you as you assess. Perhaps, for example, you'll work with a group of kids who seem like they are reading texts that are roughly M/N levels. Explain to the whole group how the running records will proceed, then ask four of the five readers to turn away from you. Then request one reader to read the first hundred words of the passage. Normally, you'd record miscues for that first hundred words, but if this is a child who reads dramatically below grade level, ask that child to read the first portion of the passage quietly and then the second half aloud while you record miscues. The children who are waiting can continue reading their books while you work with that one youngster.

When you conduct these assessments, keep in mind that you do the child no favors by putting your thumb on the scale. Allowing vague answers to substitute for a real show of comprehension, for example, does the reader a great disservice. That's like letting someone study the eye chart up close, memorizing the letters, so the person can cheat on his or her eye exam—and get glasses that don't work! The purpose of this assessment is to make sure that youngsters can succeed with their books. You want those books to provide the feedback loop that allows students to learn to read from reading. If a particular child is well below benchmark, it'd be horrible to deny him or her access to that sort of a self-correcting system. It's only when a sentence mostly makes sense, for example, that the reader can lean on that sense to figure out words that don't make sense.

It is important to realize that if you assess readers correctly and match them to within-reach books, they can make concrete, observable progress in just a few weeks. A school we know well was concerned because many of its fifth-graders were assessed at the

(continues)

MID-WORKSHOP TEACHING
Checking on Volume and Pace of Reading

Standing in the middle of the room, I called for readers' attention. "Readers, so far, you've read for ten minutes. Will you check how many pages you have read in that time?" I gave students several seconds to count their pages, then continued, "Researchers suggest that you should probably have read about seven pages—if you haven't read close to that amount, think about whether the book you are reading might be hard for you, or whether you have some habits going (like constantly rereading, or mouthing your words as you read) that are slowing you down. Then keep reading, aiming to read a little faster if need be."

start of the school year, reading at the M/N level. At the first of October, that school reassessed its students and lo and behold, in only three weeks, almost all of them had progressed an entire level. So don't worry that putting a fifth-grade student into level M books means that youngster will stay at that level for a semester!

It is important to note that you should not stop when you find what appears to be a child's just-right level (for example, they read the text with 96% accuracy and answered the questions correctly). You will want to continue to assess that child until you find his or her ceiling (that is, the level at which he or she can no longer pass the assessment). This does two things: It ensures that you have found a child's independent reading level (and not just the first assessment they were able to pass), and the running record the student did not pass will give you a great deal of insight into that child as a reader. What falls apart first? Is it the ability to decode? To comprehend a text? To think inferentially? The answers to these questions will guide the conferring and small-group work you do with these students in the works ahead.

Help students read differently, preparing to write soon about their books.

When you're not conducting running records, you'll want to help students read differently, anticipating that they will soon write about their books. Lay the groundwork for the kind of thinking they will do over the course of this unit: "All writing about reading is not the same," you might say. "There is writing to put forward the theory you've developed about a book, and to provide your readers with the evidence, reasons, and logic to persuade them that your theory is worthy. That's how one would write about reading to write literary essays. There is an entirely different kind of writing about reading that you do as you read to develop thoughtful ideas." Encourage students to flag notable passages, thinking about why these are significant, how they reveal important things about the characters and the story.

Recording Thoughts about Books

Invite children to write an entry that reflects their thinking about their reading.

"Readers, instead of talking with your partner about whatever you have been thinking as you read, will you open your reader's notebook and write an entry that captures your thinking? Make this writing about reading represent your best thinking and your best writing about reading. Get started!"

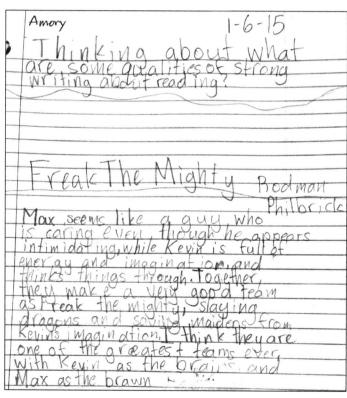

Amory   1-6-15

Thinking about what are some qualities of strong writing about reading?

Freak The Mighty   Rodman Philbrick

Max seems like a guy who is caring even though he appears intimidating, while Kevin is full of energy and imagination, and thinks things through. Together, they make a very good team as Freak the mighty, slaying dragons and saving maidens from Kevin's imagination. I think they are one of the greatest teams ever, with Kevin as the brains, and Max as the brawn.

FIG. 2–4   Amory captures her best thinking on the page.

DO MORE: WRITING ABOUT READING, IMPROVING READING WORKSHOP

Readers, today in school, you studied examples of good writing about reading. I hope you are starting to form an image in your mind of what it means to write well about reading. Remember the words of that song, "If you don't have a dream, how are you gonna have a dream come true?"

Continue to keep what you noticed in your mind, holding yourself to doing the best writing about reading you can. Make sure you read at least thirty minutes, and at least twenty-two pages. Then write!

Finally, review yesterday's list about ways to make our reading workshop more powerful. Think about one thing you can bring to school by the end of the week to help us act on that list. Can you start a collection of video trailers about books we have in the room? Can you print out maps that go with some of our books? Can you bring in a list of hot topics and come up with names of kids to lead those discussions? You may think of something that has nothing to do with our list. By the end of this week, please bring in something that makes our reading workshop the best it can be. Find time tomorrow to show me what you have brought in.

Suggestions for Making This Year's Reading Workshop as Powerful as Possible

- Put books on topics of special interest into labeled bins or shelves.
- Hold "Hot Topic" discussions on topics like making a movie of the book or possible sequels.
- Create a collection of video trailers on great books.
- Get more books in languages other than English.
- When you find or write great stuff related to a book, file it inside the back cover.
- Make a collection of great, easy books for when your mind needs a break.

ear Teacher,

We're suggesting that today you take a day off from the forward motion of the unit—just one!—to spend time with your students, learning from the performance assessments they took before the unit began. You will have decided with your team how to handle the scoring of the assessments. For your fifth-graders, you have probably decided to let them score the assessments themselves during today's class. Whether you or your students do the scoring, the most urgent message we offer you is to not delay this day, even if you feel (as you probably do!) that the children need to spend more time immersed in the unit to be able to truly analyze their prior work.

The important move today is to engage your young readers in the critical work of thinking about their own reading—and to give them some tools to do so in a way that allows them to set clear goals. The rubrics, progressions, and exemplars you'll use today provide students with clear pathways toward meeting today's exceedingly high expectations, allowing them to answer the question, "How am I doing?" even when it is being asked in relation to the black box of higher-level comprehension. More importantly, this work will help your children answer the question, "How can I improve?" Across today's lesson, you'll work to turn elusive standards into concrete, doable behaviors, ones your children are able to work toward with a sense of efficacy—"I can do this, if I work hard."

You'll find detailed recommendations for how today might go in a letter included in the Online Resources for this unit. You'll also find the resources you'll need to teach children to score their work themselves, a powerful tool that aligns to the reading learning progression.

We're sure that today's work will set you and your students up with a common vocabulary and a shared vision for the important work that is to come.

Happy assessing,

Lucy and Ali

Writing about Reading Means Reading with a Writerly Wide-Awakeness

IN THIS SESSION, you'll teach children that readers who write about their reading are extra alert, seeing more in their books.

GETTING READY

✔ If using *Home of the Brave* as your demonstration text, read aloud "Old Words, New Words," "Questions," and "What the Heck" (pages 6–12) before today's session.

✔ Be ready to distribute flags, Post-its, and colorful markers, so students can annotate their entries (see Connection).

✔ Prepare to display and read aloud "God with a Wet Nose" (pages 13–16) from *Home of the Brave* (or a selected passage from your own demonstration text) (see Active Engagement).

✔ Prepare chart "To Understand / Interpret a Story, Readers Pay Attention to . . ." on chart paper (see Mid-Workshop Teaching and Homework).

✔ Prepare Bend I anchor chart "Writing Well about Reading" on chart paper to display to students (see Link, Mid-Workshop Teaching, and Share).

✔ Prepare chart of thought prompts to display to the class, "Talking (and Writing) to Grow New Ideas" (see Share).

YOU'LL START TODAY'S SESSION by asking students to look back at the writing work they did during the previous sessions, with their performance assessment, pointing out that the reason to write about reading is to think about reading. Your goal is to value their writing about reading. During the writing workshop, you go to great lengths to drumroll the importance of students' writing. They share it with partners, they reread and assess it, there are constant efforts to improve their writing, their work is published and celebrated. Think, in contrast, of how little attention is generally paid to the writing that students do during the reading workshop. If no one is reading their writing about reading and paying attention to it, it's not surprising that often, students churn out lifeless, dull, entries.

Students need to approach reading differently when they anticipate they'll be writing afterward. If students merely read, read, read and then when they are done, crank out an entry, that writing does little to invigorate the reading that has already taken place. On the other hand, if students approach reading with a writerly consciousness, ready to take in the text with that consciousness, the anticipation that they will soon need to make something of their reading can bring heightened alertness to that reading, fostering close reading in the richest sense of the word.

If you sense that this session doesn't do a lot of heavy lifting, you are right. You are giving students time to become invested in their notebooks, writing about reading in out-of-the box, original, innovative ways. When we taught an earlier iteration of this unit, we asked students if we could take their notebooks for the weekend to study. The students were already so attached to their notebooks that they clung to them as if we'd asked to borrow a member of their family! Once we convinced them that the notebooks would be returned speedily, we left the classroom with our arms full. We were not far down the hall before we heard some students call for us. They raced to catch up, and each student gave her reading notebook a good bye kiss. The melodrama was, of course, a playful exaggeration, but it is no small accomplishment to have students wanting to give a tearful kiss good-bye to their notebooks! That's your goal for today.

Writing about Reading Means Reading with a Writerly Wide-Awakeness

CONNECTION

Ask students to study the writing about reading they did yesterday, just as they studied work in the gallery of exemplars previously, annotating what works in their writing.

"Readers, yesterday you spent some time studying the work you did on your performance assessments up against a rubric, and then using the learning progressions to revise that work and make it stronger. Will you take out a bit of yesterday's work that you are particularly proud of—something that feels like your best work? Now ask yourself which part works—and why. I'm going to distribute some Post-its and colorful markers, just as we did on our Day 2 gallery work, so you can annotate your best work and your partner's."

After readers worked for a bit, I convened the group. "You've been looking at your writing to see its powerful aspects . . . but the important thing is this: When you write about reading, the goal is not just that you produce entries that are thoughtful and provocative—the goal is that your *reading* becomes different because you read as a writer.

❖ Name the teaching point.

"Today I want to teach you that people *read differently* when they write about their reading. Writers see more, notice more, think more . . . and everything becomes grist for their thinking mill. When you read as a writer, you bring a writerly wide-awakeness, an extra alertness, to your reading. You notice stuff others would pass right by, and you make something of what you see."

TEACHING

Drumroll the fact that writers live wide-awake lives, alert to details, ready to make significance. Suggest that readers who write approach the texts they read with extra alertness.

"I want to talk to you about the way that your reading will be different this year because you'll read, knowing that afterward you'll do some really powerful writing about that reading. Katherine Paterson, the Newbery award–winning author of *Bridge to Terabithia*, was asked once, 'Why write?' She wasn't asked, 'Why write about reading?' but I think her answer has everything to do with writing about reading. She answered by telling about how she and her son had just watched a cicada bug shed its skin.

You might ask students to keep the learning progressions by their side as they annotate, aiming to use the "language of skilled readers" as they note the strengths of their writing about reading. Don't underestimate the power of this moment—as fleeting as it might be. The teachers that piloted this unit said that students were overjoyed and full of pride while marking up their own work, praising it the same way they had others' writing about reading a few days earlier.

Note that I will pull students into the importance of lesson by drawing on a quote by a famous writer, reading it reverently.

"'It came off slowly at first, and then it was almost as if the cicada bug had a waist-length zipper,' she said. 'The wings emerged, crumpled at first, then gradually they spread, and as they watched, the cicada bug twirled like a circus acrobat and then flew off, oblivious to the wake of wonder it left behind.' As Katherine Paterson stood in that wake of wonder, she thought, 'What good are straight teeth and trumpet lessons to a child who cannot see the grandeur that the world is charged with?'

"So how does that relate? What does this have to do with writing about reading?" I let the question hang in the air, hoping kids would speculate on the connection between Katherine Paterson and their writing about reading.

"I think Katherine Paterson is saying that writing helps people see and think about the small wonders that we might otherwise walk right past, like that cicada bug. And writing helps a person not only pay attention to the details but also to grow insights. Pausing to notice that cicada bug nudged her to think about how grown-ups may fret about unimportant things—providing kids with orthodontists—and forget to teach kids to notice 'the grandeur that this world is charged with.'"

Emphasize for students that if they read, read, and then afterward recall, "I'm supposed to write" and then crank out an entry, that won't lift the level of their reading. Tell them it's reading with the intention to write something that pays off.

"My point is this. If what you do is pick up a book, read, read, read, get to the end of reading and *then* think, 'Yikes, now I have to write something,' and you pick up your pen and write an entry, then that writing isn't going to lift the level of your reading. It's a waste.

"But if you go to a book, knowing from the start, 'I'm going to read this as a writer, expecting to pause over small wonders like that cicada bug,' anticipating that what you will write can turn you into an extra-aware, extra-alert reader—then that change will be as if someone turned the lights on in your reading. You'll see more."

ACTIVE ENGAGEMENT

Channel students to read like writers. Continue reading, then reread the touchstone text, then write alongside students.

"Let's try it. I'm going to read further in *Home of the Brave*. Let's all of us—you and I both, listen as writers, with that extra alertness of a writer." I opened *Home of the Brave* and read.

God with a Wet Nose

We park by the side of the fast-car road.

Walking through the snow

is hard work,

Chances are this is what most of your students are doing. By making light of it, you send another message that things will be different this year.

Again we are reading a new portion of the read-aloud in the minilesson. We feel this is important because for students to practice today's strategy, to read with wide-awake alertness, they need to practice doing this work the way they will with their independent books: with never-before-seen text and a wealth of new things to notice, rather than with text we have already read and discussed as a class.

like wading across a river

wild with rain.

The cow is near a fine,

wide-armed,

good-for-climbing tree.

To say the truth of it,

she is not the most beautiful of cows.

Her belly sags

and her coat is scarred

and her face tells me

she remembers sweeter days.

I put the book down and said, "If we weren't trying to read like a writer, we could just whirl through this part, thinking, 'There's nothing important here. This is just a cow beside a tree—an ugly cow, too,' and read right by it. But we're trying to read with a writerly wide-awakeness, seeing and noticing things that other people might read right past. So what do you notice? What feels important?

"I'm going to reread, and let me show you the text, too. This time, push yourself to see even more." I projected the part I'd read aloud onto the overhead projector and before I reread, I said, "Notice details."

"Right now, do some writing. You could link this passage to what we've already read if you want. Don't write any ol' thing. Instead, push yourself to think: 'What is especially meaningful that I'm noticing? What resonates with you, in this part of Kek's journey? When you're ready, start writing."

Children wrote for a bit. The room was quiet enough one could hear the scratch of pens.

Ask students to listen to a partner's writing and talk off of that writing, while you listen in.

After a while, I gathered students' attention and invited them to share insights that felt powerful. They pointed out that Kek seems sympathetic, observant, poetic. They realized that his observations about his new environment reveal things about his old life in Africa.

I picked up on this, saying, "Whoa. I'm realizing something. The thinking you just did is like Kek's way of observing his new world and also like Katherine Paterson's way of observing that cicada bug. You are all seeing with that special alertness."

Reading is not so tangible. Once students begin to read silently, their minds often seem closed to us. They may be thinking thoughts of profound significance. They may be calling up vibrant images as they read; their hearts may be sinking in terror and rising in joy. Who knows? This, of course, is one reason we ask them to write. It's not just to deepen their engagement with books; it's also so that they create artifacts that show us what they're thinking as they read.

Notice the way I restate what students said in a way that is both clearer and serves the intention of the lesson. Don't be afraid to say, "Oh, so what you are saying is . . ." and then take some liberties. You will do students justice by honoring and simultaneously raising the level of their words.

LINK

Point out that students will now read differently, carrying their ideas. Illustrate by reading on in the demonstration text.

"Readers, I want to make one more point. When you write about reading, that writing affects how you take in the upcoming parts of a book. I'll show you what I mean. Think of the ideas you just said":

Kek sympathizes with the cow—maybe she reminds him of himself.

Kek notices things and uses words like a poet.

Kek sees his new world in ways that show us about his old world.

"I am going to read on in the book, but here is the thing. Don't leave the thoughts you just developed behind. Keep those thoughts in mind, hold them in your hand, as you read on. Always after you write about reading, you carry those ideas as you read on, and your thinking about the next part of the book adds onto or messes with those thoughts. Try listening in that way to the next part."

My father would not have stood

for such a weary old woman in his herd,

and yet to see her here

in this strange land

makes my eyes glad.

In my old home back in Africa,

cattle mean life.

They are our reason

to rise with the sun,

to move with the rains,

to rest with the stars.

They are the way we know

our place in the world.

The room was silent. I let the silence hang. I closed the book. "Whew. A lot to think about."

Before sending readers off to read, suggest they reread their previous entry.

Shifting, I announced, "So, it is time to read. Before you read on in your book, reread what you wrote yesterday so you can carry those ideas with you, adding to them, messing with them, as you read on." Then I unveiled a new chart:

ANCHOR CHART

Writing Well about Reading

- Read knowing you'll write, seeing more.
- Read upcoming text with the ideas you wrote about in mind.

Helping Students Invest in Their Writing—and Then Make It Better

THERE'S A GOOD CHANCE that as you glanced over your students' writing about reading, you felt a bit deflated. For many students, jotting on Post-its and writing in reader's notebooks has become almost robotic, and the gallery walk alone won't have made much difference in your students' writing. Remember that in upcoming days, you'll be teaching in ways that lift the level of their writing. There are a million battles to wage: are students writing enough? Are they writing too much? Are they writing about things that help them to think deeper and more analytically about texts? Before you can tackle any of this, though, we've found that it is essential to help students *care* about their writing about reading.

Foster investment in writing.

To support students' investment in their reading notebooks, you may want to provide kids with extra cool flags, Post-its, and rainbow-colored marker pens, suggesting they can work in out-of-the-box ways to capture their thinking. That can help, but the best way to support their investment in their writing is for you to listen carefully to their ideas and respond to them. Refrain from heavy-handed coaching, for today. Instead, give students a chance to invent, to imagine possibilities, to learn from each other.

For now, you will certainly resist steering them to write with topic sentences, to cite text evidence, to use domain-specific vocabulary about literature, to elaborate before pressing on. Instead, your message will be, "Do something different in your notebook! Make it your own! Make it show your best thinking, whatever that is at the moment."

Try to see yourself as a researcher. What *do* kids do when given an open invitation to write about reading? What surprises do you see that you could never in a million years have dreamt to teach?

Know that your research will, in fact, foster students' engagement. If you go through the classroom, reading your students' work with attentiveness, they will care more about that work. So share a chuckle, nod in interest, raise your eyebrows in wonder,

reread to note more details, and know that you'll be doing a world of good. To accelerate the power of this, draw other kids in to do this too. "Listen to this bit of Nicole's entry," you can say, reading it aloud. "Doesn't that get your mind going, 'Look at the way she has already identified a repeating image and is writing to uncover its meaning. What a thought!'"

Try to compliment students for being original, for being thoughtful, for reaching for words that aren't easily come by, for trying to put something too big for words onto the page. Explicitly name what students are doing so that others in the class can learn from them and do the same.

Make sure students are writing in ways that raise the level of their thinking by helping them carry forward prior learning.

As the books your students read get more complicated, they will need new teaching to help them comprehend the book. Essential comprehension work, even such work as keeping track of characters, will need new support. Just think about what it was like the first time you tried to read a Russian novel. Remember *Anna Karenina*? Remember desperately jotting the characters' names on the inside cover, drawing lines between those who were related? Remember keeping track of time and how it was passing, and who was even alive still?

Know that when novels become complicated with multiple plotlines, back stories, and with characters who are not what they seem and who have complicated emotional lives and motivations, your students will need your help in working to disentangle the complexities of it all. The risk of rushing toward work in interpretation is that the kids either become fancy talkers whose ideas emerge only from the glossy surface of the story, or they become plot junkies who throw some themes around when required to do so.

You will want to be aware that it is all too easy for kids to read, noticing mostly the big events, unaware of the details that give a story complexity. Doing so means a reader

"Readers, we've been talking about how writers see more when they read. I'm blown away by the way you are bringing your writerly consciousness to your reading, seeing details in your texts. But let me point something out. Most of what you are seeing seems to me to revolve around one story element: characters. Will you talk with each other about other story elements, and check whether you are noticing and thinking about details related to those elements as well?"

As children talked, I distributed small copies of a revised version of a chart they knew from the fourth grade.

Ask students to share their writing about reading with the person beside them, discussing the story elements they are already thinking and writing about, and setting goals for those they'll work to think about more.

"Work with your partner to identify a story element that you haven't been thinking deeply about. Circle or highlight the element you want to notice more, so thinking about this story element becomes a new part of your goals."

As children worked, I voiced over, "Remember to draw on all you know about good reading when you are writing about your reading. Good reading should inform what you think and write about. That's what reflection and goal-setting are for! Circle those story elements you'll study more closely from this day forward so that you can remember to do the strongest reading work you know how to do." As I watched students put circles and stars around their goals, I took note of the patterns in the classroom so that I could use this data to inform my conferring and small-group work teaching in the days ahead.

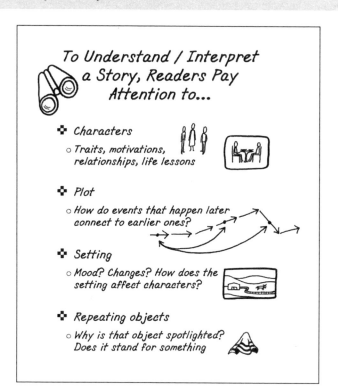

To Understand / Interpret a Story, Readers Pay Attention to...

✤ *Characters*
   ○ *Traits, motivations, relationships, life lessons*

✤ *Plot*
   ○ *How do events that happen later connect to earlier ones?*

✤ *Setting*
   ○ *Mood? Changes? How does the setting affect characters?*

✤ *Repeating objects*
   ○ *Why is that object spotlighted? Does it stand for something*

misses the richness of texts. In your conferring and small-group work, therefore, help students wrestle with those complexities. Prior to this year, when readers generally read books within the N/O/P/Q band of difficulty, their books tended to be defined by one predominate story arc. A protagonist entered the story with an overarching motivation, an enduring want, that was resolved in the end. When readers read within the R/S/T band of text complexity, however, time does not march forward. Subordinate plotlines (such as the backstory in *Home of the Brave* regarding the crisis in Sudan and the uncertain fate of his mother) can end up playing a major role in a story's resolution. In *Home of the Brave*, for example, Ganwar's pessimism and Kek's fear and the loss of his family are all directly related to the civil war in Africa, events that are offstage for the reader, yet influential to the story. The important thing is not that it occurs in this particular book, but rather that this sort of complexity is common in books within the R/S/T band of text difficulty your teaching needs to help readers work with increasingly complex novels. Sometimes this even means seeking out other sources of information—nonfiction texts, articles, and so on—because understanding the back story is so integral to understanding the plot, the characters' experiences, and more.

In Bend II, you will explicitly teach students the qualities of strong interpretive thinking and writing, but chances are, if students are carrying forward their intensive work from fourth grade, you'll see these qualities reflected in students' writing even now. Become familiar with the kind of thinking you hope students are doing by studying two things: the bands of text complexity and the Narrative Reading Learning Progression for fifth grade. After you study the fifth-grade expectations for students' work with characters, for example, then you will know to congratulate kids when you see them mulling over relationships between characters, exploring minor characters, understanding that characters are multifaceted, or considering the effect setting has on characters and their experiences. By showcasing kids who do this important work, you'll encourage more to do the same.

The way you word your responses to your students' work can further influence their understanding of what strong writing about reading entails. Think of the impact of a note such as this: "This entry blows me away! You are remembering that secondary characters are important to a story and have begun to consider their roles in your text." Or consider the message you send with this note: "I love that you have asked deep questions—and that you try to answer them. I like that you have a few possible answers and then vote on them . . . I can see your thinking in your writing."

If you find that students need more support with this work, look back at Grade 4 Unit 1 *Interpreting Characters: The Heart of the Story* and Grade 4 Unit 4 *Historical Fiction Clubs* to inform yourself (so you can remind readers) of the work they did in prior years. You may model this work in your read-aloud, as well, writing and thinking aloud for students in the ways you hope they will do on their own, while reading independently.

I updated the anchor chart to reflect our new work and asked the students to paste their new story element chart into their reader's notebooks.

Writing Well About Reading

Read knowing you'll write, seeing more.

Read upcoming text with the ideas you wrote about in mind.

Aim to notice more elements of the story.

Letting One Thought Lead to More

Channel students to rehearse for their writing, selecting one idea to develop from among various ideas.

"Readers, can I stop you? In a moment, you are going to write about your reading. Before you do, look back over what you have read so far in the book—not just what you read today, but the whole book—and think, 'What are my most important ideas?' List those ideas across your fingers." I allowed a few moments of silence for this thinking. Nudging their thinking along, I said, "Now think: 'Which of those ideas is most interesting to you right now?' Say that idea to yourself, in your own mind." Again, I let them do this.

Channel students to write, aiming to go on a journey of thought, writing their way toward new insights on their chosen topic.

"Now write about this idea. But here is the thing. After you record your first thought, try to go from that first thought to a second thought about that same topic." I gave students time to write.

"Readers, if you look back over your writing about reading, can you see that you started writing with one idea in mind . . . and now you have new ideas? If so, will you decorate the new idea? Box the new thinking or star it." The children did this.

Talking (and Writing) to Grow New Ideas

- "When I first read this, I thought . . . but now, after thinking more, I am realizing that . . ."
- "As we talk, I'm realizing . . ."
- "The thing I'm puzzled about is . . ."

"Fifth-graders, for today, will you work in partnerships, and for today talk only about Partner 1's thinking (another day, we'll switch). Use one of these thought prompts or a point from the anchor chart, if they will help. By the way, I added a new point to our anchor chart."

Talking (and Writing) to Grow New Ideas

- "When I first read this, I thought... but now, after thinking more, I am realizing..."
- "As we talk, I'm realizing..."
- "The thing I'm puzzled about is..."

Writing Well about Reading

- Read knowing you'll write, seeing more.
- Read upcoming text with the ideas you wrote about in mind.
- Aim to notice more elements of the story.
- **Push yourself to grow new ideas.**

Push yourself to grow new ideas.

 THINK ABOUT YOUR OWN WRITING ABOUT READING— AND FIGURE OUT WHAT YOU CAN DO BETTER

Readers, earlier today you set goals for your writing about reading. Specifically, you thought back over the things you've learned about story elements and set goals for the elements you'd like to pay more attention to while reading. Be sure to take your goals home with you tonight. As you read, see if you can push yourself to think and write about some new topics. If you've been thinking a lot about character, consider shifting to a study of plot in your story, or of the setting. The "To Understand/Interpret a Story . . ." chart you marked up today will help remind you of the kinds of things that are worth paying close attention to. I can't wait to see your new entries tomorrow!

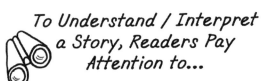

To Understand / Interpret a Story, Readers Pay Attention to...

- ✚ Characters
  - ○ Traits, motivations, relationships, life lessons

- ✚ Plot
  - ○ How do events that happen later connect to earlier ones?

- ✚ Setting
  - ○ Mood? Changes? How does the setting affect characters?

- ✚ Repeating objects
  - ○ Why is that object spotlighted? Does it stand for something

Grounding Your Thinking in the Text and Carrying It with You as You Read On

THIS SESSION picks up on a theme that has threaded through the entire series. It is important for students to learn the need to "cite evidence" that supports their ideas. The Common Core has heightened everyone's awareness of the importance of evidence. In many schools, students no sooner write or say a thought, than they think, almost as a knee-jerk reaction, "One example of this is. . . ." Typically, such a student adds the phrase, "for instance" to whatever he or she has said, and then retells a portion of the text that supports the generalization.

This session allows you to address the most obvious problems with this way of using evidence. You will help students know that a close attentiveness to the text must be part of the process of developing ideas and not something they do once they've settled on an idea. The goal is not actually for students to find some bit of the text that can validate their ideas—it is, instead, for them to grow ideas that are grounded in the precise specifics of the text.

You can't expect your students to give extremely close, word-based attention to an entire novel—no one could do that—so you'll let them know that after they generate ideas and questions as they read and home in on something worth developing, it pays off to locate particular passages that are relevant to the ideas under play, and to reread those passages extremely closely. Point out that it's when a person *rereads* a book that his or her thinking deepens. The important thing is that the work with particular passages happens when students' ideas are still under development, allowing their close textual attentiveness to inform their thinking.

Then, too, you'll teach readers that it is not sufficient to support an idea with a quick summary of an event, of the relevant portion of the plot. Instead, readers need to notice the actual words an author has used, the craft choices the author has made, noticing what the author did do and did not do, mining those very particular choices for their implications.

You do this work by convening students to think closely about the book that is threading through the unit, and then send them off to develop grounded ideas about their own novels.

IN THIS SESSION, you'll teach students that once readers find an idea worth developing, they revisit the text with that idea as a lens, rereading particular passages that inform the idea, mining them for new insights.

GETTING READY

✔ If using *Home of the Brave* as your demonstration text, read aloud the remainder of "God with a Wet Nose," "Welcome to Minnesota," "Family," pages 14–22, before today's session.

✔ Be ready to distribute flags, Post-its, and colorful markers, so students can annotate their entries (see Connection).

✔ Prepare to display and add to the anchor chart, "Writing Well about Reading" (see Connection).

✔ If using *Home of the Brave*, be prepared to read aloud excerpts from "Old Words, New Words," page 7, and "Lessons," pages 23–24 (see Teaching and Active Engagement).

✔ Prepare chart, "To Develop Ideas, Readers . . ." (see Teaching, and Homework).

✔ Prepare a chart titled "Higher-Level Thought Prompts Referencing the Text" (see Share and Homework).

Grounding Your Thinking in the Text and Carrying It with You as You Read On

CONNECTION

Ask students to give their attention to an entry they have written about their reading, considering its quality. Reference the "Writing Well about Reading" chart to help them annotate their entries.

"Readers, we've been in school for just a week, and already, your writing and thinking about reading have become deeper and more mature. Will you turn to the work you did last night (or that you selected last night as your best) and think about what you have done in this writing? Did you . . . (and I read from the list):

ANCHOR CHART

Writing Well about Reading

- Read knowing you'll write, seeing more.
- Read upcoming text with the ideas you wrote about in mind.
- Aim to notice more elements of the story.
- Push yourself to grow new ideas.
- **Use your own thinking, exploring voice.**

Use your own thinking, exploring voice.

I distributed some flags, Post-its, and colorful markers, so the kids could annotate their entries. "I know you have reread these entries and thought about what works. Do that again now, this time noting especially places where your writing grows new ideas, new thinking, which is one of the goals of this writing. Think about the parts that work—and why they work."

Ask partners to talk about their observations, then share out what you notice, including that they need to rethink the way they use evidence to support their ideas.

I gave the students time to reread, annotate, and jot, and then said, "Talk with your partner about what you notice."

> I think I should revise the idea that Mother and Fern don't have a good realationship because Mother was just worried about Fern thats all.

> I think that the old sheep is very Perswasive. For example she got Templeton to go to the fair and befoe she got him to help charlotte.

FIG. 4–1 One student jots her reflections about *Charlotte's Web*.

I listened to students talk and read their entries over their shoulders. Then I said, "As I listen to you talk and read your writing about reading, I notice that many of you come up with a general idea about a large swatch of the text. Then you put that idea on the page and try to support it by connecting it to something that happened in the story. But many of you don't use that idea to grow new insights or new ideas."

Name the teaching point.

"Today I want to teach you that once readers settle on an idea about a text worth developing, they think, 'Where does this idea live in the text?' Then they reread those selected passages extremely closely, expecting each to be a gold mine of new insights related to their initial idea."

TEACHING

Break the teaching point down into steps. Ask each partnership to work with a second partnership to apply these steps to one of the ideas the class generated about the mentor text.

"To show you what I mean, let's think about this teaching point in steps," I said, pointing to the steps written on chart paper.

To Develop Ideas, Readers . . .

- Read, generating many ideas about the text. Choose one idea to develop.
- Think, "Where does this idea live in the text?" and locate passages where the idea "lives."
- Reread a passage, mining it for new insights about the idea. Repeat with another passage.

"Earlier, we read the section titled 'God with a Wet Nose' aloud, and jotted ideas that dawned on us as we read. Now will you work with your partner and another partnership to home in on one of those ideas about *Home of the Brave* and locate passages where that idea especially lives?"

As the groups worked, I located one group that had settled on ideas that I knew would provide the class with a shared foundation for our upcoming interpretation work. I asked that group to share its thinking with the class, suggesting that for now, the entire class adopt that thinking.

Share out one group's thinking that is especially fruitful, and invite the whole class to try this work on that idea, as you scaffold.

"So class, how about if we take Caleb and Lily's and Yoon and Dominic's idea that Kek is torn between wanting to start a new life in America and longing for his old life in Africa, and then reread a few passages that will inform our thinking?

It can be difficult to convince children to reread a line, let alone a scene. Rereading with a purpose (in this case, to read closely to develop new insights) gives students a reason to go back and study a section of text.

The work of this session is incredibly important. Throughout this unit, you will help students understand that ideas live within texts, weaving and crossing along with the storyline. By asking students to take one idea and go back in search of places in the text that demonstrate that idea, you take the first step toward imparting this important message.

To Develop Ideas, Readers...

- Read, generating many ideas about the text. Choose one idea to develop.
- Think, "Where does this idea live in the text?" and locate passages where the idea 'lives.'
- Reread a passage, mining it for new insights about the idea. Repeat with another passage.

Maybe...!

"Let's reread the first passage together, so you can get guidance from me. Then I'm going to ask you to do similar work with the next passage. This is from the section called 'Old Words, New Words.' Kek is describing his relationship with Dave."

> *We are like a cow and a goat,*
>
> *wanting to be friends*
>
> *but wondering if it*
>
> *can ever be.*

I looked up and said, "How might this passage go with the idea that Kek is torn between his old and new life? Here, I'll assume that Kek is the cow (we've already said that cows are important to him—they remind him of home) and Dave, the goat." I read the passage aloud again, then said, "It's like Kek is acknowledging that he and Dave are from two very different worlds. They want to be friends but wonder if that's even a possibility. That makes me think that Kek likes Dave—he wants to connect—but he's not sure it can happen. Maybe they are just too different?" I let the question linger.

Then I said, "Readers, do you see how I looked at this passage through the lens of the idea that Kek is torn between missing his old life in Africa and wanting to start a new one in America? See how I found a new insight—that Kek isn't sure it's even possible to bridge those two worlds? That's what happens when you ground your thinking in particular passages."

ACTIVE ENGAGEMENT

Invite children to work in partnerships to try this work on a second passage (shown at right). Offer coaching tips and suggest prompts as they talk.

"Your turn to try this. Listen to this next passage. This is from the section called 'Lessons,' when Dave walks Kek through some things he needs to know."

I called out "Turn and talk!" and then walked around the room, listening in as children burst into conversation. Most picked up on the work I'd done in the teaching, adding new insights: Kek sees his world as safer, warmer, simpler. Kek isn't sure he can ever "understand" this new world. Some children remembered the first section of the book, "Snow," and recalled that Kek felt that America was cold and difficult then, too.

As they shared insights, I offered coaching tips and whispered in prompts as needed: "Remember to ground your thinking in the passage. Look at the words on the page. What is Kek doing here?" "Try saying, 'The author could have said . . . but instead she wrote . . .'"

Lessons

Number one, he says,
always lock your door.
Ganwar, show Kek what a key looks like.

In my old home,
my real home,
my father kept us safe.
We had no need for locks.

Number two, he says,
this is a light switch.
He pushes a tiny stick on the wall
and the room turns to night.

In my old home,
my real home, the sun gave us light,
and the stars
watched us sleep.

This thermostat, Dave says,
helps keep you warm.
He pretends to shiver
to paint a picture for his words.

In my old home,
my real home, we were a family,
and our laughter kept us warm.
We didn't need a magic switch
on a wall.

I nod to say yes,
I understand,
but I wonder if I will ever understand,
even if Dave stands here,
pointing and talking
forever.

Debrief. Share the value of using tentative language to understand why an author may have chosen to write passages in particular ways—and to extend an idea.

After a few minutes, I reconvened the group. "Readers, your minds were on fire! When you focused on that one idea through the lens of this passage, you ended up thinking of new things so that the initial idea—which was already big—grew.

"Thumbs up if you found yourselves thinking about the choices the author made as she wrote this part, realizing they were deliberate and wondering why she might have made them." Lots of thumbs went up.

"I thought so. I heard things like 'Could it be that . . .' or "Maybe it was because . . .' It's wise to use tentative language like that because of course, we can never know for sure *why* authors make choices, but we can *speculate*, which helps extend our thinking, our ideas. Thought prompts help us do that."

LINK

Offer students tips to keep in mind as they read on their own.

"All of this thinking and writing about your reading needs to *add onto*, not take away from your reading. As you read today, keep in mind a few things. First, think about the ideas that are already in play around your book—you know those ideas because you just reread the writing you've been doing—and carry them with you. If you think someone is mean on the outside and nice on the inside, read forward thinking, 'Why?' or, 'How will this unfold and change as the book continues?' Expect to continue thinking about ideas that are already important to you, and expect those ideas to change as you read on.

"Next, read, knowing that you'll have time later to reread selected passages in which your ideas live. So flag those passages as you read, knowing you'll come back to some of the flagged parts.

"And finally, when you note the page number on which you'll begin reading in your log, look at the rate at which you've been traveling. You've had four days and four evenings for reading, so most of you should be at something like page 200 by now, at least. If you aren't close to that, step up your reading rate and think about making more time for reading outside of school."

Name these responses even if you don't hear these exact words from students. Once you've articulated the phrases, you can be sure students will use them next time. And you'll be reinforcing the raised level of work to which students aim.

Working with Struggling and Advanced Readers

A S YOU GET TO KNOW the readers in your class, consider the books you might pair them with in Bend II. "Which of these readers can work with *Wringer*? Which of these readers can work with *My Name Is María Isabel*?" you might start asking.

As you begin to have more time to confer and lead small-group work, you'll want to divide your attention between students who could use additional support to apply today's (and other days') teaching and those who are ready for further challenges.

Support students who struggle to carry their ideas with them as they read.

Ask students, "What are you thinking about as you read?" and "Do you have any hunch about what you might write about this chapter?" A reader's responses may suggest that he is not reading with theories in mind, and instead just attending to plot.

Presumably you'll have a group of kids like this, so call them together. You might say, "I've noticed that you'll often have an interesting insight, but when you read on, you seem to leave that insight behind. Remember that being an alert reader means that when you read on, you don't just drop your first big idea in the ditch alongside the road of the story. If you have a hunch that this story is really about the destructive power of peer pressure, then as you read on you should be thinking, 'Yup, there's evidence of my idea!' or 'Wait, my theory is changing now, because I'm starting to think . . .' The ideas you have developed become a lens, and as you continue reading, you view the book through that lens."

Then you might coach children to reread their entries and Post-its and to settle on an idea they could continue to think about as they read on. Suggest they flag any new part of the text that addresses the idea they're using as a lens. After a bit, suggest they discuss what they saw in their text that illustrated, extended, or changed their initial idea. Before ending the group, remind kids that with each upcoming chapter, it is not just the plotline or the chronological timeline that unfolds, but ideas, too.

Challenge students who are ready to read and think in deeper ways.

Meanwhile, you will also have students who seem to be always a step ahead of the rest of the class. They read closely and analytically to see a *lot* in a single passage. You'll want to find ways to challenge them, to deepen their thinking.

One thing you might do is remind students of topics that experienced readers think about. You might remind these readers that authors use setting not only to paint a picture of the world in which a story is set, but also to convey the character's response to that world—and to the events that are unfolding. Sometimes characters' feelings

(continues)

MID-WORKSHOP TEACHING   Setting Up to Reread

"Readers, if you haven't flagged a passage or two that seems especially important and is related to your central ideas about the story, do that now. You needn't reread and think about that passage just yet, but flag it. Later on, this will make looking back at the text much more efficient.

"Also, I notice some of you are coming to the end of a book. Bravo! You have kept up your reading volume while thinking and writing deeply about the ideas in your story. Instead of choosing a brand-new book to read next, will you go back to a book you have read previously, a book you really loved, and begin rereading? I'm suggesting that for two reasons—in a few days, we're going to start a new bend in the unit and I'm going to set up same-book clubs, so you'll need to be ready to start a new book on Monday. Also, it's when you *reread* a book that your thinking becomes especially deep, and that's what we're after.

"Get back to work!"

match the mood of the setting, for example, a character will be sad and meanwhile it is raining outside. Other times, a character feels out of sync with the weather. In *Home of the Brave*, Kek is constantly longing for the warmth and ease of Africa, and this is contrasted with the cold and difficulty of America. Why might that be? What does it help us see or understand as readers?

You could also suggest that this group pay attention to point of view as they read. The main character's point of view is usually the easiest to follow, especially if the story is told in the first person. However, there are other characters, other points of view—and you'll want to encourage these kids to consider those, too, as they read. To illustrate this, you could refer to *Home of the Brave* again. It is told from Kek's point of view, yet a careful reader will realize that other characters' points of view are valuable to understanding Kek and his journey. They might consider Ganwar's response to America, and contrast it with Kek's. Or they could study points of view from Hannah, Dave, or Lou. Considering these different viewpoints will help readers understand the main character and the story in new ways.

As with all small-group teaching, you'll want to give this group a chance to apply this teaching to their independent reading books and to receive a bit of your personalized coaching before you send them off.

Using Higher-Level Thought Prompts

Channel children to use thought prompts that support references to the text.

"Readers, you're ready to look at the way you write about your reading with a critical eye. You're no strangers to thought prompts and how they can help push your thinking. I hear you say and write things like, 'Sarah misses her old life,' and then add, 'For example . . .' or 'I see this when . . .' or 'Another example of this is when . . .'

"Here's the thing: the thought prompts you use should push your work to new levels. When you write ideas about a text or a character without any reference to the text, these thought prompts will help. But once you shift from writing your ideas to referencing specific events in a story, you should use different thought prompts. Look at this," I said, revealing a list of thought prompts:

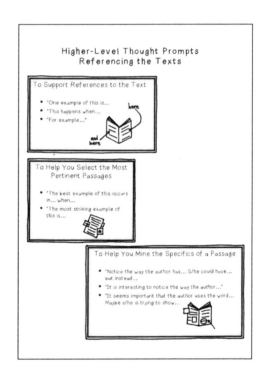

Higher-Level Thought Prompts Referencing the Text

Thought Prompts that Support References to the Text
- One example of this is . . .
- For example, . . .
- This happens when . . .

Thought Prompts that Help You Select the Most Pertinent Passages
- The best example of this occurs in . . . when . . .
- The most striking example of this is . . .

Thought Prompts that Help You Mine the Specifics of a Passage
- Notice the way the author has . . . S/he could have . . . but instead . . .
- It is noteworthy that the author uses the word . . . Perhaps s/he chooses this . . . to show . . .
- It is particularly interesting to notice the way the author . . .

"Right now, will you open up your notebooks to a recent entry and examine what, if any, prompts you've used? In places where you are pushing forward an idea by selecting a pertinent passage (I pointed to that list) or mining specifics of a particular passage (I pointed to that list), see if you've used a prompt from these lists. If not, try one now, and let it lead you to new thinking."

PRACTICE USING THOUGHT PROMPTS TO WRITE ABOUT READING

Readers, tonight for homework, continue reading your independent reading book or the book you chose to reread. As you read, continue the process you worked on today. As you read, refer to the chart you used in class and jot ideas on Post-its or in your notebook. Also, remember to fill in your reading log.

To Develop Ideas, Readers . . .

- Read, generating many ideas about the text. Choose one idea to develop.
- Think, "Where does this idea live in the text?" and locate passages where the idea "lives."
- Reread a passage, mining it for new insights about the idea. Repeat with another passage.

As you read and think and then begin to write about your reading, use familiar thought prompts, such as "I see this when . . ." or "I'm realizing . . ." to push your work to new levels. When you shift from writing down ideas to referring to particular events in a story, turn to the new thought prompts you learned in class today:

Higher-Level Thought Prompts Referencing the Text

<u>Thought Prompts that Support References to the Text</u>
- One example of this is . . .
- For example, . . .
- This happens when . . .

<u>Thought Prompts that Help You Select the Most Pertinent Passages</u>
- The best example of this occurs in . . . when . . .
- The most striking example of this . . .

<u>Thought Prompts that Help You Mine the Specifics of a Passage</u>
- Notice the way the author has . . . S/he could have . . . but instead . . .
- It is noteworthy that the author uses the word . . . Perhaps s/he chooses this . . . to show . . .
- It is particularly interesting to notice the way the author . . .

Whose Story Is This, Anyway?
Considering Perspective and Its Effects

Dear Teachers,

As you promised on Day One, you will continue to spend this bend offering students various strategies they can use to raise the level of their writing about reading, and thus their thinking about reading. Yesterday you introduced your readers to the learning progressions—one set of tools that will prove indispensable when it comes to lifting the level of their thought, talk, and writing about reading. Today, you will teach them another lesson to add to their ever-growing toolbox of strategies: considering perspective.

As students get further into their first books of the year, we think you'll agree that this is an important lesson to teach. All too often, students read through a book with little thought about who the narrator is or whose perspective they are privy to. Not only is it important for students to identify who is speaking, but also to consider the effects this speaker's voice has on the story that is being told. For a moment, consider a story about a sibling rivalry over dinner. Had this story been recounted by one of the feuding sisters, how might that be different than if it were told by their brother? Even if both gave a truthful account of what happened, wouldn't they be apt to emphasize different parts of the conversation? To imbue various words and actions with different emotions? To notice facial expressions or comments that the other may not have? You will want your students to begin considering such questions, even—especially—when the situation is not as cut and dried as the one just described. That is, we all have stories to tell, and the way in which we tell those stories is influenced by our belief systems, our prior knowledge, our feelings, our intentions, and so much more.

MINILESSON

We suggest that you begin your lesson with a story that helps students appreciate the effect perspective can have on the telling of an event, true or fictional. For your connection, you might make reference to post-recess time, when students filter back into the classroom, perhaps seeking your help with an argument that took place during their free playtime. Model telling the same story from two different perspectives: highlighting the ways in which both are true, and how they are different. You might tell students that once you were charged with settling a basketball debate: "I was running down the court and dribbling," you can begin, pretending to be one student, "when suddenly John put his arm out and knocked the basketball from me. He had a look on his face that was mean and it was like he was making fun of the fact that he could steal the ball from me. I didn't think that was very nice because John is supposed to be my friend." Then, tell your students John's perspective. Perhaps John was simply focused on stealing the ball from the other child. Perhaps he had no thoughts about the facial expression he was or wasn't making. "I was just playing ball!" he might say. "My *job* was to steal the ball away from Ryan! I wasn't trying to be mean. Really!"

Quickly shift out of storytelling mode and explain to students that neither child seemed to be lying in this scenario—they just had different perceptions of what happened. You might then explain that the same can be true for the stories they read. Depending on who is telling the story, readers might get a very different version of events. "When reading a book, one of the most important things you want to figure out is who is telling the story. Is it the main character? An unknown narrator?" you might ask. Then, name your teaching point: "Today I want to teach you that readers start a book trying to figure out who the narrator is. Once they figure out whose voice they are hearing, whose perspective they are getting, they keep in mind that every part of the story is told from that character's perspective and that other characters might imagine things differently or have different feelings."

Consider modeling this work by returning in the teaching section to a chapter in their reading and first showing students how you can try to discern who the narrator is, and then model imagining how the story might be different if it were told from another character's point of view. The initial scene in *Home of the Brave* works quite well for this. At first you can act confused, unsure of who is speaking or even what they are doing. On page 4, the narrator is referred to as Kek—your first clue! You might also show students how you had forgotten to preview the text and that going back to read the blurb on the back of the book goes a long way toward helping to clarify what is going on.

Next, you'll want to quickly model the way in which the opening scene might be different if it were told from Dave's point of view. Since he is the one meeting Kek at the airport, perhaps we would be privy to some of his internal thinking as he waits for the plane to arrive. Perhaps Dave is nervous to meet Kek? Maybe he is excited. Show students what this might look like, pretending to be Dave and looking all around the airport, not wanting to miss Kek. Perhaps he is thinking to himself, "Let's just get Kek out of this airport and then I'll be able to explain things a bit more to him." On the other hand, Dave probably wouldn't think twice about the snow or the fact that it is confusing and disorienting for Kek. Snow is a part of Dave's everyday life.

After modeling, for active engagement ask students to open their books and do the same work you just showed them. First, with their partner, they can take turns trying to figure out who the narrator is. In some cases, they may have an unnamed narrator or one whose identity is yet to be revealed.

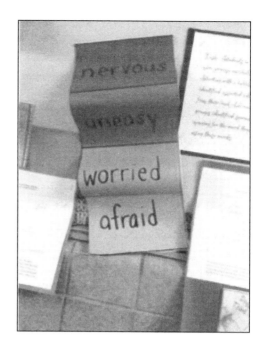

FIG. 5–2

Next, perhaps choosing just one partner, ask students to act out the initial scene in their book, imagining the ways it would be different if it had been told from another character's point of view. Is there information they might get that they don't have access to now? What *wouldn't* they know?

After today's minilesson, you will send students off to continue reading. If you noticed that particular groups of students were unable to figure out who their narrator is, you might create a link by asking them to keep this question in their minds as they read on or keep them on the carpet after the minilesson for extra teaching. For others, remind them that once they identify the narrator of a story, they can always ask, "How might this scene be told differently if it were narrated by someone else?"

CONFERRING AND SMALL-GROUP WORK

At this early stage in the unit, your conferring will still resemble a bit of plate spinning. Hopefully you have finished assessing your readers and they are each holding just-right books. Assuming this is the case, you are ready to pull small groups and conduct conferences based on today's (and the past few days') minilessons. To support today's work, you might consider ways in which students can explore multiple perspectives in their reading notebooks. Perhaps they find a scene that is particularly interesting or where there would be a range of perspectives on an event. Encourage the students to mark this scene and then do something with it. Might they make a T-chart, mapping out one character's perspective versus another's? Reread and then reenact the scene as two different characters? Or perhaps they want to write a diary entry from the perspective of a character other than the narrator, expressing his or her point of view. You'll want to encourage students to keep this work text-based. That is, it will be all too easy for them to use their imaginations and conjure up a point of view that is different from the narrator's. A little imagining, or inferring, is not a bad thing, but if they are claiming that another character would be angry, or disturbed, or otherwise, they need text evidence which shows that character is the kind of person who would react in that way. So while you are asking students to imagine what *is not* in the text, you'll still want to make sure they stick *close to* the text.

You may also find it helpful to consult the Narrative Reading Learning Progression. In the "Analyzing Perspective" strand you'll find that fifth-graders are not only held accountable for identifying the speaker in a text, but also for understanding that the narrator's perspective is only one point of view. To establish a true understanding of a story, it is important for readers to take into account the multiple perspectives that might exist. As students' thinking becomes more analytical, it will become important for them to recognize that authors make choices (such as who will narrate a story) on purpose, and that these choices affect the way readers understand a series of events.

Mid–Workshop Teaching

For today's Mid-Workshop Teaching, we recommend calling for students' attention and then sharing a few helpful tips for figuring out who is narrating a story. You'll probably find that many students are still not previewing a book before reading it. Remind students that often an unnamed narrator is introduced in the back blurb of the book. In other cases, the cover photo or title can give us clues as to the identity of the main character (who may also be the narrator). You might also mention that sometimes a narrator has not been identified. That is, stories can be told in the third person in which an unknown person tells about a series of events. In this case, most often the narrator does not have much of a stake in the story or how it is told. Finally, you might tell the students that they can ask, "Whose voice am I hearing? Whose story am I learning about?" as a way to get closer to understanding the perspective of a text. Even if a story is told by an unnamed, third-person narrator, he or she may focus more on one character's experiences and feelings than on another's. You'll want to teach your children that as readers this is an important point to notice.

SHARE

It is important for students to understand concepts such as "perspective," but also to understand that the same concept (or item, or type of character, etc.) can be represented by several synonyms. (Familiarity with a variety of terms becomes especially important in high-stakes testing, where a student may know the word *sad*, but be given an answer choice like *depressed* or *mournful*.) As much as possible, you'll want to build students' vocabulary around literary terms. You might start by explaining that words frequently have multiple meanings. For instance, the word *alien* can mean someone from outer space, but it can also mean someone who is foreign to a country. Then tell children that often people, including test-makers, will use multiple terms interchangeably. Even if they don't mean the exact same thing, it is important for students to be on the lookout for words that are similar. *Perspective*, for instance, does not mean the exact same thing as *point of view* but they are often used interchangeably. Consider starting a word bank with students to collect words that have the same *shades of meaning*, like *perspective* and *point of view*. You'll want to add to the list as the year progresses and help students to use these words in conversation as much as possible. The more you incorporate these words into the everyday language of your classroom, the more students will remember their meanings!

Yours,
Lucy and Ali

Learning to Think Analytically

IN THIS SESSION, you'll teach children that to think analytically, a person often thinks about how a subject or text is structured and divides sections into parts, then selects, ranks, and compares. This kind of analytical thinking often yields new insights.

GETTING READY

✔ If using *Home of the Brave* as your demonstration text, read aloud the remainder of "Good-Byes," "Father," "Bed," and "Brother," pages 25–38, before today's session.

✔ Display and add to chart, "To Develop Ideas, Readers . . ." (see Teaching).

✔ Prepare chart, "Questions that Can Help You Think Analytically" (see Active Engagement and Homework).

WHEN YOU ASK YOUR STUDENTS to jot about reading, some will produce ideas that dazzle you. But many will write responses that feel entirely different—naming favorite parts, commenting on a character's outfit or action, spouting off a few vague questions.

It will almost seem as if the two groups of kids are operating under different marching orders—and indeed, that is the truth. Kids in the first group tend to think analytically, and they take the invitation to write (or talk) about a text as an invitation to think analytically. Members of the second group are people who don't yet have experience thinking analytically, and therefore don't initiate that sort of thinking. They don't even know that analytic thinking is what you are calling for. As a result, when you ask them to jot or talk about a text, they tend to restate, respond emotionally, free associate, comment, note preferences.

This minilesson is one effort to let that second group of kids in on the secret. When asked to read or write about a text, they should understand they are being asked to think analytically. And doing so is a choice anyone can make. Then too, when you study our learning progressions in categories like "Determining Themes," you'll see that analytical thinking (specifically, the ability to rank and weigh evidence in support of an idea) becomes increasingly important in the fifth- and sixth-grade years. The ability to connect parts to the whole of the text is also an important skill for synthesizing within a text and monitoring for sense.

Analytic thinking could involve taking a subject (say, a book) and partitioning it, or it could involve selecting or ranking based on some criterion, or it could involve comparing (identifying similarities or differences). There are other habits of mind that constitute analytic thinking, but if the youngsters who are now commenting on texts or stating preferences or making loose connections began to do just this short list of mental operations, their writing and talking about reading would become vastly more potent.

In this session, you make kids aware that the invitation to jot or talk about a text is an invitation to do this sort of mental work.

Learning to Think Analytically

CONNECTION

Ask children to jot their thoughts about reading workshop. Then liken doing this to reading, explaining that thinking deeply, analytically is a choice.

"I'm going to ask you to do something that might seem silly—but trust me. Will you think about reading workshop and jot your thoughts down? Do that quickly."

Students did this, and then I said, "Readers, here's the thing. You can look at this classroom in a dazed, zombie-like way, or you can look at this classroom with your brain turned on full power. And the same is true of reading. I think you all realize that there is a world of difference between flying through the pages in a mindless sort of a way and really thinking deeply and acutely as you read.

"To live with your brain turned on full power, you need to choose to think analytically. And that is a choice you can make."

Notice the invitation to take part in this work. There is nothing accidental about this. In the beginning of this minilesson we hope to build up the importance of this work, suggesting it is not for the weak of heart, and then ask children to consider whether they have what it takes to do it. Of course we know they do, but we also know that their investment in the day's work is essential to its success.

❖ **Name the teaching point.**

"Today I want to teach you that to think analytically, a person divides into parts, then selects, ranks, and compares. A person can decide, 'I'm going to try thinking . . .' and then think in any one of those ways . . . and then see if that thinking yields new insights. Often it will."

TEACHING

Channel children to think about reading and writing workshop analytically, first by considering parts, then by selecting and ranking, then by comparing—and to jot their thoughts about each.

"Let's first think about reading workshop analytically. Then I'll help you think that way about *Home of the Brave* and about every book you ever read. One way to think analytically is to take a subject (say, the reading workshop) and to think about the parts of that subject. How could you divide up the reading workshop into parts and how does thinking about parts help you come to new ideas about the reading workshop? Jot your thinking."

I start this work in the classroom, thinking analytically about school, in order to take what might be perceived as abstract, complicated work and make it tangible for students. The work is still demanding, but helping students to understand it within the context of their everyday lives takes some of the mystery out of it.

As students worked, I voiced over, aiming to show them the power of this simple invitation. "I'm noticing that some of you are thinking about the reading workshop in three parts; whole group, small group, individual. Some are thinking of it in two ways; parts that are the same as last year and parts that are different from last year. Right now, try other ways to think about the reading workshop in parts."

After a bit I said, "You can also think analytically by making selections and by ranking (those two can go together). To think that way, to select and rank, will you try thinking about the parts of reading workshop that help your reading the most? Next most? The least? Or try this: which are the parts of reading workshop that you think I believe are the most helpful? Least helpful? Jot your thoughts for just a second and then I'll ask you to share."

After a minute I said, "Talk to your partner or get with another partnership if you want, and talk about the reading workshop—talking analytically. Talk about parts, ranks, and selections." The room erupted into conversation.

"Readers," I called, trying to quell the conversation long enough to insert new directions into it. "Keep talking, but this time, will you think analytically by thinking in comparisons? Listen carefully before you resume your talking. What will you compare? The parts of reading workshop with the parts of writing workshop? What's the same, what's different? Or will you compare what happens in one part of reading with what happens in another part? What are the similarities and differences between minilessons and small-group instruction? Between the reading workshop when we are reading fiction and when we are reading nonfiction? Again, turn and talk analytically."

After children did this, I reminded them that at the start of today's minilesson, I asked them to think about the reading workshop. How did they think then, when that was the charge given, and how does that compare with the thinking they were doing now, when I channeled them to think about parts, to rank and select, to compare and contrast? "My point," I said, "is that you may not realize that some people, whenever they are asked to turn and talk or to jot about their reading, are pushing themselves to think analytically . . . and some are just saying any ol' thing that comes to mind. The choice is yours—and the choice you make is everything."

I added a new bullet to our chart:

To Develop Ideas, Readers . . .

- Read, generating many ideas about the text. Choose one idea to develop.
- Think, "Where does this idea live in the text?" and locate passages where the idea "lives."
- Reread a passage, mining it for new insights about the idea. Repeat with another passage.
- **Think analytically: dividing the subject into parts, selecting, ranking, comparing.**

Notice that I repeat the phrase 'turn and talk analytically.' In my attempts to help all students feel capable of this work, I show them that the work they are doing as they are turning and talking about various elements of the classroom is indeed analysis.

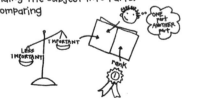

To Develop Ideas, Readers...

- Read, generating many ideas about the text. Choose one idea to develop.

- Think, "where does this idea live in the text?" and locate passages where the idea 'lives.'

- Reread a passage, mining it for new insights about the idea. Repeat with another passage.

- Think analytically: dividing the subject into parts, selecting, ranking, comparing

ACTIVE ENGAGEMENT

Ask children to now think analytically about their reading.

"You know, of course, that my real goal is to lift the level of your writing and thinking about your independent reading books. Let's practice thinking analytically about *Home of the Brave*. First, make a plan. You might say, 'I'm going to think . . .' and then decide: will you divide into parts, select, rank, or compare?"

I asked students who chose to think about parts to raise their hands. "If you are thinking about parts, how will you divide the book up? You might ask, 'What are the big, important parts of the book so far?' Or 'What have been the important parts of Kek's experience?'

"Raise your hand if you'll be selecting and ranking. You might be asking questions like, 'What passage *best* represents Kek's feelings?' Or, 'What evidence tells us the *most* about Kek's life before he moved?'

"Who will be comparing?" I asked. "To think comparatively you'll want to think of two things you can compare. They might be people, parts, settings, relationships, reactions, anything! For example, you might ask, 'How does Kek's relationship with his brother compare with his relationship with Ganwar?'"

I left those questions, generalized so that they could apply to any book, hanging on the easel.

I ask students to raise their hands so that I can make sure each student has made a choice. This also ensures that they are listening when I give them their tips for the thinking they might do.

Questions that Can Help You Think Analytically

Divide into parts
- What are the important parts or scenes?
- How does this part fit into the book as a whole?

Rank
- What passage best represents . . . ?
- What evidence tells us the most about . . . ?

Compare
- How does . . . compare with . . . ?
- How does . . . when he was . . . compare with . . . now?

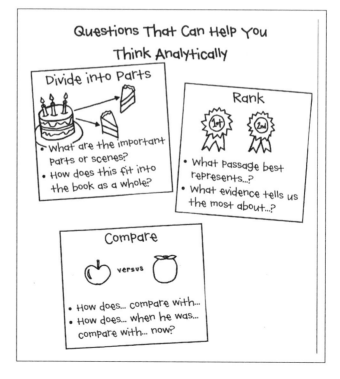

I gave children time to think and write. After they had written for a few minutes, I said, "I know I just threw a lot of suggestions at you. The truth is that when you think analytically, you'll often use some combination of these ways of thinking about the text . . . and sometimes one or another will fit your thinking best.

"Quickly, turn and tell your partner about the thinking you just did, naming which kind of thinking helped you to develop new ideas."

I listened in as Caleb shared his thinking with his partner, "I think the important parts are Kek's life in America and his life back at home. Because we keep getting the scenes where Kek remembers his old life, it gives us more information about how strange and different his new life is. It's almost like remembering his old life makes his new life harder." I gave him a thumbs up and moved on to another partnership.

"Kek knew that even if his brother scolded, he would fool around with him, too," Ben was telling his partner. "His brother wanted to make him laugh. With Ganwar, though, he never knows where he stands. He doesn't know if Ganwar means what he says, even when it's something nice."

LINK

Channel students to think analytically about their own books.

"Readers, the thinking work you've done today isn't easy, but you've pushed yourself to think in new ways and it's led you to bigger, deeper ideas. As you head off to your independent reading, make sure you take these analytic ways of thinking with you. Try them out in your books to see which strategy best fits your thinking: dividing into parts, selecting and ranking, or comparing—or maybe a combination!" I gestured to our chart, "To Develop Ideas, Readers . . . ."

"Take a minute, right now, to decide which type of thinking you'll try out in your book today." Just as I had with *Home of the Brave*, I asked students to raise their hand to indicate their decision, letting me know their plan. I took note of what students chose, so that I could follow up with them later.

"And remember that each time you begin to write about your reading, it's an invitation for you to think analytically, rather than jotting down any old idea that pops into your mind."

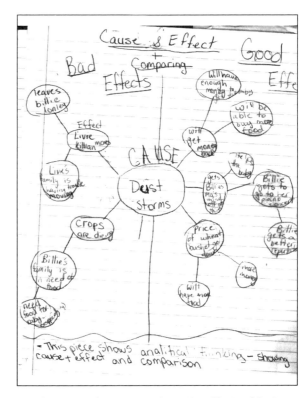

FIG. 6–1   A student writes about the effects of dust storms in *Out of the Dust,* while categorizing the effects as good versus bad.

Fostering Transfer of Analytic Thinking

THIS IS LIKELY TO BE NEW, challenging work for some students. They will need your support in applying this new work to their independent reading. You may begin today by taking a few moments to research, noticing what work students take up. Then, to move this work forward, you might hold table conferences or give table compliments—highlighting the work that one student is doing and sharing it with others. You may even want to rearrange your students for the day, inviting students who are ranking to sit together, those who are comparing to sit together, and so on. This will make it easier for you to give them tips, as well as for readers to rely on each other for help.

Lead a small group to help readers construct meaning out of the many pieces that comprise a book.

I called over a group of readers who joined me on the rug with books in hand. Denise was reading *Bridge to Terabithia*, Katie was reading *Journey*, Emma was reading *Baby*, and Lily was reading *Because of Winn-Dixie*. I started off, "Readers, thanks for joining me. The books you're reading are perfect for the work we are doing! As you've been ranking, categorizing, and comparing, you might have found that there are some parts that you're not exactly sure about. Some parts of your books might seem a bit challenging." The girls agreed that their books definitely had confusing parts.

"And it is not confusing *words*, is it, so much as confusing *parts*—chapters or whole passages." I gestured to one of the italic interludes in *Baby*. "Here's a secret. Even if you were the world's smartest person, those sections would still be confusing—because they are meant to be! Books at these levels of text difficulty—books labeled R and beyond—are *meant* to make you do a lot of work! Earlier, when a book didn't make sense, you sometimes figured it must be too hard for you. But now, keep in mind that some parts of books are supposed to be confusing. Reading can be like puzzles with many pieces that you are supposed to click into place." I mimed picking up a

piece, looking carefully at it, turning it, then fitting it into the growing puzzle. "Have you ever put together a really hard puzzle?" I asked.

The children talked. Some had, some hadn't, but they all had an image of what constructing a puzzle entailed. Lily said, "Sometimes I sit with one little piece thinking, 'Where does this go? Here? Here?'"

I agreed with Lily. "Same here! But if I can't connect or fit a puzzle piece, I don't throw it away entirely. Do you?" Lily agreed, she kept it to the side. "Most puzzlers keep the hard pieces in a special pile. And we keep picking those pieces back up, seeing if we can find where they fit. Eventually, I've done enough of the puzzle so I can snap all the pieces into place." The kids nodded at my puzzle analogy.

MID-WORKSHOP TEACHING
Readers Think Analytically about Cause and Effect

"Readers, can I stop you for a minute?" I waited until I had everyone's attention. "I hate to stop you when you're all reading so intently, but I wanted to give you one other way that you might think analytically about your books. Sometimes, thinking about cause and effect in your books can really pay off. When something important or powerful happens, you might pause and think, 'Why?' And that one little word can lead you to think back across the story and connect the events or factors that led up to something big happening. When you push yourself to think about why something happened, it can help you to grow stronger ideas about why your characters are acting and responding in a certain way, or about how parts of the book are connected. The connections you're able to find when you look closely might surprise you."

"I'm telling you this because your books will have confusing parts. You might read those parts and think you messed up because they don't make sense to you—but even adults know that sophisticated texts often leave a reader unclear about exactly what is happening or how the part they are reading connects with everything else. So my first tip to you is that it is the reader's job to know the difference between that feeling of 'Oops, I must have missed something' and the kind of confusion that an author wants you to feel, a confusion that makes you think, 'The story is still unfolding. I should keep reading.'

"And my second point is that if there is a confusing part, you will want to think of it as a puzzle piece. Think, 'How might this fit into the rest of the puzzle?' and try one possible way, in your mind, and then another. But then, if the confusing part is like a puzzle piece that just doesn't seem to click into place, put that tricky part to the side like you'd put a tricky piece of a puzzle to the side, and keep reading, thinking, 'Now does that piece fit? Now?' Often it will take many pages—even most of the book—before the tricky puzzle pieces click into place."

I asked them to each take a moment to locate a puzzling part in their own book and then share that part with a partner. I sat next to Emma and Denise so I could hear them. Emma was sharing her thinking, saying, "So, Journey has these sort of memory dream things. See, the author puts them in a different font." She showed Denise the page she was on as an example. Then she continued, "I don't really know what they mean. I don't know why the author keeps going back to them. In the memory, Journey is on his mother's lap. It must be important, because it comes up again and again, but I don't really see why yet. Except for the fact that Journey is missing his mom."

"Emma," I cut in, "it's great how you knew right away what your missing puzzle pieces were. I can tell by the way you say, 'I don't see what this means *yet*,' that you are holding onto your curiosity as you read on and that you are looking for information that will help you snap that puzzle piece into place."

After a few moments, I called for the small group's attention and shared what Emma had said. "Remember, readers, as your books get more and more sophisticated, there will be parts in which the author intends for you to be confused and unclear about what's happening. Emma found that for her, some of those parts seemed to be flashbacks that her main character has from time to time. These tricky structure moments, like jumping around in time, are another thing you'll see more of in level R, S, and T books, and she is so wise to ask, 'Why did the author put these parts here?' Read the puzzling parts very carefully, like you are turning them this way and that in your mind and trying to fit them into the bigger picture. But remember, the answer might not be in that part. It might be in the rest of the book, so ask, 'What might this have to do with the whole message the author is trying to say?' And know that rather than leaving these parts *out* of your writing about reading, they can be some of the richest parts to write about."

Sharing Our Best Work and Learning from Others

Explain to students that they will have the opportunity to create a gallery of their own analytical writing.

Readers, some of you chose one kind of analysis, like ranking, and spent the workshop diving deeply into a study of your text through that one lens. Others chose to jump between one or two types of analysis, often finding that one kind of thinking led to another. For instance, Tobie created a huge timeline in his notebook where he marked the key moments in Gilly Hopkins's life. He's only about halfway through the book, but was able to ask himself questions like: 'How does this part fit with the others? How does it fit with the book as a whole so far?' As he did this, he realized that the major events in Gilly's life can be divided into two *categories*—moments when she is helping herself and moments when she is hurting herself (so far, there are way more of these moments!). What Tobie did, and what I think many of you will begin to do as you continue on with this work, is to realize that one kind of analytical thinking is rarely a dead end. Instead, one kind of thinking often leads you to another, and another, and another.

"For the end of today's workshop, I'd like to give you the opportunity to share the work you did today. Will each of you take a moment and turn to a page in your notebook where you tried some of this new work? If you have several entries or Post-its to choose from, pick one that you are particularly proud of." I gave students a moment to do this.

"Leave that entry open on your desk so that we can do a little gallery walk. Let's each grab a pack of Post-its and something to write with. When I say 'go,' travel to another desk and study the work that another reader has done. Try to wrap your mind around what, exactly, they did as a reader and a thinker. Focus on something you find interesting. Then, jot a few notes to yourself so that you can add this method to your repertoire of ways to think and write deeply about your reading.

"We'll have about five minutes to do this, so I'm hoping that each of you will have the opportunity to study the work of two or three of your classmates. Ready? Go!"

At the end of the workshop, I reminded students to take home the Post-its they jotted during the gallery walk to use for homework.

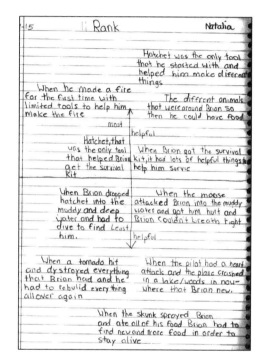

FIG. 6–2 Natalia ranks the events and objects in *Hatchet* from least to most helpful.

PRACTICING ANALYTICAL THINKING

Readers, tonight, continue to think analytically about the books you are reading. Below you'll see a copy of today's chart to help you remember the different ways you might think and write about your reading. You'll also want to refer to the Post-its you jotted during today's gallery walk. They will give you new ideas for the work you can be doing.

Questions that Can Help You Think Analytically

Divide into parts
- What are the important parts or scenes?
- How does this part fit into the book as a whole?

Rank
- What passage best represents . . . ?
- What evidence tells us the most about . . . ?

Compare
- How does . . . compare with . . . ?
- How does . . . when he was . . . compare with . . . now?

One word of caution: we have been studying ways to think and write about our reading, and all of this new learning is incredibly important to your growth as a reader. That said, the volume of reading you do each day is also very important. We can't get better at something if we don't do much of it, right? So tonight, and always, be sure to keep a careful eye on the amount of time you spend reading and the number of pages you read. One rule of thumb that can be helpful is this: for every ten minutes spent reading, you should get through about eight pages of text.

Session 7

Having Second Thoughts

Revising Writing about Reading

I N THIS SESSION, you remind students that for readers, as for writers, revision is an integral part of the meaning-making process.

In writing, you've taught your students that revision means, quite literally, to re-see. You've helped them learn that after writing with abandon, flash-drafting to generate thoughts and to put them onto the page, it is important to pause, step back, and return to those initial thoughts to revise them. Your students have learned, in the writing workshop, that the revision process allows them to take their early thoughts and mold them as a sculptor molds a piece of clay. More importantly, you've helped your students learn that the real work of revision involves not just prettying up or clarifying those initial theories—but rethinking them, seeing new possibilities, finding logical holes that weren't evident earlier, exploring connections that had initially eluded them.

Now you help your students know that revision of reading involves similar work. You'll help your students know that although reading, like writing, requires times when they open the floodgates, progressing with abandon through the text, it is equally as important to stop, step back, and to return to the initial "read" so as to rethink that first draft work.

There are lots of ways for readers to shift from passion-hot to critic-cold, to borrow Ciardi's terms for a meaning maker's shift as that person goes from pulling in to pulling back. This session simply proposes one impetus for doing this. Today, you teach your students that it can be valuable to study the work of another reader, naming out the admirable qualities of that reader's work, and then to return to one's own work, this time ratcheting up the level of it by working under the influence of the mentor text. Students will study one strong piece of writing about reading to name and note the ways they can lift the level of their own.

In the final part of this session, you will teach students that having a partner read their writing about reading with a critical eye can help them revise and improve their writing. Partners can notice parts that are strong and other parts that might benefit from clarifying or expanding thinking or adding evidence.

IN THIS SESSION, you'll remind children that when people aim to improve their writing about reading, they revise their work, relying on examples of what constitutes powerful writing about reading.

GETTING READY

✔ If using *Home of the Brave* as your demonstration text, read aloud the remainder of "TV Machine," "Night," "Mama," "Sleep Story," pages 39–50, before today's session.

✔ Distribute one example of student work, Sam's writing about *Wringer*, to every foursome in the class. Also display a copy of the example so you can demonstrate marking it up (see Teaching and Active Engagement).

✔ Display anchor chart, "Writing Well about Reading," with new bullet point (see Share).

Having Second Thoughts
Revising Writing about Reading

CONNECTION

Remind students that at the start of the unit, they studied examples of effective reading entries, and talked about decreasing the gap between their writing during writing and reading workshop.

"You'll remember at the start of this unit that you studied a few examples of effective writing about reading, annotating those entries and thinking about what constitutes effective writing about reading. That day, we talked about how writing about reading shouldn't feel altogether different than the writing you do about other things—about a day at the carnival, or at your grandma's farm. Whether you are writing about what you did, saw, heard, as a reader or as a friend or as a cousin, you are still trying to capture your experiences, thoughts, observations, memories, musings . . . the works . . . on the page.

"Since we talked, your writing about reading has been much more full of life—and more full of yourself, too. Right now, go back and look at the first writing about reading you did, before we even started this unit, and will you contrast it with the best recent writing about reading you've done. Get ready to talk about whether your work is getting better—and how it is getting better." I gave children a minute to identify the entries they were going to think between and to read them, noting the difference, then asked them to tell each other what they noticed.

They talked while I listened in and took notes, aware that any student who didn't see notable improvements needed to be on my to-do list. Then I interrupted. "Readers, what I am hearing is that even though we haven't been back in school very long, you have already started having that growth spurt as readers that we talked about earlier. You'll remember that I told you at the start of this year that the way for you to become dramatically better as readers this year is for you to work with deliberateness toward specific goals. The goal of lifting the level of your writing about reading is one of those goals that can actually lift the level of your thinking about reading, so it is a big deal."

As mentioned earlier in this unit, there is nothing more empowering to students than to remember that they have control over their growth as learners. No doubt, as students look at their writing about reading from the beginning of the unit through their most current work, they will see progress, which will spur them on to make even more as we enter Bend II.

❖ **Name the teaching point.**

"Today I want to remind you that when aiming to write well about reading, it's important to remember that revision is the most important way to ratchet up the level of your writing. And to revise any text, it helps to have an image of good work in mind. In this instance, it helps to have a sense for what constitutes potent, vital writing about reading."

TEACHING AND ACTIVE ENGAGEMENT

Explain to students that revisiting a piece of writing about reading can help them to see more, and to raise the level of their own writing about reading even further.

"I know you have already been thinking a lot about ways to lift the level of your writing and thinking about your reading. The work we did yesterday—realizing that you can choose to think analytically—can be transformational. But I'm greedy, and I want even more for you as readers and writers about reading. So, let's press on and see how studying examples of potent writing about reading can help you revise your own writing about reading.

By having the class return to the same writing about reading, I avoid the need for students to orient to a new piece of writing and offer them a chance to see more this second time. I have also purposefully chosen a piece that bears the imprints of several of the lessons in this bend. I know there will be plenty for the students to notice.

"I've brought out part of Sam's writing about *Wringer* again, though I know that this time you will be able to see even more in it than you did just a few days ago. Will you again study this writing about reading, and this time, will you flag places where the writer has done something you think you could also try?" I distributed one copy of the student work to every foursome, channeling kids to clump into small groups.

Ask students to read Sam's entry in their groups, sharing what they notice with each other.

"Read this entry with your partners and see what you notice in this bit of writing about reading." I circled the meeting area, voicing over what students noticed so others would be able to notice the same. "You'll want to read it closely," I said. "Ask questions like, 'What has Sam done as a reader here?' 'What about here?' Feel free to jot on your copy of the entry and annotate it with what you are noticing."

I briefly called for the students' attention: "Jared and his group noticed that Sam started with a jot, and then wrote long about it, growing his idea. And Dominic's group noticed that it feels like this writer is writing to discover, not just to prove a point. Nice thinking.

"Emma and her partner noticed that the writer stated his idea, that Beans, Mutto, and Henry have a popular group in the neighborhood, but then gave evidence from the text. Like here, where he writes 'I think this because . . .' or here, where he says, 'For instance . . .'" I said, underlining these phrases on the copy displayed at the front of the room. "But this

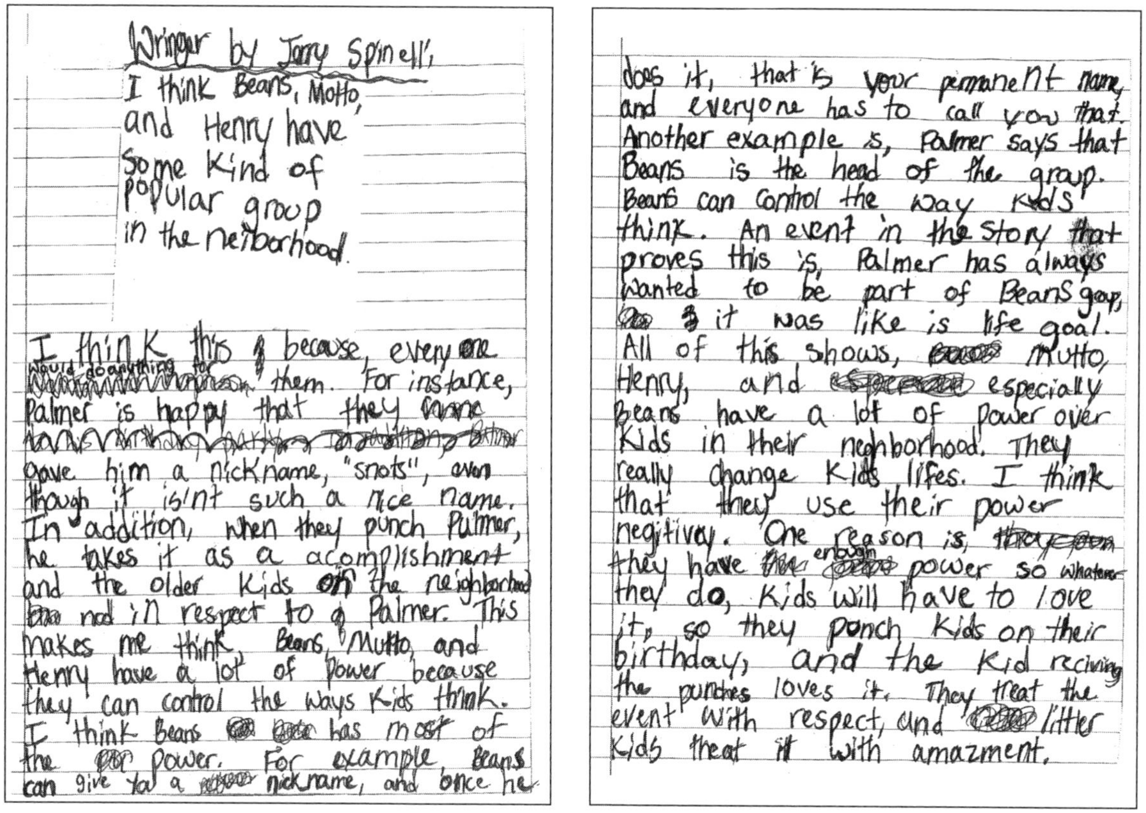
Wringer by Jerry Spinelli

I think Beans, Mutto, and Henry have some kind of popular group in the neiborhood.

I think this because, every one would do anything for them. For instance, Palmer is happy that they gave him a nickname, "snots", even though it isn't such a nice name. In addition, when they punch Palmer, he takes it as a acomplishment and the older kids in the neighborhood nod in respect to Palmer. This makes me think, Beans, Mutto, and Henry have a lot of power because they can control the ways kids think. I think Beans has most of the power. For example, Beans can give you a nickname, and once he does it, that is your permanent name, and everyone has to call you that. Another example is, Palmer says that Beans is the head of the group. Beans can control the way kids think. An event in the story that proves this is, Palmer has always wanted to be part of Beans gop, it was like is life goal. All of this shows, Mutto, Henry, and especially Beans have a lot of power over kids in their neighborhood. They really change kids lifes. I think that they use their power negitivey. One reason is, they have enough power so whatever they do, kids will have to love it, so they punch kids on their birthday, and the kid reciving the punches loves it. They treat the event with respect, and litter kids treat it with amazment.

FIG. 7–1 Sam's writing about *Wringer*

writer didn't stop there, did he? He used another prompt, 'This makes me think . . .' and then 'All of this shows . . .' to grow his idea even further. We know how to do that, don't we?"

I continued to move among the groups, coaching into what they noticed and voicing over key points to ensure the whole class was taking notice of them.

Call the students back together, emphasizing a few more key points.

"Readers, I like how specific and reflective your conversations were. You thought hard about the decisions you can make as a reader. Some of you feel you can raise the level of your entries by using more prompts to extend and challenge your thinking. Others of you realized that you have many ideas, much like Sam, but that you aren't spending enough time thinking about how those ideas connect. Others realized that they have a tendency to write long, thoughtful entries, but that these entries would be stronger if they were grounded in details from the text."

LINK

Channel students to use what they learn from student exemplars when they revise their own writing about reading.

"Readers, today you see how important revision is . . . not just as writers, but as readers, too. One way to revise our writing about reading, our thinking, is by studying the work of other readers and asking, 'What has this reader done that I might try, as well?' Today, as you continue to read and write, will you take some time to revisit some of the writing about reading we studied when we started this unit? This time, try to see more than you did the first time around. See if you can't learn a thing or two from these writers about readers. Then use what you learn to go back and revise the writing about reading you've been doing."

I voice over to help others along. By sharing the work that one or two proficient groups are doing, I set others in motion—giving them ideas for the kinds of things they might be noticing. As you voice over, be sure to especially point out things students have learned to do in this bend (like the use of prompts to extend thinking and add evidence).

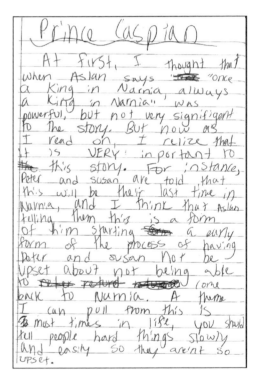

FIG. 7–2 Christopher revisits his intial thinking

Helping Students Find Ideas that Are Worth Exploring

A S YOUR STUDENTS BEGIN their independent work today, ensure that they are taking on the work of big revision. Some children will be intently studying and annotating the mentor pieces, while others will set to work revising their own writing. You can expect, though, that some students will have trouble assessing which ideas feel like bigger ones, spending time revising ideas that won't pay off. If there is a group of children doing this, you'll likely want to work with them together. When I convened Joseph, Deena, and Tyler, I began our work together by saying, "Readers, I called you together today because I noticed that sometimes it can be tricky to decide which ideas are worth pursuing. Remember, you are trying to grow *big* ideas. Let's try something. I'm going to say some ideas about *Home of the Brave*, and I want you show to me with your arms whether the idea is a *big* idea" (I struck an Atlas-like pose with outstretched arms) "or a little one" (I pinched my fingers together).

"Kek doesn't know what snow is." The children pinched their fingers together, and I did as well. "Kek yearns for his old life—he is confused about what has happened and what will happen next." Again I let the children lead and then joined them in signaling that this idea was big. "Kek is nervous to start school." I let children make the small gesture. "Ganwar is unhappy," the children kept their fingers close together. "Kek feels a hole in his life—a hole that was once filled by the love of his mother, father, and brother." The children signaled big. "Kek feels like he didn't appreciate Lual while he had him." Again, the children stretched out their arms.

"Here's a tip. Usually—not always—for an idea to be big, it needs to pertain to more than just one character. So our ideas like 'Kek is nervous to start school,' are important observations, but they will be bigger ideas if you think not only about one character but between the characters. For instance, what role does Ganwar play in his nervousness? Does he help? Or does he make things worse for Kek?

"Let me show you what I mean using another entry of Sam's about *Wringer*. In this bit of writing, Sam is growing his thinking about the main character, Palmer, by examining how the secondary characters, Beans and Dorothy, act toward him. Sam noticed that

Beans makes Palmer do things that Palmer doesn't feel comfortable doing, like leaving a dead muskrat on Dorothy's doorstep. Dorothy, on the other hand, makes Palmer feel safe so Palmer can be who he really is. As a result, Palmer actually acts like a completely different person when he is with Dorothy than when he's with Beans.

MID-WORKSHOP TEACHING POINT
Revisiting Key Parts of the Text to Spur Revision

"As you study the writing about reading around the room, many of you are finding new ways to lift the level of your own reading entries. I can't wait to take a closer look at what you've done at the end of today's workshop! Many of you are realizing, however, that revision is not just about noticing what another reader has done. Once you've noticed something you can improve upon, like gathering more evidence to support an idea or pushing yourself to see new possibilities, you need to take out your books and take a closer look! Let's say you are revising a theory about two characters' relationships. You don't just want to think about it in your head. No way. Instead, open your book to the key scenes where those characters interact, revisit the parts of the text that gave you your initial idea, and use the text to help revise your thinking.

"Apply what you learned in recent minilessons. Do you recall the question, 'Where does this idea live in the text?' You looked for evidence to support your idea—but even more importantly, you mined those relevant passages to develop new insights related to your initial idea. So remember to do that now. Your new insights will help you revise your writing about reading with fresh ideas that are grounded in the details and specifics from the text. You could also continue the analytical thinking that you just did in the previous minilesson. This will result in more powerful writing about reading."

"Then Sam took his thinking to the next level. He asked himself, 'What does this make me realize about Palmer's relationships?' Now as he reads, he's keeping a theory in mind that the way Palmer acts with Beans is that he becomes the person he thinks his father would approve of, and the way Palmer acts with Dorothy is that he becomes the person he wants to be but is afraid of being. Sam used his thinking to make a prediction that Palmer is not going to be a wringer like his dad and like Beans because his relationship with Dorothy is going to help him see who he really wants to be.

"By starting with his thinking about the main character, and then thinking about how other characters treat that character, Sam did some truly amazing work. I'm going to jot a couple of those questions Sam asked himself as he read and thought today. I'm sure that, by using these questions, you can grow some fantastic ideas."

- How do other characters act toward my character?
- How does my character act differently with different characters—and why?
- What am I realizing about my character's relationships?

I asked children to apply these questions to their own books. "Take a minute to look back at the thinking you've been doing about your character and see if you can use these questions to push yourself toward a bigger idea." After a moment or two, I said, "Get with your partner again and share how your thinking is growing as you take other characters into consideration." I motioned toward the questions I had jotted, saying, "You can refer to our questions as you talk."

Bean's makes Palmer do things he's not comfortable with. Dorothy makes him feel safe and he can be himself.

FIG. 7–3

Letting Partner Feedback Spur Our Revisions

Praise students' revision work and give them an opportunity to share it with their partners.

I revealed our anchor chart with today's teaching point added on:

ANCHOR CHART

Writing Well about Reading

- Read knowing you'll write, seeing more.
- Read upcoming text with the ideas you wrote about in mind.
- Aim to notice more elements of the story.
- Push yourself to grow new ideas.
- Use your own thinking, exploring voice.
- **Ratchet up the level of your writing about reading through revision.**

Ratchet up the level of your writing–REVISE!

"You've each been working hard to revise your writing about reading today. Will each of you take a moment to share a bit of the revision work you did with your reading partner? Don't just open the page and show it to them. Take a bit of time to explain what motivated you to change your work and how you went about doing it."

I listened in as students discussed the changes they had made, admiring the flaps, marginal additions, and Post-its they'd used to add and change their ideas.

Explain that partners can be an important part of the revision process.

"We all know that it can be hard to look at our own work and see the places where our thinking doesn't quite add up, or where we'd benefit from adding a bit more evidence or some more of our own thinking. You've done a wonderful job being your own critics, but remember that you also have partners who can help you out. An important part of being a reading partner is giving constructive feedback. This means reading your partner's work with a critic's eye, noticing and naming the parts that are strong, and pointing out the parts that would benefit from a bit of work."

I asked each student to partner-up and sent them off to work together, analyzing each other's work and giving constructive feedback.

At the end of share, I instructed students to take home the feedback from their partner so they could use those tips to work on their homework. I also asked them to take home their club book and the revision they began working on in class.

 ## ACTING AS YOUR OWN CRITIC TO REVISE MORE

Readers, tonight for homework, continue reading in your book to meet your reading goals. (You may be reading your club book or independent reading book.)

When you finish reading, go back to the revision you began in class today about your club book. Refer to the feedback your partner gave you in class. Use this feedback to continue revising your work. Then read over your revised writing with a critical eye. Act as your own partner, your own critic. You may be asking yourself questions like these:

- Is this idea supported by evidence from the text?
- Am I thinking and writing analytically? Am I comparing or pointing out cause and effect?
- I have new insights from my reading. Did I weave them into the ideas in my writing?

If you prefer to work on a different piece of writing, go through a few recent writing about reading entries in your notebook. Choose one that you feel has some interesting ideas, but needs more work. Then apply your partner's feedback, as well as your own critical thinking, and start revising.

Launching Interpretation Book Clubs

IN THIS SESSION, you'll remind students that as readers sharpen their reading and thinking skills, they are able to see more significance in a text and to trust that they notice things for a reason.

GETTING READY

✔ If using *Home of the Brave* as your demonstration text, make sure you have finished Part One of the text (through page 50), before today's session.

✔ To prepare for launching book clubs, think about a rough seating chart for the meeting area and be ready to call kids into sitting in clusters with their club mates. Plan to provision each club for the rest of this unit with books relating to that club's topic and at the appropriate level of text difficulty. You'll need a copy of each book for each member (see Connection, Active Engagement, Conferring and Small-Group Work, and Share).

✔ Prepare to read aloud an excerpt from "Paperwork," pages 53–54, *Home of the Brave* (see Active Engagement).

✔ Prepare to introduce Bend II anchor chart, "Drawing on All You Know to Read Well and Interpret Texts" (see Mid-Workshop Teaching).

✔ Be ready to display chart, "Creating a Constitution for Your Club," and provide copies for each student (see Share).

✔ Provide a club folder to each club to keep its constitution and other club documents (see Share).

T HIS SESSION launches a new bend. For this bend and the one that follows, your students will study interpretation by reading great literature in small book clubs that will last for the rest of this unit. They'll work toward the fifth-grade level of the "Determining Themes" strand of the Narrative Reading Learning Progression. Prior to this session, you will have decided upon the composition of your clubs, bringing four readers together. You will have selected books that merit close interpretive reading, providing each club with multiple copies of a terrific book, one that all club members can read. Ideally, you'll have taken into account some kids' suggestions for club membership, and you'll be able to give each club some choice from among several titles.

Because club members will read and reread a single book in sync during this bend, devoting about a week and a half to it, the choice of text is especially important. (A club of less experienced readers may instead work with a set of two closely linked books, as books at lower levels of text complexity can generally be read within a few days' time.) The important thing, however, is that the club members are excited to work together and have energy for the book you've sent their way. For help with choosing books that merit the sort of close reading this bend calls for, see the online resources for this unit. There you will find a list of book titles that have proven especially rich and engaging during an interpretation unit of study.

By studying the skills and strategies of interpretation while reading, writing, and talking together, club members will come to identify themes that are important in their books, trace the progression of themes as the book progresses, and eventually think *across* books with their clubs. In the final bend of the unit, you will help members of each club read other texts that highlight similar themes, thinking across those books.

For now, however, you'll rally your youngsters to approach the books they'll be reading for the next week or two, expecting to see significance. In this session, you will remind students that reflective readers don't just rush from here to there. Instead, they pause to read important passages closely, expecting to grow ideas about texts and their lives. The work of interpretation is very much a part of what it means to be a reflective human being. This is an especially important message today because your students will begin to read books that you've channeled them toward because these books are especially laden with meaning.

"Readers pause to read important passages attentively, expecting to grow ideas about texts and their lives."

Reading interpretively won't be new for your students, nor will the "Determining Themes" strand of the learning progression, and your intention will be for this session to call forth all that your students already know about this work. Although they'll draw upon some knowledge of interpretation, this is complex and demanding work. The speculations will increase significantly this year. Fifth-graders need to be able to see multiple themes in a story, to select supportive evidence for each, and to see the craft as well as the content of a story as evidence for a theme. Throughout their upcoming school career and again in college, teachers will continue to teach the skills of interpretive reading, adding layers of complexity to this instruction. You'll be given a chance today to watch what your students do when invited to read interpretively, and to tailor your instruction in response.

Launching Interpretation Book Clubs

CONNECTION

Return to the earlier talk about fifth-graders having growth spurts and ask students to think and talk about the changes they've seen in themselves thus far.

"Readers, I will call you to the meeting area in clusters, and these clusters will be your reading clubs. I have a rough seating chart in mind for the meeting area—plan to sit together for today and for the next few weeks both during the minilesson and during reading time. Meanwhile, you and the other club members will be reading a book in sync together, a book that is as rich as *Home of the Brave*. You'll write about that book like before, only you'll also be writing for each other, as well as talking. I know this will help you continue on with the reading growth spurt you've begun.

"Right now, before we get deep into this minilesson and this bend, will you think about times in your life when the chance to read and talk about and study a book with others has helped you get to be a stronger reader?" I left a long moment of silence. "Think about specific things that made that one time of shared reading so valuable." Again I left a stretch of think time. "Remember those times when you and your club begin working together," I said.

Use an anecdote to illustrate the point that one way readers grow is by learning to see more of significance in a book.

"As we start the second bend in the road of this unit, I want to talk about one of the most important ways you can grow as readers. To explain this kind of growth, I want to tell you about a story my friend Mary shares about attending a baseball game with her friend, Jack, who is a huge fan.

"Mary doesn't know *anything* about baseball. This was her first pro game ever, and frankly, it bored her. She phoned me two hours into the game and said, 'This game is soooooo slow! I'm just sitting here, waiting for them to do something. The score is still one to nothing.'

"But Mary told me after the game that at the seventh-inning stretch, Jack had turned to her and said, 'Oh my gosh, this is so exciting—I can't stand it!'

"Naturally Mary looked back at him like this"—and I made a "huh?" look. "Not wanting to confess she found the game totally boring, she asked, 'What's the best part for you?'

The new seating arrangement is a wonderful way to signal that the students are entering a new chapter in the unit. You are giving them a heads-up that expectations are growing. Soon you'll bring out the "Determining Themes" strand of the learning progression, and that also will signal that your expectations are rising.

"Jack went on and on about the pitcher's amazing fastball and the heads-up plays by the shortstop. Then he talked about how the batter who'd just been up always knew which pitches to swing at and when to lay off—and how once he was on base, he'd spotted the perfect moment to steal a base.

"Listening to Jack, Mary realized that because she doesn't know anything about baseball, she hadn't had the eyes to see. She realized that for a baseball expert, everything matters."

Clarify how your anecdote relates to your fifth-graders and their reading.

"I'm telling you this because it is all too easy to read books the way Mary watches baseball games. Younger kids might read the first part of *Home of the Brave* and say, 'Nothing much has happened. It's just about a kid who comes to the United States and likes cows. That's all.' But you are developing the eyes to see *so* much more in a book—and now you can bring those eyes to more books."

Name the teaching point.

"Today I want to teach you that as readers sharpen their reading and thinking skills, they develop the eyes to not only *see more* in a text, but to *make more significance*. They pay more attention as they read because they trust that they notice things for a reason and expect to make something of observations others just pass by."

This could really be the teaching point for the entire bend, the entire book!

TEACHING

Suggest that reading and living interpretively are similar. Help children think of an experience that was saturated with meaning.

"When I talk about seeing more in a book, I'm really talking about reading interpretively. The important thing for you to realize is that *reading* interpretively and *living* interpretively are similar—and you already know what both of these feel like. Let me help you think about a time you lived interpretively."

"Think about a time when you were with someone you really cared about, and you knew this was probably your last time together." I gave them half a minute to scroll through their memories. "Or think about a time you were in a place that really mattered to you, and you knew you were leaving it and just had a minute to see things one last time." Again I left some silence.

"If you can't recall such a time, imagine it. On the last day before your best friend moves away, you share your snacks, like always. But on this day, she opens her bag of chips and . . . what? Maybe the chips fall to the ground and you both laugh, rummaging around for a chip that is safe to eat. They are just potato chips, after all, but whatever happens with those chips, on that day, will seem so huge. It will be like an omen that represents something important about the friendship."

You'll see that the method of this teaching section is not the usual. You talk to the kids more than you demonstrate. You do coach them to do some mental work, so the best term for the method of teaching in this section is "guided practice," but either way, it is unusual.

Liken the experience you've described to reading, referring to books the students know from previous years.

"What I want you to realize is that you are thinking interpretively. Readers do this. Once a book becomes extra meaningful—which usually happens after you pause to ask questions like, 'What's this really about?'—then the little things in the story suddenly become more meaningful. Think back to *Number the Stars*. Do any of you remember the brown leaf that Annemarie finds floating in the sea near Uncle Henrik's house? If you don't, imagine it. Imagine that as those families try to flee the Nazis by sailing across the sea, they see a brown leaf floating. It becomes more than what it first seemed. Interpretive readers think, 'Maybe that leaf has come from across the sea, from Sweden, where Jews are free.'

"Or think, in the same novel, about the Star of David necklace that Annemarie has hidden in a safe place until it is time for her Jewish friend, Ellen, to wear it again—it is not just a necklace that she has hidden. What is it? What does it mean?

"So today, as you read, think about the meanings that you are finding—no, think about the meanings you are *making*. We'll do this work together with the start of the next section of *Home of the Brave* . . ."

ACTIVE ENGAGEMENT

Read more of the read-aloud book, asking kids to listen interpretively, letting the details take on significance. Remind them to draw on what they learned in fourth grade. Then channel readers to join you in reading a passage from the class read-aloud interpretively.

"Readers, we're starting a new bend in our unit. We are also starting serious work with the "Determining Themes" strand of the learning progression." I guestured toward an enlarged copy of it. "And we are beginning a new part in *Home of the Brave*. Later, you'll start your club books, too. So right now, we're working with beginnings, and beginnings are always ripe for interpretation. To get ready to listen and talk, position yourselves so you are facing your club mates. Members of each club will probably want to make yourselves into a little circle." I waited for them to do this.

"I'll be reading the beginning of Part Two, *Home of the Brave*. The African proverb that opens the part goes like this:

> *You only make a bridge where there is a river.*
>
> *—African Proverb*

"Whoa." I reread it. Then I read on:

> **Paperwork**
>
> *Dave comes for me the next day.*
>
> *He has snow in his eyebrows.*
>
> *We drive in the red rattling car*

In the fourth-grade Unit 4 Historical Fiction Clubs, *children read* Number the Stars—*so this reference is to that book. If your kids didn't read that book, you'll make other associations. The bacon that is cooked in the first chapter of* Charlotte's Web *is bacon for a reason. Meanwhile the main event of that chapter revolves around whether the runt of the pig litter will be allowed to live. Or will he become bacon?*

to a new place.

Refugee Resettlement Center, Dave calls it.

It's warm there,

with many chairs

and many more people,

all colors and shapes.

It's my job to answer

a bored lady's questions.

Her fingers bounce on

a machine with many buttons

while she stares at a bright box.

Her fingernails are shiny red,

the color of blood,

and I feel sorry

for her bad fortune.

I lowered the book, then said, "Clubs, you'll need to decide how to talk and listen so that everyone feels heard. Ready?" The children nodded yes. "Get ready to talk about the beginning of this new part of the book. What are the 'floating leaves' kind of detail that you see in this passage—details that others might miss but you notice, because you are reading interpretively?"

As children shared ideas, I circled the room, reminding them of rules of club conversation etiquette—to listen attentively while someone talked, to build off the talk before offering a new idea altogether. I also took note of what they were saying, using this to assess the level of their interpretive skills at this juncture in the unit.

I listened in as Caleb and Lily's club spoke. "I notice that Kek sees *everything*," began Lily. "He notices the snow on Dave's eyebrows and all the colors and shapes of the people."

I prompted them to think more deeply. "How does this connect to what we've noticed about Kek before?"

"It's like he's a little kid who doesn't know the names for anything. Like instead of saying that he sees a woman typing on a computer, he says that her fingers bounce on the machine with buttons," said Jonas.

Caleb chimed in, "Yeah, but I can't tell if this is scary for him or if he is okay. He acts pretty brave."

As students talk, take this opportunity to notice the level of interpretive work they are doing on their own. For instance, a student who simply notices that Kek has arrived at a Resettlement Center might benefit from some teaching around the kinds of things worth paying attention to. A student who notes Kek's intuitiveness (noticing that the lady is bored, for instance) or the way he is drawn to the shiny red nails as a symbol of blood will be well primed for the lessons that follow. Know, too, that continuing to do this work in book clubs will exponentially increase the work students are able to do.

"And he even feels bad about the lady with the red nails," added Lily. "He says they are like blood. I wonder if they remind him of the blood in Africa, like that woman he sees in his dream with the dress that is covered in blood. But Kek doesn't talk about that. He just feels bad for the woman with the red nails."

LINK

Channel students to transfer the reading, thinking, and writing they've been doing with the read-aloud text to their own club texts and independent reading books.

"You are seeing so much in *Home of the Brave*! Your hard work in writing about reading has made each of you into an extra-alert reader, thinker, writer. So the challenge will be to read your own books with the same alertness and eagerness you've brought to this book," and I tapped *Home of the Brave*.

"Club members, talk for a moment about your plans for reading today. Choose a stopping spot for your reading. If some of you reach that spot earlier, and some of you will, then that person rereads and jots to prepare for talking."

"As you begin your new books today, remember that beginnings are often chock-full of meaning. These are complex books, and a lot of your mental work today will involve getting to know the characters, setting, and plot. But remember to also read closely, interpretively. The challenge is for you to see, and to make, significance. Take notice of those brown leaves instead of letting them float by you."

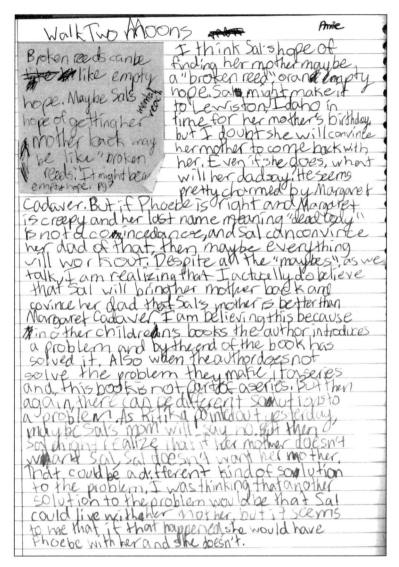

FIG. 8–1   Annie writes to see more in her independent book, *Walk Two Moons*.

Using Guided Reading, Scaffold Readers to Move Up a Notch

AT THE START OF ANY NEW BEND, there are a few things you must do. First, be sure that with the emphasis on new work, readers don't forget to use what they have learned so far. Then, you need to race around the room, recruiting kids' energy for the new work. And finally, the start of a new bend—especially one that launches new books and kicks off book clubs—gives you an opportunity to support a group of readers to move toward a level of text difficulty that is a bit of a stretch.

In tomorrow's session, we'll describe ways to get this new bend's work underway, while also reminding readers to continue doing what they already know how to do. For now, we want to emphasize that this is a golden opportunity to help members of at least one club tackle a book that is a notch harder than the texts they've been reading on their own. You might start by reading the "Understanding Bands of Text Complexity" chapter in *Reading Pathways*.

In your guided reading session, start with a book introduction, providing enough of the plotline so that as kids read parts of the book, they can hang what they learn onto what they know about the overall plot. To craft a book introduction, it often works to think about the story elements, perhaps using the template: Someone wanted . . . , but . . . , and so . . .

In addition to summarizing the text, it can help to point out genre characteristics, reminding readers of the implications for their reading. For example, for a historical fiction book, you might tell readers, "You already know about how historical fiction texts usually go and what this means for your reading." The setting is important in this genre. Also, when the story begins, trouble is often brewing. Readers should try to understand the conflicting forces behind that trouble and to consider how different characters react. Do these differences come only from characters' personalities, or do the differences also reflect the characters' race, social group, age, job, or economic status?

You may also want to point out some new challenges for readers now that they are reading more difficult books. You might say, "It used to be that the setting was presented in the first chapter. Now the setting, like the characters, unfolds across the whole book."

A book introduction should last only last two or three minutes, and then you'll want to channel readers to start reading. As children read, you can circle from one to the next, tapping on shoulders to signal, "Read a bit to me" or "Tell me what you are thinking." You will coach into their work, lifting the level with lean prompts. You might say, "Tell me about the characters and what you've learned about them so far." Or you might ask a question to check comprehension: "Why do you think he's so mad?" Both of these ways of talking about the text will give you a window into a reader's ability to make meaning.

As you listen to readers, think of ways they need help. You may decide that though it is great for readers to read interpretively, they first need to collect information about the characters and the setting. Readers may need to pause to recollect all they have learned, making sure they are grasping what they read. If the text is passing by undigested, have readers pause to reread more alertly and think as they read.

Keep in mind that a little bit of talk can make a big difference when done at the start of the book. So you may ask readers to pause to resurrect the text together. Point out that as they read on, their club should set stopping points. When club members reach that point, the rule of thumb is that the reader pauses till others catch up, thereby allowing them to support each other's retelling of the text.

"Readers, you are still taking in a lot of information and tacking the details of the book up onto your mental bulletin boards. But remember, you don't need to *wait* to interpret. You aren't reading this book like Mary watched that baseball game, waiting for the plotline to unfold. Just as Jack knew enough to see significance in the little things about baseball, you know enough about how stories go to see little things as significant. Read alertly to see what stands out, realizing the author probably made those things stand out on purpose. Maybe there is something quirky about the setting or a character—think, 'What could this signify?' 'Why is this here?'

"Do you spot a recurring object, a repeated line? Mark it and plan to talk about it. Remember that especially at the start of a book, everything matters. If you sped through the first part, trying to understand the plot and get acquainted with the characters, go back and reread. You'll want to be ready to bring *something*—just a simple thought or a seedling idea—to your club conversation.

"I started an anchor chart for Bend II with this bullet point," I said, gesturing toward the new chart. "Remember that you already know so much about how to be strong readers, so draw on that knowledge as you do the work of this bend and this unit. In your upcoming club work, you will also draw on the knowledge and ideas of others."

ANCHOR CHART

Drawing on All You Know to
Read Well and Interpret Texts

- Read alertly to notice what stands out and find the meaning in specific details.

Drawing on All You Know to Read Well & Interpret Texts

Read alertly.

See details as meaningful.

Setting Up Book Clubs

Ask students to meet in clubs and to construct a shared "constitution," club name, and more.

"From earlier work in clubs, you understand the power of club work. Last year, when you launched your Historical Fiction book clubs, your teacher reminded you that our nation was formed by an elite club of sorts. Thomas Jefferson, Ben Franklin, John Adams, and others gathered in a room in Philadelphia to talk over the plan for the new nation. Perhaps the most important thing they did was to write the Constitution: the set of cohesive principles and rules that would guide the new country.

"Now, I want your clubs to take a bit of time to form official groups. Think of a club name and perhaps a logo or image to represent your club. (Similar to our sports teams, the Cougars, represented by the image of a cougar claw.) Then, agree on how your club will work. I've written some questions to consider on this chart. You'll remember this chart from your *Historical Fiction Clubs* unit last year," I said as I handed out copies of the chart to students.

As children worked, I coached them to think about the questions on our chart and move quickly to deciding on a Constitution.

"In the past," I said, "many of you found it helpful to begin your club by considering the logistics of how your club might run. For instance, what will be the expectations about coming prepared to club meetings? How will your club manage things if a member doesn't do the reading or the writing for a meeting? How will you decide what to talk about each day?" Start discussing and making decisions.

I interrupted for a moment. "I want to clarify the third bullet on the chart. To plan your reading, think about how many pages to read before each meeting. When you begin a book, will your club chunk out all the text, or will you decide on chunks each day your club meets?"

The room filled with talk, and I moved among the clubs. When I heard club members dreaming up punitive consequences for infractions, I suggested they think first about ways to be in solidarity. "If a club member doesn't come prepared one time, maybe for the next night's homework, could you find ways to remind that person? Are there ways to support and nudge before you get into punishments?"

Creating a Constitution for Your Club

- What will you call your club?
- What will your rituals be—your ways of working?
- How will you plan your reading? (number of pages, chunks)
- How will your club plan and organize writing about reading?
  - Forms of writing (Post-its, letters, notebook entries, charts)—decide on your own or let the club decide.
  - Binders—use your own club binder or a shared club binder.

Wrap up the first club meeting by handing a folder to each club.

After a few minutes of talking, I intervened. "Readers, I am handing a folder to each club, so you can keep your new constitution and other shared documents in it. Once you've put your club name and logo on this folder, put your folder into your club's book basket and get started reading."

READ WITH WRITERLY ALERTNESS, PLANNING TO BRING WHAT YOU SEE TO YOUR CLUB

Readers, for homework, you'll read and also write about your reading. You will probably be reading your club book for a bit, and then perhaps your club may have decided that you also keep another book going—that's up to your club.

But the important thing is that either way, you will be reading as someone who writes about your reading. So that means you need to read with that extra alertness, extra wide-awakeness, that writers have.

Over the last week or so, you have done a lot of writing about reading. Think about how your writing has changed as a result—but also, equally important, how your reading has changed. When you know you are expected to see detail, to note things that others would fly right past, you read differently.

The great thing is that you'll be able to bring your writing to your club tomorrow, and to use that writing to help others see more in your text as well. Plus, the more you see early on in the book, the more you will carry with you as you continue to read. So tonight's reading and writing will be important.

Characters—and Readers—Find Meaning in the Midst of Struggle

TODAY YOU WILL TEACH YOUR STUDENTS to pay close attention to one element of a story—characters—in a way that ripples into larger ideas about the book as a whole. In the last session you asked them to begin reading their new books closely and interpretively, and you probably found them paying close attention to character. You can embrace that focus today, even though the real goal is interpretation, which requires a focus on many elements of a story.

Most students are starting fantastic new books. Could you imagine reading *Wringer* and *not* thinking about Beans and Mutto? Reading *Bridge to Terabithia* and *not* thinking about Jess and Leslie? These books are written in such a way that alert readers are bound to connect with the characters who are brought to life in them. Your teaching will be powerful when you are in sync with your students' thinking and can guide them to new pathways. Your students are bound to be thinking about *who* is in the story, what those characters want most, what frightens or excites them, how they interact with other characters. So yes, this session embraces the natural focus on character.

This session also uses work with characters as a stepping-stone toward a more in-depth study of interpretation. In the days ahead, you'll want to carry strands of the Narrative Reading Learning Progression with you in your conferring and small-group work, to help you envision the trajectory students can take as their thinking about characters becomes more complicated and eventually yields ideas that bridge character issues, relationships, and theme.

In today's minilesson, when you ask students to think about Kek, you'll use what your students notice to nudge them toward more sophisticated theories about the story as a whole. You'll ask them to think more universally about their ideas of Kek and to consider the author's possible larger messages about the main character and his challenges, uncovering larger truths and lessons—meanings—that are tucked into this one boy's story. The challenge for today will be to help readers transfer that learning to their own books, doing similar work as they read, talk, and write about their reading.

IN THIS SESSION, you'll teach students that to think thematically, readers sometimes name the problem that a character faces, and then think about the lessons the character may learn or what the author may want readers to know.

GETTING READY

✔ If using *Home of the Brave* as your demonstration text, read aloud the rest of "Paperwork," "Information," "School Clothes," "Once There Was . . . ," "New Desk," "Ready," "Cattle," "Lunch," and "Fries," pages 54–80, before today's session.

✔ Use students' ideas to write a chart in class, "When We Study Character, We Can Think About . . ." (see Connection and Conferring and Small-Group Work).

✔ Prepare to read aloud an excerpt from "Night," pages 43–46, *Home of the Brave* (see Active Engagement).

✔ Use students' possible themes to write a chart in class, "Possible Themes in *Home of the Brave*" (see Active Engagement).

✔ Display and add to Bend II anchor chart, "Drawing on All You Know to Read Well and Interpret Texts" (see Share). ✍

Characters—and Readers—Find Meaning in the Midst of Struggle

CONNECTION

Explain to students that they can focus on one element of a story, like character, and use that to see more in a story as a whole.

"Yesterday, and throughout this unit, many of you probably found yourselves focusing on the characters. Year after year you have learned more complex ways of studying character. This work has yielded complex theories, reams of writing about reading, and rich partner and club conversations. Today we will return to all that you have learned about character, adding one more strategy to your repertoire.

"Will you take a moment and tell your partner what you *already know* about studying characters?" I gave the students a moment to talk, jotting the strategies I heard on a chart. I called the students back together and asked them to turn their attention to the chart.

When We Study Character, We Can Think About . . .

- Their feelings and traits
- How they change
- What they want (what motivates them)
- How they respond to difficulty
- The ways they are complicated
- The ways they act with different people
- The ways they act in different contexts or situations
- How they are on the inside versus the outside

Call students back together, congratulating them on their depth of knowledge.

"Whoa, you know quite a bit about studying characters. The poet Maya Angelou once said, 'I've learned that you can tell a lot about a person by the way he/she handles these three things: a rainy day, lost luggage, and tangled Christmas tree lights.'" I let the quote sit in the air for a moment and then went on. "What Maya Angelou seems to be saying is that you can learn the most about a person in times of trouble. When a person has a problem, the way in which they deal with it can speak volumes about the person. I'd also add that in those moments when a character deals with trouble,

In fourth grade, students went on a similar journey, from studying character to making interpretations. They learned how characters can be complicated, acting differently in different contexts and relationships. This work led to determining patterns in a character's feelings and actions, especially her desires and obstacles and how she achieves or overcomes them. Then students were asked to connect this to life lessons: what was the author trying to teach about life?

Students should have an armload of strategies for studying character. By asking them to turn and talk, you help them to conjure up memories of those strategies, as well as to benefit from the recollections of their peers. You chart the strategies so that students can feel the weight of their past learning, and can use the chart when they need reminders on what to focus on. You will be gleaning knowledge from your own students. It's fine if your chart looks slightly different from this one.

you also learn about the big messages a book is trying to teach. Those moments are not only windows into the character as a person but also into the larger meanings of the story."

❖ Name the teaching point.

"Today I want to teach you that sometimes readers think thematically by first naming the problem that a character faces, then asking, 'What lessons does the character learn from (that problem)?' or 'What might the author want me to know about that problem/issue?'"

TEACHING

Ask students to think with you about the character in the class read-aloud, thinking about the problems the character faces, the lessons learned from that problem.

"Let's try that work by thinking about Kek. In *Home of the Brave*. Hmm." I looked at the book, flipping through pages, as if just then beginning to think about Kek. I knew that in the silence, students were turning their minds to him as well. "Doesn't it seem like Kek faces a ton of problems?" I asked. "List some of them with each other."

As the kids talked, I listened for just a bit and then stepped forward. Nodding, I said, "I agree with what you were saying. He is in a strange, new place—the language is different, the snow is cold. He's lost his family and he worries about them."

I turned through the chapters we had read, visibly mulling over ideas, clearly inviting children to think along with me. "I know some of you were saying that Kek is not just an immigrant, feeling misplaced, he is also a survivor of war. He is all alone, without his parents. He is homesick. I know that by the way he stares longingly at the cow."

ACTIVE ENGAGEMENT

Ask students to help as you consider the ways in which Kek deals with his problems and the larger themes or messages his reactions convey.

"I'm afraid I did the easy part. I listed the problems Kek is facing, but the real challenge is asking, 'What lessons does the character learn about (the problem)?' In other words, are there larger lessons or messages or themes that Katherine Applegate is trying to teach us through Kek? *That's* hard!

"Let's reread a part of 'Night,' and as I read, will you think about what the author might want us to think or learn through Kek. If ideas pop as I'm reading, jot them in your notebook. Later, you'll talk to your club." I began reading.

"Turn and talk to your club. What might Katherine Applegate want us to know or think about the issues in this book based on the way Kek deals with them?"

Are you glad that you're here, Ganwar?
I ask.

He breathes in and out, in and out.

This is a good land, he says.
There's great freedom here.
But even when you travel far,
the ghosts don't stay behind.
They follow you.
You come here to make a new life,
but the old life is still haunting you.

We don't say anything for a few minutes.
Finally Ganwar speaks.
They're all gone, Kek.
They're dead.

I want to hate Ganwar for his words.
But I am too weary for anger.
Already there are so many people to hate,
too many.

Not all, I finally whisper.
Not Mama.

He sighs. It isn't good to fool yourself.
I've learned that much.

Hope isn't foolish, I say.
If I can make it all the way here,
then anything can happen.
He shakes his head.
Crazy boy, Ganwar says.
Hoping doesn't make a thing come true.

[. . .]

A man does not give up, I say.

A man knows when he's defeated, Ganwar replies.

I wipe away a tear
with the soft cloth in my hand.

I don't answer.
I am afraid of what the answer might be.

Immediately the room was abuzz as students shared their thoughts about Kek and Ganwar. "It's like Kek won't even think about negative things," said Katie. "He just *has* to have hope."

"I think Katie's right," added Tobie. "It's like he just can't let his mom be dead. He has to hope. Otherwise, he'd be all alone."

I called for students' attention. "Readers, listen carefully because I'm about to ask you to do some hard work. When thinking and talking interpretively, readers don't just talk about one character. Instead, they apply what they notice about one person to the world, to all people. To do this, it may help to start your sentence with 'Sometimes people . . .' or 'Sometimes in life . . .'

"Katie, can you get your club started in taking what you notice about Kek and making it about *all* people? Try using the prompts 'Sometimes people . . .' or 'Sometimes in life . . .'" Then, I asked each club to resume talking, this time using the language of interpretation. As I circled among the clubs, I heard the beginnings of themes and jotted them on this chart.

FIG. 9–1   This is one class's theme chart for *Home of the Brave*.

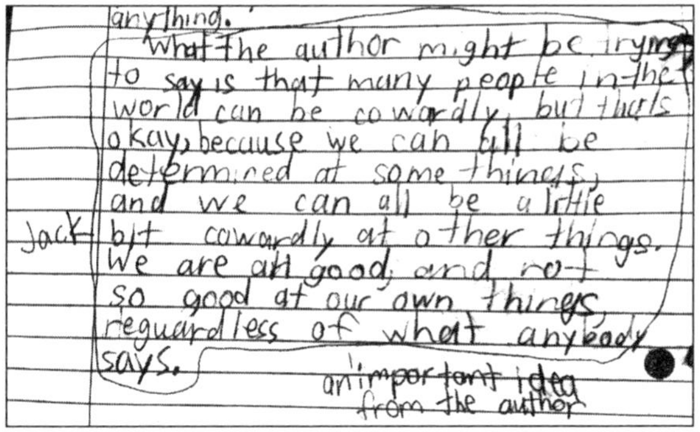

Possible Themes in *Home of the Brave*

- Sometimes people need to hold onto hope.
- Sometimes other people want to take your hope away, but you don't have to let them.
- Sometimes, even when things are bad, you need to believe they will get better.

FIG. 9–2   Jack thinks about larger life lessons in his book club book.

LINK

Remind students that they can take on the lens of character to develop interpretations.

"Readers, I can't wait to see what you come up with in your reading and conversations today. Two things. First, before you read on today, will you reread what you wrote last night? Keep that writing out and as you read, see if you can add onto or extend any of those ideas.

"And secondly, remember that one way to develop interpretations is to name the problem a character is facing, then ask: 'What lessons does the character learn from (the problem)?' 'What might the author want me to know about this issue?' You might use sentence starters such as, 'Sometimes in life . . .'"

I sent students off to read.

The Close Link between Assessment and Teaching

AS STUDENTS READ, you'll want to check in on what they are doing so as to do your usual routine of assessment-based instruction. You'll want to make a habit of checking the writing about reading students do each night, as this will provide valuable information about the progress they are making in the unit. When students are writing about characters, it will help you to keep the learning progression for character theory work in mind, noting where a student is on that progression and nudging them toward the next steps. For example, if students are noting a single character trait, you can applaud that the student has inferred that trait (presumably the author didn't come right out and label the character) and has found places in the text that provide evidence of the trait, and then you can build on that by suggesting the student might take the next step and realize that characters are complicated, they are multidimensional, and look for other traits. (See the Literature Reading Continuum in the online resources to help inform your understanding of the trajectory of skill growth students are undertaking in this unit.) Because your ultimate goal is to support interpretive reading, no matter what the student notices about a character, you may want to help the student mull over why the author made the character be that way. "You are right that both the son and the father are wearing blue in this story—what do you think led the author to make that decision? What connotations does that color have for you? Why not red? Purple?"

If appropriate, consider going back to the chart you created with students in today's connection, using it to ground the work you help these students do around character.

MID-WORKSHOP TEACHING   Looking for Places Where Characters Seem to Realize Something or Change

"Readers, today you practiced thinking about how a character faces problems, asking, 'What lessons does the character learn from the problem?' or 'What might the author want me to know about this issue?' By now, you and your club mates should have a starting sense of the problem(s) the characters are facing in your club's book. Quickly, turn and tell someone in your club what you've found."

After kids talked for just a minute, I stepped in. "Readers, some members of the *Esperanza Rising* club were just saying that their character, Esperanza, is unhappy, struggling with loneliness. They know the problems, but can't see a life lesson. Are any of you in the same boat—you can name a problem your character encounters, but you haven't seen the character learning a lesson about it?" Many kids agreed that they were stuck on the same challenge.

"I gave the *Esperanza Rising* club a tip that might be helpful: when you are looking for lessons, after you name a big problem, then find a place where the character realizes something related to that problem, or where something related to that problem shifts. Reread that part closely. There are usually lessons to be harvested from that part.

"Remember that conversation between Kek and Ganwar when Ganwar keeps trying to convince Kek to give up. At the end of that passage, Kek begins to cry a bit. That's a shift because it is the first crack in Kek's determined hopefulness. From that one place in the story where things shift, we learn some big truths about Kek and his need to hold onto hope.

"So return to reading now, but as you read, watch for the shifts that suggest a character is changing in relation to a big problem."

When We Study Character, We Can Think About . . .

- Their feelings and traits
- How they change
- What they want (what motivates them)
- How they respond to difficulty
- The ways they are complicated
- The ways they act with different people
- The ways they act in different contexts or situations
- How they are on the inside versus the outside

You will probably also see readers who are thinking about the life lessons that can be learned from ways characters handle their problems. These students might well talk about somewhat clichéd ideas like "Friends help you" or "Anything is possible if you just keep trying." Celebrate that effort, as long as those ideas do seem to match the text. Again, you may use the Narrative Reading Learning Progression, noting first where a student falls along the progression of "Determining Themes" and then deciding on appropriate (and attainable) next steps for that student. For instance, if a student tends to simply name a topic (this book teaches friendship) rather than a lesson or theme, you may teach him or her to ask, "What lesson does the character learn about (the topic)?" If a student is beginning to identify a more complex lesson in a story, you may teach him or her to keep an eye out for multiple lessons or themes. And, of course, as students determine themes, you'll likely need to remind them to ground their thinking in text evidence, especially quotes directly from the text. You may need to help students see that some details (those that relate to the central problem, for example) are often most important in determining the theme.

Here are some questions that you can teach students to ask themselves and others:

- What is the character's central problem in this scene? How does that relate to the theme of this story?

- Which of the details about _____ seems most important to the reader's understanding of him or her? How do those details help convey a theme?

- Which detail in this scene best helps to show a theme in this story?

- What moments seem most important to this story? Do they reveal something about what this story is really about?

Writing and Talking about Texts to Uncover Life Lessons, Challenges, Important Shifts

Channel kids to decide whether they will talk or write today, and then help them get started talking if they chose that route.

"Readers, I'm going to ask you to get together with your club and decide whether you want to talk today or to continue reading and writing about your reading. If you haven't read at least twenty pages today, you probably should continue reading because you definitely don't want a day to go by without reading at least that much!

"If you do meet with your club, will you take a moment at the start to talk about how your talk should go? Please remember that what you don't want to do is to hop from one person to the next without taking time to develop and learn from each other's thinking. So you probably will choose a way to start—maybe someone has ideas he or she thinks could spark a good conversation—and then stay with those ideas. But you could also begin by laying out some of your writing about reading—Post-its and entries and so on. Then read silently for a bit, before saying to yourselves, 'Okay, what should we talk about?'"

Spend time conferring with clubs, especially with clubs that include kids who could use a boost.

I meanwhile pulled in to work with a group of readers who are working below benchmark, reading *The Hundred Penny Box*. I asked them how they wanted to spend their club time, and they decided to first recall and organize their Post-its. While doing this work, they invented a chart that used plus signs and equal signs to show how one idea plus another idea led them to a new idea. Although I was glad they'd made a tool that encouraged them to accumulate their ideas, closer inspection suggested that despite the plus signs, the students hadn't actually synthesized their ideas. Instead, they had restated the text.

Taking hold of the page on which they'd used an addition sign to link their Post-it notes, I read the sequence of work as I might read a sentence.

"Readers, what I am noticing is that your first idea—'Aunt Dew is annoyed . . .'—pretty much restates your original thinking. Reread what you have written and see if you can spot how you repeat yourself." The boys read their work over. They then added to their big idea verbally: Aunt Dew doesn't want to throw away her stuff, including the Hundred Penny Box, *because* those things are important to her.

It was a start! I said, "You are on to something! And this is important to the whole of the story, isn't it? We know the author wanted the reader to think about the importance of that box because she chose it as the title for her book. So you are the kinds of readers who know how to determine what's worth growing a theory about. This is huge!"

I then suggested that the club might discuss the idea among themselves briefly. "Sometimes when people talk about an idea—like when we talk about an idea we discover in *Home of the Brave*—the idea grows," I pointed out. I knew the chances were greater that the idea would grow if I endorsed it. To get them started, I repeated what they'd said and added 'because . . .'

"Aunt Dew is annoyed that Ruth is throwing stuff away because that stuff matters to her. *This is important because . . .*" I gestured for the kids to continue and they did. Marcus continued, "Because the pennies mean a lot to her."

"And . . ." I coached.

Spencer added, "The pennies represent her whole life." The boys exchanged glances, and laughed.

Again I said, "And . . ."

Soon the club members had added, "And Ruth didn't realize they were important, and throwing them away was kind of like wiping her out." "Aunt Dew would have nothing if she didn't have her box full of memories."

That was a beautiful, sophisticated idea and metaphorical, as well. I repeated Marcus's words and then restated the teaching point of the conference.

"Well done, readers! I want you to take away some key learning from today," I said, gesturing to the new bullets on the anchor chart.

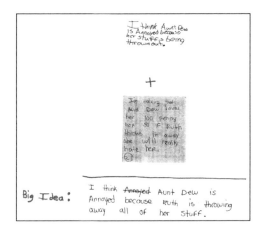

FIG. 9–3

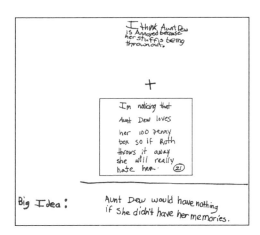

FIG. 9–4

ANCHOR CHART

Drawing on All You Know to Read
Well and Interpret Texts

- Read alertly to notice what stands out and find the meaning in specific details.
- **To uncover a life lesson or message from a story, name a big problem or challenge faced by the main character.**
- Look for a moment when something related to that problem shifts—a realization, feeling, or relationship.

Uncover life lessons or messages:

Name a big problem or challenge faced by the main character.

Look for a moment when something related to that problem shifts.

TAKING THE LEAP: FROM A CHARACTER'S BIG PROBLEM TO A BIGGER TRUTH ABOUT LIFE

Readers, tonight's homework is due not tomorrow, but the day after that. For tonight and tomorrow, continue reading your book club novel. As you read, jot to answer the questions you learned to ask today. What are the challenges, the problems, that the main character is facing? Where in the story is the main character facing that problem or challenges? What life lessons can be learned from the way the character responds to those difficulties?

After you have found a few passages where the main character is facing a big problem, will you reread those passages three or four times, thinking about the decisions the author made. Ask, "Why does the author have the character doing . . . ?" "What do I notice about this passage . . . what stands out?" "How does this connect with earlier parts of the text?" "What message might the author be trying to communicate?" "What lesson about life is the author trying to teach?"

Write a two-page entry about what you notice and think. What might the author be saying about not only that character, but about people, in life?

Seeing a Text through the Eyes of Other Readers

IN THIS SESSION, you'll teach students that when people read with others, they end up seeing more than they would have seen on their own.

GETTING READY

✔ If using *Home of the Brave* as your demonstration text, read aloud "Not Knowing," "Home," "Time," "Helping," "How Not to Wash Dishes," "Not-Smart Boy," "Magic Milk," pages 81–106, before today's session.

✔ Be ready to show "*My Name Is María Isabel,*" a short video clip of a book club discussion. A link to this video is available on the online resources (see Active Engagement).

✔ Prepare a chart titled "How Club Members Learn from Each Other's Ideas," with points to be completed in class (see Active Engagement).

✔ Display and add to Bend II anchor chart, "Drawing on All You Know to Read Well and Interpret Texts" (see Link).

✔ Display chart, "Passionate Interpretations Might Say . . ." (see Mid-Workshop Teaching).

IT IS NO ACCIDENT that this unit combines book clubs and a focus on interpretation. One of the most important things you can do to help kids grow as interpreters of literature is to help them read closely, in the company of others, coming to learn that other readers see the same text differently—even seeing more in that text. So, though your minilessons will be instructive, the fact that kids are reading beautifully written books in the company of a reading club will be even more instructive.

Do you hear the "But . . ." looming, the qualifier that comes next in this prelude? Because of course, there is nothing automatic about kids learning to interpret through participation in book clubs. For that to happen, there are a number of conditions that need to exist—and probably none matters more than the fact that kids actually listen to each other, expecting their own take on a text to be changed by hearing what other readers make of that same text.

This session, then, is a bit of a "Kumbaya" one. Its intent is to build community. But you'll be talking up the intellectual, not the social, value of listening. Your message won't be that kids need to listen to be polite. No, this time, your message is that texts are rich enough and multidimensional enough that to read them with depth and intensity, readers need to learn from the perspectives of others.

You will tell kids that book clubs can actually change how a person reads. It's true, you know! I absolutely find that I read with my reading club mates perched on my shoulder. Whether the book I am reading is one that will be shared in my book club or not, I see any book through the eyes of my book club colleagues. I promise you, that is exactly what will happen if you participate in a book club. Try it!

Seeing a Text through the Eyes of Other Readers

CONNECTION

Set students up to understand that people read differently when they read with others and share ideas. Readers carry the ideas discussed with them as they read, seeing new text through that lens.

"As we go through life, there are moments we experience that change us forever. Some of these are happy experiences—participating in a concert, going to summer camp, making an invention with a friend. Other experiences, like losing someone we care about or being hurt, can scar us. But all of those moments stay with us. It is as if they travel with us through the rest of lives.

"Being a part of a book club can be that way, too. Your life is different if you are in a book club—you find that your book club is present whenever you read. Maybe you come to a descriptive passage and almost do your usual skimming past it—but then you think, 'Katherine's probably *loving* this part' and you read the passage after all, and find yourself almost loving it, too.

"Once you've been in a book club, you read with your club mates perched on your shoulder. I've been reading *Game of Thrones* with lots of friends, and even more friends are watching the series. Every Sunday night, we text each other, and every Monday, we talk about what just happened. Often one person will see something the rest of us missed, and that opens up all sorts of new ideas.

"After a major character was killed off, I said, 'I'm so sad that Ned died. I'm mad at the author for that.' Another book club member said, 'But he *had* to die, because now all these other characters are empowered.' Her thought *floored* us. Since then, we have been reading differently, based on this idea that sometimes, authors write in a way that a character *has to* die." I looked at the kids, aware that Harry Potter readers who had grappled with Dumbledore's death knew exactly what I meant.

❧ **Name the teaching point.**

"Today I want to teach you that the best part of reading with others is that it changes you. You end up viewing the text through the eyes of others, and therefore seeing more than you would otherwise have seen."

By comparing participating in a book club to something as gigantic as summer camp, you implicitly talk up the significance of the work your kids are doing.

TEACHING

Tell students about reading a book in a parent-child book club, explaining that the kids and the parents saw different things in a book. Use this story to point out that complex texts deserve to be seen with multiple lenses.

"I want to do something unusual today. I'll use the time to tell you a true story about a book club I once participated in. It differed from yours because it was a parent-child club. We all read *Charlotte's Web*, and then we met to talk. How many of you have read *Charlotte's Web* or seen the movie? Thumbs up, if so."

As expected, most thumbs went up.

"When our club got to talking about *Charlotte's Web*, one kid said that he learned life lessons from the book and everybody in the club agreed. Then that kid added, 'This book teaches that you shouldn't give up, you come through in the end.'

"Now, will you think about *Charlotte's Web* and decide if that makes sense?" I gave the kids a minute to think. "I'm asking because here's the thing—half the group acted like that was crazy and said, '*What?* You think this is a survival story. It's not that at all. It's a love story.' That is, half the people in the club thought *Charlotte's Web* is the story of loving someone so much that you'd do anything for them.

"I'm wondering if you are figuring out what happened in that book talk. It went like this. The *kids* thought *Charlotte's Web* is the story of a little runt, Wilbur, who almost gets himself killed and manages to survive, against the odds. But the *grown-ups* thought this book is about a generous spider named Charlotte, who so loved her friend that she gave her life for him.

"Which is right?"

The students talked. After a bit, I asked, "So readers, which is it? A story of self-sacrificial love? A survival story?"

As expected, the kids said it was both, agreeing that it made sense that the parents first saw the story one way, the kids first saw it another way. But more to the point, it's *both*, and the good thing about being in a club is that this way readers end up seeing stories in more ways than one.

Flip back to the current situation, conveying that you are sure your kids will find club mates who interpret books differently. Suggest that those different views can be enriching.

"I can promise you that someone in your club will start talking, and you'll think, 'You think *that's* the important part about this book? Geez. I see it *totally* differently.'

"I suggest that you make your next question be, 'What made that particular thing seem so significant to you?' And expect the answer to that question to come from the text—'It was repeated,' 'It was unusual and stood out,' 'It seems

Any well-written book that is open to multiple interpretations will work for this teaching moment. Just make sure it is a book all of your students have read—even if it's a picture book—so they can all participate.

In reality, most books are about multiple themes; Level 5 for "Determining Themes" requires students to find and support multiple themes in a text.

Louise Rosenblatt suggests that the meaning of a book is created through the interaction of the reader and the text. She calls that a "transactional" experience, meaning the text will mean something different, at any moment, to each reader. The glory of reading being transactional is that each reader will bring the book of himself or herself to the text they share, and that means they will see different things in it.

to have been highlighted'—and also from that reader's life. Your goal will be to listen longer to each other, to devote more energy to following each other's line of thinking, and—here is the last point—to be willing to read the text with that other person's ideas in your mind (not just your own ideas) and to see the text in a new light because of doing that.

"You won't always take on that other reader's perspective. But you want to be the kind of reader whose own thinking is affected by the thinking of others around you."

ACTIVE ENGAGEMENT

Show students a short clip of a book club talking, asking them to name out the ways in which the readers allow each other's thoughts to affect their own.

"Let's watch students talking about a book on a short video clip. Notice that these readers are not only *telling each other what they already thought* about this book, they are also changing their thinking as they listen to each other. One person says something, and you can almost see the next kid take that person's idea seriously and try to go farther with that idea." I unveiled a blank chart, and said, "Be on the lookout for the specific things you see these kids doing that shows they are learning from each other and are changed because they are in this conversation."

I showed the video, in its four-minute, thirty-one-second entirety. When it was over, I said, "Talk with your club mates about what you saw these students doing that showed they were learning from each other. Be specific, citing exact parts of the conversation." As the clubs talked, I moved among them, recording what I heard on the chart as generalized, replicable moves.

How Club Members Learn from Each Other's Ideas

- Readers give examples of their own and each other's ideas.
- Readers restate each other's ideas in their own words.
- Readers allow others' thoughts to change their own.
- Readers add onto what each person says, growing a larger theory together.
- Readers use their writing about reading to fuel their talk.

LINK

Remind students that they want to be the kind of readers and book club members whose thinking is affected by those around them.

"Readers, I began our minilesson by pointing out that people can be changed by life experiences—a summer camp, a performance, a trip, an injury, a family event. And then I pointed out that readers can be changed by belonging to a book club.

Your chart will be based on your own students' ideas and will look slightly different, of course. Feel free to incorporate some points from our example chart into your class chart if you think your kids missed a key point or two.

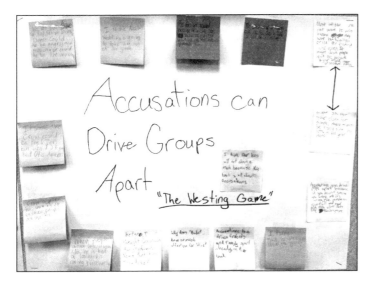

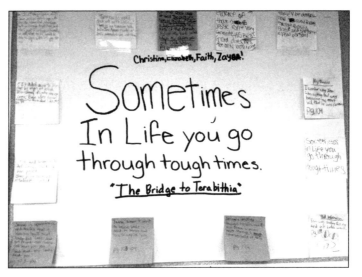

FIG. 10–1 *The Westing Game* club collects their best thinking so they can talk off of it.

FIG. 10–2 *The Bridge to Terabithia* club prepares to talk about their ideas.

"But for that to happen, you can't go into a conversation, planning to report on the ideas you already had when you were reading and that's it. Instead, you need to go into that club, expecting to hear something, to learn something, that makes you read differently—and not just today, but always.

"And later, I'm hoping that your conversation is one that changes your thinking. It may help to refer to our anchor chart as you read, think, and talk. I added a point that summarizes what we've been discussing today. Get started, reading."

ANCHOR CHART

Drawing on All You Know to Read Well and Interpret Texts

- Read alertly to notice what stands out and find the meaning in specific details.
- To uncover a life lesson or message from a story, name a big problem or challenge faced by the main character.
- Look for a moment when something related to that problem shifts—a realization, feeling, or a relationship.
- **Be open to seeing the text differently through other readers' eyes and deepening or changing your interpretation.**

Be open to seeing the text differently through other readers' eyes.

Helping Individuals and Clubs Prepare to Meet

Confer with individuals as they read.

As you confer today, look for strengths that each child can offer to his or her club. If you can identify the ways that individual readers approach a text and highlight the perspectives that they bring to a book club (especially for readers who may be insecure about their contributions), there will be big payoffs later. For example, if you ask a reader what he is noticing and he says that this book reminds him of another book, celebrate that reader's ability to compare and contrast. "I love the way you read, thinking not just of this *one* book but of similar books—and how those comparisons help you notice what's special about this book. Keep thinking between this book and others and share those ideas. That's going to be a huge contribution to your club."

Similarly, celebrate readers who notice the language authors use, or who think not only about plot and character but also about setting, or who think not only about the details of a setting but also about the *tone* and *mood* those details create. Celebrate readers who think about minor characters as well as major ones, or who consider the relationships between characters. Over and over, say, "I love that you are the kind of reader who . . . Do you have any idea how rare it is for a fifth-grader to be the sort of reader who is alert to . . . ? Your tendency to notice . . . is a real gift. Always cherish your tendency to do that." Naming the work that each student is doing (even if they are just beginning) motivates them to continue that work and replicate it. Just as importantly, it helps give each reader a sense of identity and purpose as a reader.

Confer while students talk in their clubs.

Later, you will want to listen in as students take turns sharing the reading they have done, encouraging other club members to be active listeners and learners. "You might want to jot down what Deena is saying," you might whisper to one group. "She says she reads closely when the action slows down, when the author moves into 'descriptive mode.' That's a smart thing to do, don't you think?" Move on to the next group, listening in and offering similar thoughts on members' contributions. "Interesting," you might say, "Jared knows that authors use description on purpose. Katherine Paterson could have said that Jesse simply chose not to wear sneakers. Instead, she writes that the bottoms of Jesse's feet 'were by now as tough as his worn-out sneakers.' Jared is smart to wonder what the author is trying to tell us about Jesse. Maybe each of you could look for more places where this author uses descriptive language, flag it, and talk about what it means tomorrow."

You'll also want to point out how they bring their own experiences to texts. "You see different things in a text," you might say, "because you come from different perspectives. Some of you come from big families, some from small families, some with siblings, some not. You bring that background to your reading. For example, Denise feels close to her older brother, and he recently left for college. Now, when she reads *Shooting the Moon*, Denise understands how it feels to miss a brother, and this helps her understand Jamie in a way that others of you might not.

"Then too," you might teach students, "you also see different things in a text because there is far more to see than one person can possibly notice. Each of us tends to home in on certain things in texts. Some of you automatically see the issues hiding in this story. Others may notice what the author has done in terms of craft that you could try as a writer. Or you could be a painter with a keen sense of beauty—and notice how profoundly the setting affects various characters."

"Readers, as many of you finish reading your books and wrap up the unit, I have a tip to help you get yourself ready to talk and write about your books. You should prepare to share your thinking about what the book is really, really about—and also share your own reaction to the book. If you look at mentor texts of interpretations, such as the book reviews in *The New York Times* or essays published in famous magazines like *The New Yorker*, you'll find that great responses to literature nearly always discuss why the reader loves the book. A writer almost never takes the time and effort to write about a book they detest. Most of the time, people who write for newspapers and magazines only *want* to inform their readers about books they think are important or that evoke a special emotional response.

"In many well-written reviews and essays, you'll see sentences such as, 'The truly beautiful thing about this story is . . .' or 'The reason I love this book is . . .' or 'The most unforgettable moment in this story is . . .' or 'Something incredible that happens is . . .' Can you appreciate how intense, how passionate, those sentences are? If a reader who is writing about these books uses these sentences, she wants others to *love* the book, to find it deeply significant. I've written some of those sentence starters on a chart. They might help you ratchet up the ways you are thinking about your books.

"Readers, as you read and as you think back over books you've finished in preparation for sharing them, you can be collecting things to love. A good interpretation shows that the reader cares and wants others to care, too! It can be emotional. It can be excited. It can use literary language. It invites others to see new things, to find new parts of the novel to love.

"So off you go, back to work, reading in ways that allow you to fall in love with this book—and to convey that love to other readers."

Passionate Interpretations Might Say . . .

- A beautiful thing about this story is...
- The reason I adore this book is...
- An unforgettable moment in this story is...
- Something incredible that happens is...
- One of the lasting images that I'm going to carry from this book...
- Years from now, I know I'll remember how...

Holding State-of-the-Art Book Club Conversations

Invite one reader from each book club to share ideas at length, and coach other members of each club to listen and talk off of the one person's ideas so those ideas become well developed.

"Readers, now it is your chance to have your own book club conversation. Will one person start, and lay out the ideas you have been thinking about? That one person who shares your thinking—plan to talk a while. Share your thoughts, show your club members places in the text that helped you grow this idea, explain why the idea matters to you.

"And listeners, will you do everything you can to encourage the club member to talk at length, to explain his or her thinking, to really communicate ideas. I'm going to watch for ways you make it easy for the presenter to talk at length.

"Then . . . you know what to do. Pick up that person's idea and go with it . . . add to it, find more examples, generate questions related to it, talk about why it matters. If the conversation becomes repetitive or loses energy, switch and hear a second reader's ideas, and again talk at length about that."

SESSION 10 HOMEWORK

 ## TAKING THE LEAP, CONTINUED

Readers, for homework, continue last night's assignment. Keep reading your book club novel. Keep jotting answers to these questions: "What are the problems that the main character is facing?" "Where in the story is the main character facing that problem?"

After you locate passages where the main character is facing a big problem, reread them, mulling over the author's decisions. Think about these questions: "Why does the author have the character doing . . . ?" "What do I notice about this passage . . . what stands out?" "How does this connect with earlier parts of the text?" "What message might the author be trying to communicate?" "What lesson about life is the author trying to teach?"

Last night, you began writing a two-page entry. Continue working on the entry. Be ready to share it with the class tomorrow. Remember that you want to take the leap to figure out what the author might be saying about not only that character, but about people, in life.

You may also want to think about what you learned today from other readers. What do other readers notice in terms of language, plot, setting, characters? Where do some readers pause in their reading? Is it when the author moves into descriptive mode? Or when the author chooses to explain something in a particular way? Also, think about different readers' life experiences and how those experiences color the way they read.

Linking Ideas to Build Larger Theories and Interpretations

I T USED TO BE enough to help kids break the code and to support them in the five pillars of No Child Left Behind laws (phonics, phonemic awareness, fluency, vocabulary, and comprehension). Now it's clear that kids need to learn to read interpretively—doing high-level intellectual work on the run as they read.

In this unit, you move your readers along a trajectory of growing ideas about books. To better understand this trajectory, especially in relationship to developing themes, we hope the Narrative Reading Learning Progression is a helpful tool, as there is no doubt you will continue to have a range of learners in your classroom. Some of them do not yet feel comfortable generating their own ideas about a text, so they often do little more than retell the text, not even replacing any of the author's words with their own. One of your goals during the remainder of this unit will be to help these readers go out on the thin ice of developing their own tentative, exploratory theories.

Of course, a number of your readers do already grow insights as they read, and your work will be to help them to progress from developing insights about a part of the text (these tend to be insights about a character) toward growing interpretations that are overarching enough that they pertain to many important dimensions of the text.

The challenge lies in helping students to find an idea they can stand behind and speak about at length. The idea must be one that says something important, and holds meaning and weight. During today's lesson, reminding your class about the work done by a former student, you will teach students one way to develop an idea that is large and meaningful—by looking across our jottings in a text, starting with a thought prompt, "I think this book teaches us that . . .", noticing patterns and connected ideas, and using them to build a larger theory.

IN THIS SESSION, you'll teach students that readers link ideas together to build larger theories or interpretations, aiming to uncover a larger truth or lesson.

GETTING READY

✔ Before today's session, read aloud "Wet Feet," "Bus," "Lou," "Cows and Cookies," "Night Talk," in *Home of the Brave*, pages 107–27.

✔ Provide giant Post-its to students so they may record ideas (see Connection).

✔ Display Sam's notes on *Wringer* (Figure 8–1) (see Teaching).

✔ Display and add to Bend II anchor chart, "Drawing on All You Know to Read Well and Interpret Texts (see Link).

✔ Display "Questions to Ask to Grow Seed Ideas" (see Mid-Workshop Teaching).

Linking Ideas to Build Larger Theories and Interpretations

CONNECTION

Ask students to share the ideas they are developing about their club books from their homework.

"Readers, I'm going to ask you to share your interpretations of your club books. But before you begin, will you each reread your homework and mark the part in your writing where you capture your ideas about the novel's big ideas, the lessons the author is teaching, or the author's message?"

I gave children a moment to mark up their writing. Then I said, "I'm going to ask one person to read the portion of your writing where you try to capture the novel's ideas, and the rest of the club, without talking, you have the responsibility to capture your friend's thoughts onto a giant Post-it that I'll give you.

"Then another club member will read his or her ideas about the novel's big idea. The listeners—all of you working together but without talking—you have the job to decide, 'Is that a somewhat new interpretation, a new thought about the novel?' If so, make a new Post-it, and again capture the person's main thoughts on it. But if the second person to share has ideas that are almost the same as the first person's ideas, just listen for what new additions the second person brings and doctor up that first Post-it."

Pretty soon you will have a few Post-its that capture multiple ideas about the novel—with different readers presumably seeing different themes and life lessons in the same book.

As you listen, take note of which kids are thinking and speaking in interpretive ways and which are just stating facts or simple ideas about characters' traits or emotions.

Before all children had time to read, I stepped in. "I love that you are paying attention not just to *who* is in the book and to *what* is happening, but that you are also writing things like, 'This seems important because . . .' and saying, 'Sometimes in life . . .' I know you haven't all had a chance to read portions of your writing yet, but we're going forward anyhow. I want to show you some ways readers continue to think about a book after they grow some great ideas about a text."

❖ Name the teaching point.

"Today I want to teach you that readers link ideas together to build larger theories or interpretations. As they think about how ideas might connect, they ask, 'Could there a larger truth or lesson here?'"

TEACHING

Share the work of a student who developed several smaller ideas about a book. Ask students to look across the ideas and think about how they connect, before sharing the interpretive work the student did.

"Readers, I love that you are uncovering more than one idea in a book. That's what good readers do, and it is something most of us learn to do by reading in the company of others, like you are doing, and bringing not only your own thinking but also the thinking of other members of your club to your book.

"What I want you to see is that readers pause and ask, 'Do some of these ideas connect to each other or fit together in ways that add up to an even larger idea?'

"For example, let's take a look at some of Sam's thinking about *Wringer*. Only a few of you have read *Wringer*, but you'll remember studying Sam's writing about reading when we began this unit. Only this time we are not studying Sam's work to get inspired to write about our books. Instead, we are studying the way that Sam gathered ideas about *Wringer*, reread those ideas, and then thought about whether he could make something bigger out of them. Let's take a look at his jots."

> Palmer is different when Beans is around. Beans acts like the gang leader, luring Palmer to do bad things.
>
> Palmer is different when he is around Dorothy and when he is around Beans. Dorothy brings out his kinder side and makes him nicer.
>
> Palmer's dad wrings the necks of pigeons. His dad likes Palmer's relationship with Beans better than his relationship with Dorothy.

"What connections between these ideas do you see?" I asked, "What questions do these ideas, taken together, raise? Turn and talk."

The students talked. Some thought that Palmer was influenced by other people—for the good, with Dorothy, and for the bad, with Beans. Why doesn't he figure out his true self and act that way? Most wondered why a father would want his son to hang out with people who are bad influences. Maybe Palmer will have to choose between his dad and Dorothy, between his bad side and his good side.

I nodded, and told the students that they'd done the same sort of thinking that Sam had done, only Sam went one step further and thought that maybe one thing *Wringer* is *really* about—a larger truth—is that as we grow up, we have to decide the kind of person we want to be and that choice isn't always easy.

Today's teaching will be a method we refer to as "example and explanation." This means that rather than demonstrating a strategy for your students, you are showing them an example of it, and then unpacking and explaining that example for students. This method works especially well when you have a strong exemplar or story that can serve as a model for students.

ACTIVE ENGAGEMENT

Ask students to recap the work they just did before trying it with their own book club books.

Then I said to the class, "Can you retrace your footsteps, thinking about what you just learned about how to interpret a book?" I gave them a moment to do this. "Now, will you and your club try to do similar work, starting with the ideas that you have already recorded as a club?"

The kids talked, and I coached into one club after another, saying things like, "So first Sam reread ideas that he's gathered about the character's problems and relationships. Next, he noticed patterns across those ideas. Then, he asked, 'What questions do these raise? What life lessons could be learned from this?' Do that same work now. Look across your jottings—the ones you have recorded in your notebooks or elsewhere. What questions do they raise? What life lessons can be learned?" I listened in a bit longer, helping their thinking along, before moving on to another group.

> **ANCHOR CHART**
>
> ### Drawing on All You Know to Read Well and Interpret Texts
>
> - Read alertly to notice what stands out and find the meaning in specific details.
> - To uncover a life lesson or message from a story, name a big problem or challenge faced by the main character.
> - Look for a moment when something related to that problem shifts—a realization, feeling, or a relationship.
> - Be open to seeing the text differently through other readers' eyes and deepening or changing your interpretation.
> - **Connect ideas to form bigger theories, asking if there is a larger truth or life lesson to be learned.**

Connect ideas to form bigger theories.

LINK

Remind students that one way readers build interpretations is by linking similar ideas together to build larger theories and then asking, "Is there a larger truth or lesson here?"

"What you have done is to develop ideas that relate to almost the whole of your books. Your ideas, like Sam's, function like umbrellas. The ideas are so big, the whole story fits underneath it.

"Sam was able to use his umbrella idea to predict how the book will end, a prediction based less on his knowledge of the plot and more on his sense of what the author seems to be trying to say. Palmer will have to choose whether he wants to wring pigeons' necks like his dad and Beans do, or whether he wants to be a different, kinder sort of person, like Dorothy.

"Today, in your own reading, don't just stop with small, Post-it-sized ideas. Instead, see if you can connect ideas to form larger theories and then ask, 'Is there a larger truth or life lesson here?' I've added this key point to our anchor chart," I said, gesturing toward the chart.

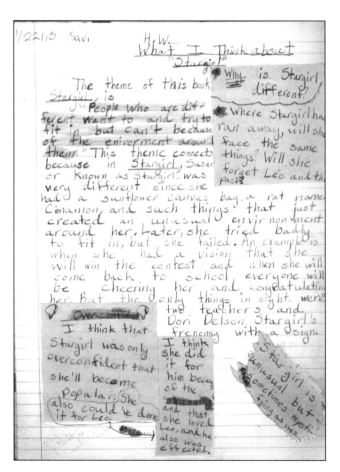
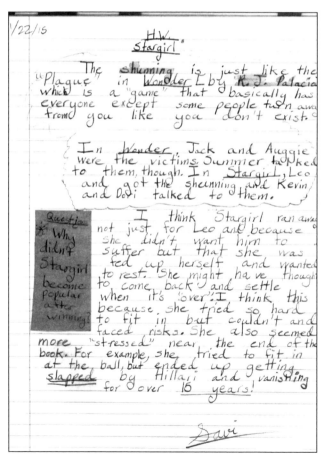

FIG. 11–1 Savi explores her ideas and questions about *Stargirl*.

Using Thought Prompts as a Tool for Revising Theories

WHEN YOU APPROACH CHILDREN who are, you hope, reading with their theories in hand (and also with theories they've picked up from listening to their club mates, too) you may find that some of your children aren't quite sure what you mean by "expecting their theories to change." They may not grasp what you mean by letting an idea morph because they are accustomed to having an idea, then locking that thought in their minds, recording it, and, if anything, searching the text for evidence. You will probably want to do some small-group instruction to help these youngsters learn that they can hold an idea loosely in mind—almost writing it in pencil—expecting that the idea will evolve as they talk and read some more.

When I convened such a small group, they'd each already developed a couple of different theories about their books and they were now reading forward, mining their stories for parts that supported those theories. I told them that I'd gathered them together in part because they were each reading particularly wonderful books, and with books like those, I thought they could generate even more complex theories. I pointed out that I would generally do that by writing, and that I had some thought prompts that I often used to nudge me to write in ways that made my thinking deeper and more complex. I knew that as soon as we got going in this work, the students would recognize what I was doing as a strategy they'd used within the essay-writing unit of their writing workshop.

I suggested the students each record one of their theories on the top of a clean page in their notebooks and I explained to the group that I was going to call out thought prompts. After I said a phrase, I wanted them to record what I said and use it to help themselves keep writing and keep thinking. I knew my interjections would not be timed to allow them to finish every previous thought, so I let them know that when I threw out a phrase, they'd need to stop whatever they were writing (and thinking), skip a line, and quickly record whatever I said. "You'll be writing fast and furious," I said. "I won't stop for you to catch up."

I asked them to reread the thought they'd recorded at the top of their page, and then I extended their thought by saying, "To add on . . ." I made sure the lilt in my voice rose in a way that helped to convey that they were going to say more about their first thought.

As children wrote alongside me, I peeked at what they were writing, knowing that what I saw would help me choose what I'd call out next, and letting their pace influence my timing. At some point, I noticed a few children would write just one sentence and then wait, so I said, "Keep your pen moving and your mind moving 'til I call out something else." When I noticed children's thinking becoming repetitive, I was especially apt to insert a thought prompt. "This is making me realize . . ." or "This is true because . . ." or "The important thing about this is . . ."

At the top of Emma's page was her theory that Leslie (in *Bridge to Terabithia*) is having difficulty fitting in with the other kids at school because she is so different. Then Emma had written, "To add on . . . Leslie is new to the school and no one is really accepting of the new kid, especially when she isn't like the other girls. She is more athletic and would rather play with the boys but they don't want to play with her because she beat them all in a race and it's like they can't handle it. The girls don't like the way she dresses and her short . . ."

I called out, "This makes me realize . . ." Emma pushed up her knobby red plastic bracelet and continued to scrawl: "This makes me realize that the other kids in school don't know what to do around her. It's like she makes them uncomfortable so they push her away."

After a few other thought prompts, I lifted the entire enterprise by saying, "This may fit with my other theory (the one you've kept close at hand) because . . ." Then I added a parenthetical tip. "Take your other theory and try to connect it with what you are writing right now." To get them started, I said, "Let me say the prompt again. This may fit with my other theory . . . because . . ."

"Readers, have you ever read over all your entries, all your thoughts about a book and thought, 'I'm not sure *any* of my ideas are good enough to be called an interpretation'? If you have had that feeling, you have just experienced what every writer in the world experiences *all the time*.

"Here is the truth. There is a reason that writers say they usually begin writing with 'a seed idea.' How big and impressive are seeds? Have you ever gotten a packet of marigold seeds? They are so small they look like dust. They start as almost nothing.

"So stop fretting if your ideas seem obvious or inconsequential. Remember last year, when we read *The Tiger Rising*, and we started out with just the idea that Rob was wimpy? That's a pretty obvious idea, but it gave us a place to start, a place to put our feet. As we read on, we used our theory to help us go deeper. For example, we asked ourselves, 'Is *wimpy* really the right word to describe his behavior?' 'What seems to be making Rob act like such a wimp?'

"My point is that it is just fine to start with a small or ordinary idea, as long as you think of it as a seed. Then think more about it. Ask questions."

Questions to Ask to Grow Seed Ideas

- Is this really true?
- What is the precisely right way to say this
- Why is this so?
- How does this connect with other parts?
- So what's the life lesson: In life, . . .
- Try again: Sometimes when people . . . they . . . because . . .

"Here is one other tip. You should be growing a bunch of ideas—not just one. And whenever possible, you think between those ideas, attempting to make them something bigger."

By now Emma was, in fact, writing fast and furious—and in ways that struck me as pretty impressive, given the fact that she'd entered the year as a child who read fast but didn't think in response to books with any sense of fluency. She wrote, "My other theory is that Jess isn't the kind of son his dad wanted, so both kids aren't fitting in

somewhere. Jess's dad wanted a tough kid because his dad doesn't know what to do with a son who'd rather draw and play with a girl." Then Emma reread her first set of ideas, in which she'd written about peers rejecting Leslie, and now she added, "It's like Jess's dad is pushing Jess away just like the kids are pushing Leslie away. And when his dad does that it makes Jess feel like he isn't a part of the family."

Leslie is having difficulty fitting in with the other kids at school because she is so different.

To add on she's new to the school and no one is really accepting of the new kid especially when she isn't like the other girls. She is more athletic and would rather play with the other boys but they don't want to play with her because she beat them all in a race and it's like they can't handle it. The girls don't like the way she dresses and her short

This makes me realize that the other kids in school don't know what to do around her. It's like she makes them uncomfortable so she they push her away.

My other theory is that Jess isn't the kind of son his dad wanted, so both kids aren't fitting in somewhere. Jess's dad wanted a tough kid because his dad doesn't know what to do with a son who'd rather draw and play with a girl. It's like Jess's dad is pushing Jess away just like the kids are pushing Leslie away. And when his dad does that it makes Jess feel like he isn't a part of the family.

The bigger idea I am having now is that both Jess and Leslie are on the outside in some way and their friendship makes them feel less alone. But I think Jess has it the worst because feeling on the outside of your own family is worse than being on the outside of friends

In other words, Jess and Leslie are left out, Jess at home, Leslie at school. My new theory is that it is because Jess and Leslie are left out that they go to each other.

FIG. 11–2   Emma uses thought prompts to nudge her thinking forward.

I called out, "The bigger idea I am having now is . . ."

Emma recorded my thought prompt and kept writing: "The bigger idea I am having now is that both Jess and Leslie are on the outside in some way and their friendship makes them feel less alone. But I think Jess has it the worst because feeling on the outside of your own family is worse than being on the outside of friends."

After I prompted, "In other words . . . ," Emma wrote, "In other words, Jess and Leslie are left out, Jess at home, Leslie at school."

After I interjected, "My new theory is . . . ," she wrote, "My new theory is that it is because Jess and Leslie are left out that they go to each other."

I gathered the group back together, and we shared out our new theories, and then I restated the techniques I hoped they'd begun to learn, pointing out that they, too, could draw from the chart of prompts and that the most important thing was for them to understand that their big ideas would change, becoming more true.

Following and Staying with Ideas

Ask clubs to start talking before stopping them to impart one last tip.

Clubs, I don't want to say anything just yet. Pull together and start talking." The students looked at me curiously, then quickly recovered and sought out their groups.

As the clubs met, I circulated among them, trying to sense what I could say that might do the most to lift the level of their talk. After a bit, I asked for all the clubs to leave their books and notebooks where they were, and for everyone to gather in the meeting area for a quick conversation.

Once they'd convened, I said, "Readers, earlier we talked about the fact that at some point in your work with a book, it is important to reread all that you've said—the different insights—and to think, 'How might these different ideas go together, how might they be built into something more?' You watched Sam build his ideas from 'Palmer gets in more trouble when he is around Beans' to 'In life, there comes a time when we need to decide what kind of person we want to be.' We talked about how you can do this same work by trying to see connections between your different ideas and then thinking about how they apply to life.

"So here is my new tip. One of the best ways to become accustomed to connecting ideas is to learn how to talk in ways where different people all contribute to one line of conversation. This means keeping your ideas close together and letting each connect to, and build, on the next. What I noticed just now is that your talk sounded a bit like your ideas were scattered in different directions. One person said something about one topic (and I cupped my right hand and reached far off to the right, pretending to hold an idea). Then someone said something about this topic (and I cupped my other hand, again pretending to hold an idea and reaching far off to the left).

"Your talk will go better—and your interpretations will get better—if you try, when you are talking, to build a tower of ideas. I'll show you. Start by thinking right now of ideas you have about *Home of the Brave*. Okay, in a conversation, one person says something." I gestured to one child and said, "Say an idea about *Home of the Brave* as we all know that book":

> *Kek holds onto a little piece of cloth, because it is from home.*

Then I said, "Now the rest of you have a challenge. You can't just say any ol' idea. You have to find a way to connect whatever you want to say to the idea that is already on the table, so your idea goes on top of the first, like a tower. Try it," I said, and gestured for a second child to speak.

Kek holds onto hope like he holds onto that little piece of cloth.

Then I channeled the clubs to continue talking, and again I moved among them, coaching and supporting. After a few minutes of talk I reconvened the students. "Readers, today and always, try to imagine that you and your club mates aren't just talking, but are building something together. Each of you holds a few small ideas, like little Lego pieces, and your goal is to link and connect those pieces together until you make something of them—something bigger and grander than the little piece you started with."

SESSION 11 HOMEWORK

 # LINKING SMALL IDEAS TO FORM LARGER ONES

Readers, tonight, as you read, continue to practice the work you started today. As you read, allow yourself to have thoughts about characters, their relationships, the plot, whatever it might be. At a certain point, however (maybe after you've accumulated a few Post-its or when you feel like you've got something bigger to say), take your Post-its from your book and spread them out before you. Ask: "Do these connect in some way? Can I make something bigger out of them?" Then, see if you can write long for a few minutes, pushing yourself to make something more complex out of those little Lego pieces!

A couple days ago, I taught some of your classmates a few questions they could ask themselves when trying to develop big ideas. They found them helpful, and I thought they might help you as you work to take something small and make it big.

As you look across your Post-its, you can ask yourself:

- What is the character's central problem in this scene? How does that relate to the theme of this story?
- Which of the details about _____ seems most important to the reader's understanding of him or her? How do those details help convey a theme?
- Which detail in this scene best helps to show a theme in the story?
- What moments seem most important to this story? Do they reveal something about what this story is really about?

Reading On, with Interpretations in Mind

I F YOU'RE READING THIS BOOK, chances are, you are a reader. So it's safe to ask you to think about a novel you're reading now. Maybe it's *The Goldfinch* or *The Girl with the Dragon Tattoo*. Call to mind the beginning of the story. Consider what you were thinking about then, what seemed important. Then think later in the book. Consider what other characters became important, or what issues revealed themselves, or what you were paying attention to. Notice how your thinking expanded as the story evolved.

As an experienced, fluent reader, you do this work naturally. Earlier in this unit, during Bend I, you helped readers to notice whatever they attended to in a story and to stay with that, developing it into a line of thought. For instance, if a reader of *Becoming Naomi Leon* jotted a few ideas about the meaning of soap carving, you encouraged her to reread (even just to skim) to find other places where soap carving—and anything else, like soap carving—emerges as significant to Naomi. Perhaps that student made a timeline, noting the different times soap carving was mentioned and what it seemed to signify in those moments, or drew a quick sketch of Naomi carving soap sculptures. Either way, you helped that student take her initial observations and stay with them, forming theories.

In this session, you will remind readers to follow multiple theories, and to make sure that each of those ideas expands as the stories they read expand. Otherwise, they may hold onto one or two ideas they had at the beginning of the story, and then ignore the parts of the story that don't fit with those ideas. So you want them to learn to continually, habitually revise their thinking, and at the same time, expand that thinking.

Today, you will teach and then encourage students to follow their ideas as if following a through-line in a story—letting their initial ideas stay with them from one page to the next, changing and morphing as they read on. Perhaps just as importantly, you'll want to remind students to do this work in ways that allow their voice and personality to shine through on the page. This way, developing interpretations becomes more than just an act of good reading, but a way of bringing themselves to the parts of a book that truly matter.

IN THIS SESSION, you'll remind students that readers wear their interpretations like a pair of glasses, reading on in the text with their ideas in mind, gathering evidence and deepening their theories.

GETTING READY

✔ Before today's session, read aloud "Cowboy," "Working," "Ganwar, Meet Gol," "An Idea," "Field Trip," "The Question," "Apple," pages 131–54, from *Home of the Brave*.

✔ Prepare to share or display examples of written notes from a few students that show how they generated important, provocative ideas from reading a text, and then connected those ideas to more than one place in their books (see Connection).

✔ Prepare chart paper with this sentence written on it, "Hope can help people survive hard times and go on" (see Teaching).

✔ Be prepared to read aloud excerpts from *Home of the Brave*, pages 62–64 (see Teaching).

✔ Consider displaying an excerpt from *Home of the Brave*, page 65, using chart paper or a document camera (see Active Engagement).

✔ Display and add to Bend II anchor chart, "Drawing on All You Know to Read Well and Interpret Texts" (see Link).

✔ Provide a copy of the "Inferring Characters" strand of the Narrative Reading Learning Progression to each student (see Conferring and Small-Group Work).

✔ Prepare to show a chart titled "Thought Prompts to Help You Grow Complex Ideas . . ." (see Mid-Workshop Teaching and Homework).

✔ Be ready to provide a large sheet of construction paper for each club, along with Post-its and markers so club mates can connect different ideas (see Share).

Reading On, with Interpretations in Mind

CONNECTION

Share examples of a few readers from the class who have generated provocative ideas as they read.

"Readers, I've been thinking a lot about the work you did yesterday and the important, provocative ideas you are beginning to generate about the books you are reading. It seems to me that these ideas are not just the kind that can be applied to one book, but to other books, to your lives, and to our world.

"When the *Bridge to Terabithia* club read yesterday, they began to notice the importance of running for the main character, Jesse. In fact, they began to notice that running means *different things* in different parts of the book! Erin came up with this idea." I put up Erin's notebook page for the class to see.

"Joseph used writing about reading to capture a larger interpretation he was having about *Locomotion* by Jacqueline Woodson." I put his Post-it on the overhead.

You'll want to spotlight the work of a student who has not simply had an idea, but thought about that idea more than once in the book. Use this connection as an opportunity to highlight the beginnings of the work you will teach students to do today. If you can't find an example from your own class, simply put up the pieces we've chosen to show, explaining to students that they are the work of another fifth-grader.

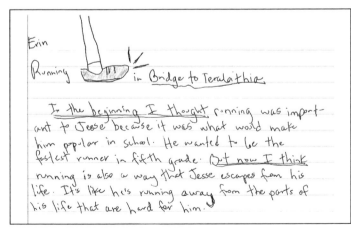

FIG. 12–1 Erin tracks the symbolism of running across *Bridge to Terabithia*.

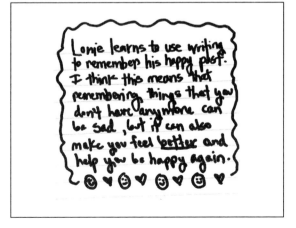

FIG. 12–2 Joseph turned what he noticed about the main character, Lonnie, into a larger interpretation.

"Both Joseph and Erin took something that could seem small to a younger reader (writing about memories and running), and turned them into something much larger by thinking about what those activities meant to the character."

❖ Name the teaching point.

"Today I want to remind you that once a reader has developed an interpretation about a book, it is important that he or she *stay with that idea*. As readers, you can wear your interpretation like a pair of glasses, as a lens, and read on in your book looking for more places that fit with or change your idea."

TEACHING

Tell a story that shows the importance of mental flexibility.

"Do you know any crossword puzzle lovers? I do. One of my friends loves them, and even I like to do them occasionally. To be successful at solving a crossword puzzle, it helps to think of possible answers, not final answers. I use a pencil to fill in the words so I can easily change my first answer as I continue working. My friend writes his solutions in tiny script in the corners of the boxes until he's sure of them.

"Crossword puzzle lovers know what readers know—it's important to be flexible, to expect that as new information comes in, our initial ideas will change and grow. That's why we call these interpretations we're developing *theories*. Theories are important—grand, even—like the theory of life on other planets. But theories are still open for exploration. As we read, we don't just set out to prove our theories. Instead, we read on, gather more information, and revise as we see new things."

Model this work by taking an idea the class developed in read-aloud and showing students how you read a bit of a chapter with the idea as a lens.

"One interpretation, one theory, we've developed as a class is about hope—how hope helps Kek move forward, how he hopes to find his mom. But when we studied the scene between Kek and Ganwar (who doesn't have hope and tries to convince Kek that it is silly to hope), we weren't sure if the author was telling us that hope is a good thing or a bad thing." I revealed the following, written on chart paper.

> Hope can help people survive hard times and go on.

"I'm going to hold this idea in my mind. Like all good interpretations, it leaves some room for change. As I read on in *Home of the Brave*, think along with me. What about this idea of hope? Is it a good thing? A bad thing? Will our interpretation about Kek and hope hold true, or will it change as we gather new information?" I began to read, rereading the chapter we'd read the previous day.

While students will have learned a thing or two about this kind of work in fourth grade, your fifth-graders will almost certainly not have mastered this difficult skill. That, of course, is why you are highlighting the art of interpretation in this unit, and also why teachers will continue teaching interpretation in middle school, in high school, and even in college.

If you question your students' familiarity with crossword puzzles, you might bring one in to show them as you talk, or change this story to something of your own.

Some days you will choose to read a new portion of text in your teaching or during the active engagement. More often, however, you'll revisit portions of text you have already read. This allows students to focus on the strategy at hand, rather than the plot of the story.

In the bathing room
I look hard in the shiny glass.
I wonder if I look
like an America boy.

I'm not sure if that would be
a good thing or a not-good thing.

I paused a moment to make sure students were thinking along with me. "Hmm, that's an interesting way to end this chapter. He isn't sure if he wants to be an American boy or not. That seems to connect to this idea about hope and whether it is a good thing or a bad thing . . ." I continued reading.

Once there was . . .

The next morning,
I don't know what I am feeling.
I'm excited, yes,
because to go to school and learn
is a fine honor.
[. . .]

But sometimes there would be
singing, or a story
or numbers on our fingers and toes to count.

I liked the stories the best.
Once there was
a lion who could not roar . . .
Once there was
a man who sailed the sea . . .
Once there was
a child who found a treasure . . .
The stories would lift me up,
the words like a breeze beneath
butterfly wings,
and take me far from the pain in my belly
and the tight knot of my heart.

The students raised their hands in the air as I finished reading the text. "I can see you are thinking a lot about this and its connection to hope." I reread the lines "Once there was a lion who could not roar . . . Once there was a man who sailed the sea . . ." as if to mull them over.

"Gosh," I said. "Even when Kek was back in Africa he was a dreamer. Earlier we read how he couldn't always go to school because he was too ill with 'the fever.' Other days the teacher couldn't come because of the 'men with guns.' Life

This move shows students that I am actively thinking and rereading while giving those that may not have zoomed in on those particular words a chance to do so.

was not easy, and Kek would have tight knots in his heart, but he loved the stories." I looked back at the text. "Where does it say that? Hmm . . ."

A child piped in to read aloud this part of the text:

> . . . the stories would lift me up, the words like a breeze beneath butterfly wings, and take me far from the pain in my belly and the tight knot of my heart.

"You are right! Life wasn't easy for Kek in Africa either, but stories helped him to feel better. Maybe it isn't hope that helps Kek so much as being *a dreamer*. When he hears stories about how people overcome tough times, he dreams about overcoming tough times. He feels better, happier."

Debrief, pointing out the way in which your interpretation of the story is evolving. Highlight the fact that, as a class, you grew a theory, an interpretation, then read on expecting it to change.

"Thank goodness we went back and did some rereading! Do you see the way that I wore our interpretation—our ideas about Kek and hope—as a pair of glasses, of sorts? I read on, expecting to revise our theory as I read. As a result, our interpretation is beginning to evolve and deepen."

ACTIVE ENGAGEMENT

Read the last portion of the chapter, giving the students an opportunity to try the same work.

"Now it's your turn. I'm going to reread the last bit of this chapter to you. As I do, think about the ideas we've developed about Kek. Does this next part of the book change those ideas? Add onto them?" I began reading aloud.

> I hope they will have stories
>
> at my school.
>
> If they don't know how,
>
> perhaps I can teach them.
>
> It isn't such a hard thing.
>
> All you must do is say
>
> Once there was . . .
>
> and then let your hoping find the words.

Consider having this last portion of text, if not the entire chapter, available for students to see. You might write the chapter out on chart paper, or put the text under a document camera. This will ensure that students can refer to explicit words and phrases as they talk.

"Turn and talk in your clubs," I said urgently. The students' voices erupted and I listened in as Katie, Tobie, Jenn, and Ben talked.

"Did you guys notice that it says the word *hope* twice in this part?" asked Jenn.

Tobie looked at the text with a surprised look on his face. "I didn't even notice that! He is even hoping that they will have stories. He's a real hoper." The club giggled at Tobie's use of the word.

Tobie continued, "I think the last two lines are the most important. 'Once there was . . . and then let your hoping find the words.'"

I coached the listeners in the club, encouraging them to nudge Tobie to elaborate.

"What do you mean by that?" asked Ben.

Tobie thought for a minute. "Well, it's like you can start with the words *once there was* and then you can make up any story you want. Maybe Kek could say, 'Once there was a boy who lost his whole family . . .'"

Jenn added, "It's a story, so you can make it end any way you want. At the end he can find his mom!"

"How does this connect with our ideas about Kek's hopes and dreams?" I asked.

Katie spoke up. "When I read, I sometimes forget about everything that is stressing me out. Maybe for Kek he can tell stories and forget about his worries. He can hope for anything he wants and get it. So this is more evidence for our idea that Kek is a dreamer and that he needs hope."

Call the students back together, summing up some of what you heard.

"As I listened in on your conversations, I heard many of you saying that this last part of the chapter supports our idea that Kek is a dreamer. Hope is what helps him get through each day."

LINK

Remind students of the day's strategy and send them off to read, think, and write in ways that nurture their interpretations.

"I'm hoping that today's lesson will remind you of something important," I leaned in to accentuate the importance of the words to come. "An interpretation is not something a person has and then leaves on one page, in one part of a text. Instead, it is important to develop your interpretation. One way to do this is to wear your interpretation like a pair of glasses, and to read on with your interpretation in mind. When you do this, you are bound to find places where your

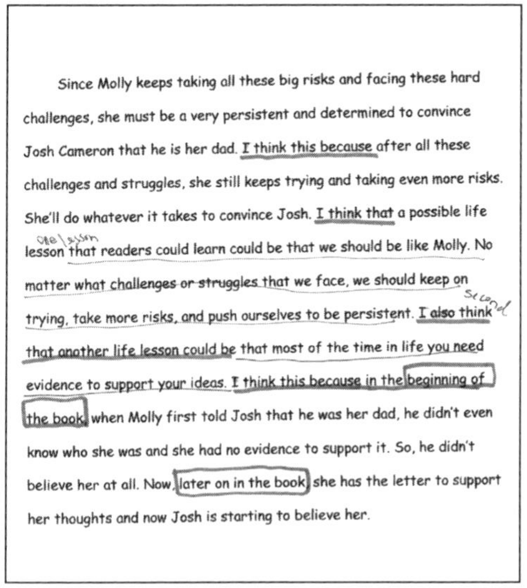

Since Molly keeps taking all these big risks and facing these hard challenges, she must be a very persistent and determined to convince Josh Cameron that he is her dad. I think this because after all these challenges and struggles, she still keeps trying and taking even more risks. She'll do whatever it takes to convince Josh. I think that a possible life lesson that readers could learn could be that we should be like Molly. No matter what challenges or struggles that we face, we should keep on trying, take more risks, and push ourselves to be persistent. I also think that another life lesson could be that most of the time in life you need evidence to support your ideas. I think this because in the beginning of the book when Molly first told Josh that he was her dad, he didn't even know who she was and she had no evidence to support it. So, he didn't believe her at all. Now later on in the book she has the letter to support her thoughts and now Josh is starting to believe her.

FIG. 12–3 A student uses the learning progression *and* thought prompts to push her interpretations to a Level 5.

initial thinking deepens, develops. Let's promise each other that as we continue to read on, we'll wear this interpretation as glasses and deepen it even more." The students shook their heads, agreeing with the idea. "I've added this point to our anchor chart so we won't forget."

> Drawing on All You Know to Read Well & Interpret Texts
>
> Read alertly. See details as meaningful.
>
> Uncover life lessons or messages: Name a big problem or challenge faced by the main character.
>
> Look for a moment when something related to that problem shifts.
>
> Be open to seeing the text differently through other readers' eyes.
>
> Connect ideas to form bigger theories.
>
> Read on, using your interpretation as a lens.

ANCHOR CHART

Drawing on All You Know to Read Well and Interpret Texts

- Read alertly to notice what stands out and find the meaning in specific details.
- To uncover a life lesson or message from a story, name a big problem or challenge faced by the main character.
- Look for a moment when something related to that problem shifts—a realization, feeling or a relationship.
- Be open to seeing the text differently through other readers' eyes and deepening or changing your interpretation.
- Connect ideas to form bigger theories, asking if there is a larger truth or life lesson to be learned.
- **Read on, using your interpretation as a lens, gathering evidence and finding places where you can add to or change your initial thinking.**

Read on, using your interpretation as a lens.

"Determine the page that will be your stopping spot today, and see if you as a club can read with a shared lens, a shared pair of glasses. That will make it likely that you will have plenty to talk about when you meet later today."

Pushing Students toward Higher Levels of Interpretation Work

TO TEACH ANY SKILL, from prediction to envisionment to inference and interpretation, it helps to have a sense of how that skill develops in readers. If you keep in mind a progression of interpretation work, this can help you confer and lead small groups. On this day, and as you continue to teach interpretation, you will want to take note of the level of work done by a child and then be able to answer the question "What's next?" to teach toward that goal with clarity and specificity.

Use learning progressions to guide interpretation instruction.

When you nudge children to grow ideas as they read, many will start with ideas about characters. Some will sum up an entire character in a single generic term: Kek is sad; Ganwar is mean. For them, it is a step ahead to reach toward more specific terms, for instance, Ganwar is hurt or pessimistic. You can coach them by saying, "Can we be more specific? What exactly is he like?" Give them miniature word walls to help internalize the work of taking a millisecond to think, "Wait. What is the precisely true word?" Remind readers that often it helps to use lots of words to say what you mean, and to entertain possibilities. Maybe Ganwar acts mean because he has been hurt by the world or because he wants to help Kek. Maybe he doesn't see the point of hope and thinks that Kek is naive for holding onto it.

The "Character" strand of the Literature Reading Progression may help here. Determine where students fall on the continuum and then help them to work toward the next level up. For instance, for a student who is developing grade 3 inferences and interpretations, begin by teaching him or her some fourth-grade sentence starters. "Characters in books like yours are complex," you might say. "When we talk about them, we want to consider the ways they can be different at different times or with different people. For instance, we might say: 'My character has different sides to him or her. On the outside . . . but on the inside . . .' Or, 'My character does things for lots of reasons. For example, sometimes . . . but sometimes . . .'" And for the student

mastering fifth-grade thinking, you might offer scaffolds such as: "I have several theories about my character's motivations. On the one hand . . . but on the other hand . . ." Or "These two characters are in constant conflict, but they have some similarities as well."

Of course, once readers are growing complex ideas about characters, you'll help them to think about the meanings contained in their books as wholes. Readers should first think about what the main character is learning. Kek learns that even when things are at their worst, you can find happiness in small things. So a reader might say, "One theme is that Kek learns that even when things are scary and new, you can find happiness in small things." Help these readers find several places in the text that support that theme. For Kek these joy-filled things are those that remind him of home: a piece of cloth, memories of his family, the cow, storytelling. Suggest that students put a sticky note containing their big idea on their desk as they read, and later to put it in the center of a club meeting as something to talk off of. Some clubs might make a "conversation board" that contains a blank space at the center for children to put the sticky note that is "in play" in a book club discussion.

Eventually you will want to help students reword the theme so that it is broadly applicable. Prompts like, "This is important because . . ." or "In life . . ." can help. You can also coach children to try deleting the character's name so that instead of "Kek learns that even when things are scary and new . . ." you say, "Even when things are scary and new . . ."

Once students are caught up in this work, they'll be ready for today's work and the lessons that follow. You'll aim to teach children that there are multiple themes that exist in a text, that themes open up and change as we read on, and that various parts of a text can support different, even contradictory ideas.

"Readers, can I interrupt you? During today's minilesson I spoke about how as a reader, you carry your interpretations with you. Now I want to remind you that you also carry all of the skills and strategies you've ever learned as a reader. One strategy is using thought prompts to expand your thinking. Some of you are starting to jot down some of your ideas, so I wanted to remind you that thought prompts can help you extend ideas, gather evidence, and challenge your own thinking." I pointed to the chart of prompts I had hung. "Use these prompts to explore and expand your thinking as you prepare to meet with your clubs."

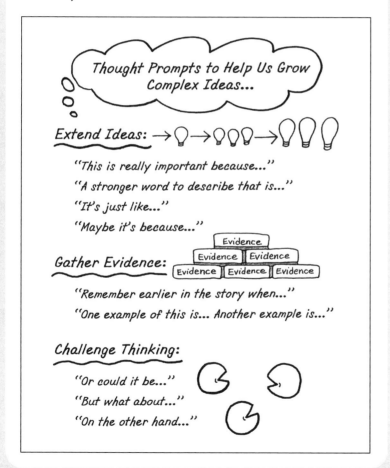

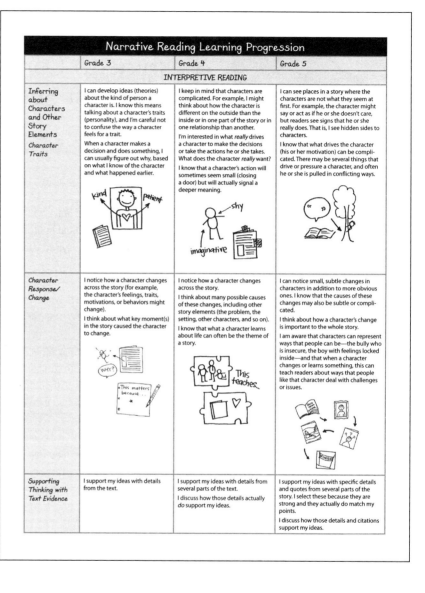

Pushing to Connect Interpretations that at First Seem Unrelated

Prepare students to meet with their clubs.

Readers, before I send you off to meet and talk in your clubs, I want to leave you with a tip that will help your conversation be the best it can be. Today, I saw many of you rethinking your initial interpretations. Some of you opened up your interpretations to fit with new information from your reading. Others revised your interpretations completely or started new lines of thinking.

"When you meet with your clubs in a few minutes, you may find that while you all started today's workshop with similar interpretations, many of you will be bringing new, smarter thinking to the table. When you were young readers, just starting out with partnership and club conversations, you learned to use prompts like 'I agree . . .' or 'I disagree . . .' to respond to each other. While these are still thoughtful ways to engage in conversation, today I'll ask you to do more complex work to bridge your ideas. While at first it may seem that someone has very different ideas, thoughtful readers let these different ideas soak in and then push to see connections between another's thoughts and their own.

FIG. 12–4

"I've put a large piece of construction paper at each meeting spot. I'd like each of you to choose an interpretation to bring to the table. It may be an extension of the work you began after today's mini-lesson, or it may be an entirely new idea. Before beginning your conversation, put your Post-it onto the large piece of construction paper. Then (and here's the hard part), as a club, try to talk *across* your ideas and look for connections. You might say, 'I think that this idea connects to this one because . . .' or 'I'm wondering which part of the text we can study to investigate these two ideas that seem so different.' Use markers, Post-its, or other tools from our supply center to build connections between the ideas you have as a club. I think you'll find that many theories can be true and can even exist together under a larger, overarching idea."

TALKING TO DEVELOP YOUR IDEAS

Readers, you've become accustomed to the pattern of reading and writing about reading every evening. That pattern is important—a sort of breathing in, breathing out. But to write and think well, sometimes one has to step back and not write. Sometimes one needs to fill the well. So tonight, I'm hoping you'll have a conversation about the reading you do, but don't write. You can confer over the phone with a club member, or in person with a family member, or you can have a conversation across the Internet or even with yourself!

Please, as you confer, use the thought prompts that we studied today. Try to use them in ways that help you to have an especially provocative, brave, important conversation.

And if you want, when the conversation is over—flash-draft the best ideas you came to so they don't get lost!

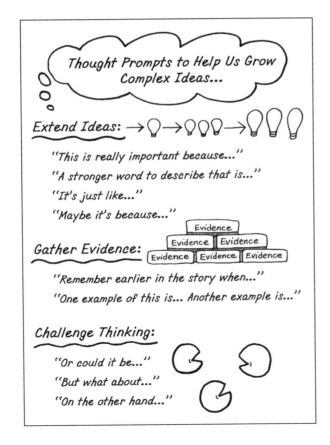

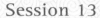

Debating to Prompt Rich Book Conversation

Readers Have Different Viewpoints, Defending with Claims, Reasons, and Evidence

IN THIS SESSION, you'll teach students that readers can debate differing viewpoints on a provocative question about a book they have both read. In a debate, each reader supports his or her side with evidence to persuade the other person.

GETTING READY

✔ Before today's session, read aloud "Grocery Store," "The Story I Tell Hannah on the Way Home," "Library," "Going Up," "Hearts," "White Girl," "Scars," "Bad News," "No More," pages 155–83 in *Home of the Brave*.

✔ Prepare a list of possible debate topics related to *Home of the Brave* on chart paper so that the class can decide which ideas are or are not debatable (see Teaching).

✔ Provide small groups with white boards or chart paper and markers to collect evidence (see Active Engagement).

✔ Provide groups of students with copies of pages 20–22 ("Family"), 32–36 ("Bed"), 43–46 ("Night"), 60–62 ("School Clothes), 123–27 ("Night Talk"), 138–45 ("Ganwar, Meet Gol" and "An Idea"), and 178–83 ("Bad News" and "No More"). These passages have been carefully selected to support one side or another of the topic chosen for debate during the minilesson (see Active Engagement).

✔ On chart paper, create a list of key phrases to present a position in a debate (see Active Engagement).

✔ Prepare chart, "Suggestions for Generating Provocative Debatable Ideas about Texts" (see Link and Conferring and Small-Group Work).

✔ To assess readers and note areas in which kids need support, prepare a box chart (see Conferring and Small-Group Work).

✔ Prepare and display a debate protocol chart, "Let's Have a Club Debate" (see Share).

THIS SESSION propels the work you have done on talking and writing about reading to another step, channeling students to explore the power of debate as a way to capture, defend, and develop ideas. Today's emphasis on argument as a way to wrestle with texts is very much in keeping with most global standards. George Hillocks, Jr., a distinguished proponent of argument, once wrote, "It's clear from observing students in various contexts that although students may intend to present an argument, they often see no need to present evidence or show why it is relevant; they merely express (usually vague) opinions." One way to recruit students to see the need for evidence is by engaging them in debates around their ideas.

Of course, debate is only possible if the ideas are provocative, and it takes some work for students to learn to grow provocative ideas. It would be hard to organize a rousing debate over the claim, "Kek is lonely," but an idea like, "Kek's hopefulness makes him more lonely" would certainly be open to debate. So the session begins with you teaching students to weigh the questions they have been asking about their club book, selecting one that is especially provocative and open to debate. Then you set students up to take a contrary position on that question and to find supporting evidence to persuade people of their view. As kids hunker down to find evidence to support and also to persuade others of the validity of their claims, you will challenge them to prepare to argue their own position—and to anticipate arguments their opponents may make and ways they can respond to them.

As students become skilled at debate, they learn not just to *defend* their initial ideas but to *develop* those ideas. So in this session, you will use debate and argument as a way to teach students the importance of talking about ideas, elaborating on their positions, and of selecting evidence that is the most persuasive.

Debating to Prompt Rich Book Conversation

CONNECTION

Give students a vision for how debate can hone critical thinking by using an example from popular culture.

"I recently overheard a conversation between two children—and it made me think of you and your reading. I was waiting in line at the grocery store, and I was behind a mother and her two daughters, who must have been about five and seven years old. They were talking about the movie *Frozen*.

"The older girl said, 'I want to be Elsa for Halloween this year. She's my favorite character.'

"The younger sister said, 'Well, Anna's my favorite character.'

"The conversation could have ended there, but the mother intervened with an interesting question: 'Which character do you think is stronger?'

"Both girls started talking at the same time:

"'Elsa is stronger—she's so powerful and then she figures out how to control it which made her even stronger!'

"'Anna is stronger—she had to follow her sister through the snow and find a way to help her. She almost died but even when she was dying she still fought for her sister.'

"As the girls kept going, back and forth, I thought: 'Wow, they are having to think really hard to debate each other. It's a lot better thinking than when they just said what character they liked the best.' This made me think: debate can be great for pushing our thinking about reading."

❖ **Name the teaching point.**

"Today I want to teach you that when different readers read the same book, they often develop different viewpoints on provocative questions related to the book. The differences of opinion can spark a debate. In a debate, each person (or each side) presents his or her position and then supports that position with evidence, aiming to persuade the other person, the other side."

One of the jobs that a connection accomplishes is to provide the motivation for a session. This connection tries to say, "The work I am teaching you to do will help you think more critically— and it is work that exists in the world outside school. This is authentic work that will pay off."

TEACHING

Teach children that debates can only occur around a provocative idea that can be argued from both sides. Channel students to test whether ideas you suggest qualify, and to generate others.

"I've been noticing that oftentimes when you and your partner talk about the same book, you have different positions, but instead of seeing those moments of difference as invitations to debate, you just shrug them off, saying, 'Oh well, we disagree.' Because my aim is for you to participate in the world of literate conversations, I want to show you how readers often seize upon a difference of opinion as an invitation to debate, just as the girls in the grocery store were able to say so much more once their mother prompted them to debate.

"Let me lay out the steps for engaging in debate, and walk you through those steps. Later you can do this on your own.

"First, you need to have differences of opinion about a text you both know. But you can only have differences of opinion if your idea is not an obvious idea that *anyone* reading this book is apt to have. The idea needs to be a brave, thought-provoking idea, so that informed people might think differently about it. The idea needs to be provocative—and defensible. That is, for there to be a debate, there needs to be a disputable idea and two competing claims.

"Coming up with brave, provocative ideas is one of the hard parts of this—but you'll learn to do that in time. For now, let's practice thinking about whether an idea is debatable. I'll give you some opinions, some topics, for you to think about. For each opinion, give me a thumbs up if you think this is an idea that could be debated. Give me a thumbs down if it is either too obvious, if the idea really isn't a topic that someone could take 'a side' on, or if it would be hard to defend with evidence." I pointed toward the easel and went through the ideas one by one, the students assessing whether the ideas were debatable, with a thumbs up or a thumbs down.

> Kek is sad. (no, too obvious)
>
> Kek misses his mother. (no, too obvious)
>
> Minnesota is a good place for Kek. (yes, open to debate)
>
> Kek is sadder than Hannah. (yes, open to debate)

"Before we go on, with the group of kids near you, try to brainstorm some other debatable ideas about *Home of the Brave*. When you generate an idea, give it a test—see whether there would be evidence supporting either side."

I listened as children talked, and after a few minutes began adding to the list above, drawing from debatable claims I heard them make (and ignoring the less effective ones, for now).

> Ganwar is a good teacher for Kek.
>
> It is a good idea for Kek to try to fit into American life.

In this part of the minilesson, you are not exactly teaching all children how to generate debatable ideas, but instead you are letting some children carry the ball for others. Given that some may have experience with this from last year, there will be some kids who are ready to practice this independently, but be aware that you are providing some kids with shoulders to ride on.

Kek and Ganwar are complete opposites of each other.

Hannah hates her mom.

Demonstrate how to develop an evidence-based argument for or against one of the claims related to the read-aloud. Take the side that is harder to defend for yourself, leaving the other for the class.

"Before you can participate in a debate, you need to decide upon your positions, whether you are for or against an idea, or in debate speak, pro or con. You know how you take positions on a baseball team (the catcher, the first baseman) and those positions tell you where to stand on the field. Well, you take positions in a debate too. And a thoughtful reader decides on his or her position by reviewing the evidence.

"Take this claim—'Ganwar is a bad influence on Kek.' To decide what position you want to take, pro or con, think over the book, review your notes, recall your ideas. We'll do that really quickly for now, just so you get the idea, though in real life it takes more time. So do some quick research and decide: where do *you* stand on whether Ganwar is good or bad for Kek?" I flipped through the pages of the book, driving home the fact that successful arguments rely on evidence, not just opinion.

I looked up from the book. Gesturing to show that I was listing evidence across my fingers, I said, "I'm remembering how Ganwar teaches Kek how to dress so he won't get teased. And I'm also thinking about the part when Kek gets Ganwar a job on the farm—Kek seems happy then."

Debrief in ways that enable students to try what you have just done.

Pausing to name what I'd done, I said, "Readers, you see that first, I reviewed the evidence to decide on my position, and then I collected evidence from the book to support my position. The evidence is not from my own ideas about how cousins should treat each other, but from the book. Some of you might take a different position, though."

ACTIVE ENGAGEMENT

Channel the class to work together to gather evidence to support the opposing side, distributing relevant passages from the text and white boards or chart paper to help them collect evidence.

"Now, see if you can take a position different than mine. Will you and the kids near you collect some evidence that Ganwar is *bad* for Kek? While you shore up your position, I'm going to be looking for more evidence of *my* position—and if some of you want to come help me with my side of this debate, come on up here."

This is work that students may have begun in fourth grade. If they haven't, you might add some everyday examples to your initial list: practicing outside of the text may be clearer at first. But even if students recognize this from last year, it's worth giving them more opportunities to practice. Really, this is about forcing oneself to question assumptions and see the other side. For example, when I first read the part when Ganwar tells Kek that it's pointless to try to fit in in America, I thought, "Ganwar is so bad for Kek." And much in the book seems to confirm that Ganwar is a negative influence on Kek. But then, I see that Ganwar is struggling too, and that his friendship is important to Kek, and that makes me wonder, "Is that really true?" and I realize that this is totally debatable.

In deciding on the position that you will take in this debate (or any debate you do with your students), try to remember that you want to model the tougher position. Usually one side of the debate will be easier to defend than another, and your instinct will be to take the most obvious position as your own. Don't do that—leave that one for the kids. In this instance, I've got to forage about a bit for evidence that Ganwar is good for Kek, so that is the position I'm taking.

I purposefully chose two examples that might support different reasons later in the lesson: the first example connects to how Ganwar is a teacher for Kek; the second connects to how Kek becomes a kind of teacher for Ganwar—this latter point will later be found to be not as strong in supporting Ganwar's influence on Kek. In this way, I was setting up future work.

"I know you don't have the book and you need to actually cite the text in a debate, so I have copies of a few pages you may want to review." As I said this, I distributed assorted passages (carefully selected to provide the support students needed) to kids scattered about the carpet, knowing children would huddle around those pages. I also passed out a few white boards and markers, so that some individuals could act as scribes, capturing the ideas of the group.

"We're going to do this really fast, so just take three minutes to gather some evidence—help each other. You can record your evidence on your white boards—but don't let me see it before the debate."

For a few minutes, I worked with my advisors to collect boxes-and-bullets style notes, arguing that Ganwar is good for Kek. I jotted my notes on chart paper, half-pretending the children arguing the opposing side wouldn't see the notes (while knowing they would, and wanting them to emulate the format). Meanwhile children gathered notes defending the other position.

Set children up to participate in a bare-bones debate protocol. Give them phrases that they can use to state and defend their positions.

"Okay, time for the debate. Each side needs to present your position, and your evidence." I showed where I'd written some key phrases on chart paper:

I take the position that . . .

My first reason for this is . . . My evidence for that is . . .

My second reason is that . . . My evidence for that is that . . . Also, . . .

Recruiting a child who'd helped develop my position, I said, "D. J. and I will go first, and then can we have a volunteer to represent the other side? You all can whisper suggestions to your representative when it is your turn to argue your position." The children volunteered Anna to articulate the opposing view; she busily got her argument together, and D. J. and I started laying out my side.

Pointing to the chart paper template, which gave key starting phrases as cues, D. J. started:

"I take the position that Ganwar is good for Kek."

I touched one finger to show this would be reason #1, and then touched the words on the template that D. J. read. "My first reason is that he gives Kek realistic advice on how to act in America. My evidence for that is that when Kek is getting dressed, Ganwar lets him know that he has to dress differently or he would get teased. He picks out jeans and a T-shirt so Kek will fit in."

Then I took over, touched a second finger and again, the template, and said, "My second reason that Ganwar is good for Kek is that Ganwar reminds Kek that Kek is not the only one who has gone through terrible loss. My evidence is that Kek often thinks about what Ganwar has gone through as a way to understand how sad Ganwar seems. Also, when Kek gets

You can easily supplement white boards with any kind of paper for kids to jot evidence on.

book club debates
I take the position that Ganwar is a bad influence on kek

My first reason for this is that Ganwar is Shooting down all of kek's idea making kek pecimistic and ruining his self esteem. My evidence for this is that when kek says his mother is alive, Ganwar says she's dead.

My 2nd reason for this is Ganwar is being a bad role model. My evidence is he had a smoky smell he has with his friends Very Shady, smoking?

A Long Walk To Water
My position is they should have left him behind

1 My first reason for this is that children get tired easily. My evidence for this is Salva said that children get tired and the soldier said he wasn't a "man" and couldn't work.

2 My second reason is that they thought that he would be safe where he was. My evidence for this is that the barn is Shelter and he has water nearby and the women to take care of him also there is a war going on around him.

· can do thing strong, Smart, house

· charged by adrenaline
· legs are short
· girls
· dangerous

Ganwar the job on the farm, it is as a way to help Ganwar feel a sense of belonging. Helping Ganwar feel better helps Kek too. He says, 'For a moment, as Ganwar and I hum one of the old songs, we are where we belong in the world.'"

With my help and help from classmates, Anna launched into her argument: "I take the position that Ganwar is bad for Kek, because he is constantly telling him that there is nothing to be happy about in America. *Plus* he is clearly jealous of Kek, and tries to make it seem like Kek's job is not a good idea."

I flipped quickly to the pages from "Night Talk." "And the evidence is . . ."

Here you'll want to make sure the example from you and your helpers contains all the parts—the position, the reason, and the evidence.

Anna nodded. "And the evidence is when Ganwar tells Kek, 'This isn't our country.' It's like he's trying to make Kek feel bad for getting a job, even though he's really jealous."

LINK

Channel students to generate provocative, debatable ideas from the club books they've been reading.

"Remember I began today's minilesson by telling you that I read bestsellers a lot because I like to engage in the book talks that buzz around me. When I read books that others are reading, I'm apt to get into big conversations—and often, into debates—about those books.

Before you go off to read today, will you meet with your club quickly—here on the rug—to come up with a debatable idea that you will read to think about today?

Today's link is a bit more extensive than most. This will be an important time to assess how students are faring with generating debatable questions. Don't be afraid to steer them in the right direction if they are struggling.

As students moved to sit in club formations, pivoting to sit in circles rather than facing front, I suggested the children start by trying to generate provocative ideas about their books. I gave them a list of suggestions to help.

Suggestions for Generating Provocative Debatable Ideas about Texts

- Could you debate which character in your book is more powerful or is happier, or is meaner . . . or some other characteristic?
- Could you debate what the main character draws on, above all, to get past his or her troubles?
- Could you debate which obstacle is the most difficult for the main character?
- Could you debate whether the setting helps or hurts the character?
- Could you debate which secondary character has the greatest effect on the main character?

Some of these suggestions are deliberately repeats from the work students did in fourth grade, and some are extensions. This work is tricky enough that practicing the same work in more complex texts will itself be a new challenge, and yet you also want to add new paths of thinking for students who are ready.

Tell children that they should be able to debate their own position—and also the opposing one.

I then told the children that true debaters are able to argue for either position. I shepherded them to approach their debate with opposing positions in mind, reading in such a way that they gathered evidence to support their position. As clubs began to settle on ideas, I suggested that they make a new page in their reader's notebook, with the debatable idea at the top, and space to collect for both sides of the argument.

Quickly assess if each club truly has a debatable claim as a focus for today's reading.

I moved from club to club, glancing over shoulders and quickly reading their ideas to determine which were okay as debate topics and which would be too obvious, or just too one-sided, to really spur rich debate. As soon as a club showed me an idea that would work, I released that club to go back to their seats and read. I asked the clubs that still needed support in generating provocative topics to stay on the carpet for a small-group lesson.

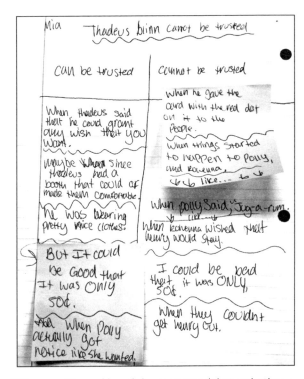

FIG. 13–1 Mia and her club prepare to debate whether a character can be tested. By the end of the period, they have collected ample evidence for both sides.

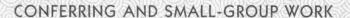

Assessing How Students Find Debatable Topics and Prepare for Debate

YOU HAVE SENT YOUR STUDENTS OFF with a mission today and you will want to be careful not to pull them away from that mission. So, likely, today you will not choose to engage in longer conferences, asking a reader to discuss all she is doing and thinking with a text. Instead, you may want to use your conferring and small-group work time in a few different ways: coaching into readers' abilities to develop debatable ideas and prepare for a debate, and then supporting readers in their preparation.

To start, you will want to quickly support the clubs that are still on the carpet in coming up with debatable topics. You will want to refer to the chart you have already revealed, "Suggestions for Generating Provocative Debatable Ideas about Texts," this time taking more time to think through each suggestion. Tell readers that as you go through the suggestions together, they should think about how they can make that sort of question work for their texts.

You might also offer some additional generalizable questions that readers would be able to apply to their texts. For example, you might say, "I know if I were using *Home of the Brave* and creating a debate, I could also discuss the question 'Is Kek strong or is Kek weak?'" (When you name the question, you can extend your hands out like a scale and show that you have two sides to that scale.) Then coach readers, "Could you debate if a character in your text is strong or weak?" More than likely, your students will be able to debate whether a main character (or minor character) is strong/weak. "Characters are flawed and complicated, which is part of what makes for a great story."

If a student seems to have a sense of a possible question but may be struggling to articulate that question clearly, you might decide to provide support by naming it: "So it seems like you are saying one debatable question for your book might be . . ." (and then name the question as simply and as clearly as you can). Being a little heavier-handed in your conferring and small-group work today can ensure that your students all have debatable questions that will work. Note to yourself who needed the most

support and set a goal of working with those students to strengthen their ability to generate debatable questions with more independence in the future.

After you have addressed this, you can turn to assessing how the other readers are doing in their preparation for debate. You will want to see how your readers go about figuring out what is worth arguing in their texts and their support for those positions. No doubt you will see students having some predictable trouble, and it is worth doing some assessment now to create future small-group work. You'll want to compare notes with teachers from other grades who are also supporting debate, perhaps thinking about some ways that teachers across the school can collect data on what kids are and are not able to do as debaters. You may find that teachers in many grade levels find it helpful to note the areas in which kids need support, using a form like this to quickly plan small groups. The fourth-grade teacher may be using something very similar, but finding that a greater percentage of students are in the first couple of boxes.

Needs help reading with a focused question in mind	Needs help distinguishing reasons/evidence	Needs help finding evidence from across the text
Needs help finding evidence on both sides of the argument	Needs help explaining how evidence supports position	

Doing this assessment work can help you figure out what supports your readers need going forward to help them use text evidence to back their position. It is worth spending the time today to do this assessment, since it can help you to see a trajectory of

(continues)

MID-WORKSHOP TEACHING   Preparing for Debates—Deciding Sides and Prioritizing Reasons and Evidence

Challenge readers to divide their clubs evenly, into two members for each side of the debate.

"Readers, as you continue to read, remember that in a very short while you will be debating with your club about the idea you have selected. It's probably helpful at this point for you to decide sides—which people in your club will present one side of the argument, and which will present the other? At least one person in each club needs to take on each side—I'm hoping you can divide up the sides mostly evenly, with two people on each side. This means some of you may have to take on a side that you don't personally agree with, for the sake of argument. This doesn't mean you have to change your mind, just that you are willing to try this out. Right now, figure this out with your club, then put a star by the side of the debate that you will present during our share time today."

I moved quickly between clubs, urging students to not take this too personally, and to quickly decide on sides. I made a point of publicly congratulating students who took a risk and chose sides that were difficult or ones they did not agree with. When most clubs had decided, I added another layer to their reading work.

Ask students to read forward or reread analytically, prioritizing reasons and evidence.

"Okay, now you have your lens! During the rest of reading time today, you will either reread or read forward, all the time gathering reasons and evidence to support your side of the debate. If I were supporting the idea that Ganwar is good for Kek and I got to the chapter 'No More,' I would want to collect quotes like, 'Ganwar keeps going to the farm. But he doesn't say anything to me about it.' This seems more supportive of my side than when Kek helped Ganwar get a job, because it's more directly about Ganwar being kind to Kek. I would put a star next to this and make sure I talk about it in my debate. As you reread or read, be sure to star your reasons and evidence that feel the strongest."

small-group work and conferring that will be needed for your readers. This assessment may also help to inform your teaching of later Literary Essay and the *Research-Based Argument Essay* units in your writing workshop if you are using the Units of Study in Opinion, Information, and Narrative Writing series.

Of course, you'll also want to support your readers in preparing for their debates, and that will mean addressing some of what you are seeing. Some of these concerns will be more immediate—for example, coming up with evidence to support a position.

For these students, model how you reread parts of a text using your position as a lens, looking for details that stand out. Push students to not just find a part, but to note the exact details that they think support their position.

For many students this work will be challenging, and you'll surely see that there are clear paths for future small-group work and conferring. You may be working with groups in which:

- You bring several quotes from the read-aloud to the group, supporting them in prioritizing which examples best support one or the other side of the debate.

- You work with readers who are ready to tackle forming more nuanced questions and positions.

- You work with readers to find debates within the story itself—for example, Ganwar and Kek have an ongoing debate about whether hope is a good or a foolish idea.

All of this work can come in the future. For today, you have made sure to assess the strengths and needs of the class and have ensured that each of your students has a provocative, debatable idea about his or her text.

Debating to Lead to More Complex Thinking

Ask clubs to caucus to plan for team debates within clubs.

"Okay, clubs, the time has come! You will now have a chance to debate your provocative ideas. Here's how it will work."

I unveiled a chart titled "Let's Have a Club Debate!"

Let's Have a Club Debate

1. Read to gather reasons and evidence for both sides of the debate.

2. Caucus with your same-side club member(s): plan your strongest reasons and evidence in box-and-bullets style. Decide who will present and who will support.

3. Present! Each side gets one minute to present strong reasons and evidence. One person presents at a time. Same-team partner may whisper in or write notes. Opposite side takes notes.

4. Caucus again! This time, compare notes and decide which of your opponents' points were strongest—how could you talk back to them?

5. What are we thinking now? Plan with your club for how to read on tonight, carrying this debate with you into your reading and into your writing about reading. Write a rebuttal response to bring in tomorrow.

"You've already completed Step 1. Right now, talk with your same-side club partners. Caucus! This means make a plan for your presentation—what will be your best reasons and evidence? Who will be your first presenter? Rehearse a little and practice being convincing—use your voice to state your case strongly."

Teachers, this is a modified version of the Debate Protocol. If you are teaching the Units of Study in Opinion, Information, and Narrative Writing, you will see this protocol in full in Grade 5 Unit 4 The Research-Based Argument Essay. Some students may have experienced the full protocol last year. Either way, it's fine—but be aware if this is new to students. It is a lot to pack in and students are not rounding out the experience with an actual rebuttal. You may decide to turn this session into two, giving more time to this work and expanding it to include an opportunity for additional caucus and rebuttal.

One child from each side presents to the club.

"Are you ready? It's time! Side One—you will have one minute. Only one person from your side will present. Your same-side partner can coach you in writing or whisper in if you need help or run out of things to say before the timer goes off. Be sure to take notes when you are not presenting—you will need these for your rebuttal. Ready, set, go!"

I didn't interfere with students' presentations. At times I mimed whispering or writing to partners who were sitting by as their presenter floundered. This spurred them to throw a lifeline to their presenter and help them say one more point or offer another example. At one minute, I called time and had the groups switch to present the opposite side.

Caucus again to plan rebuttal.

"Debaters, this is a crucial moment. Meet with your same-side partner again. This time look carefully at what your opponents said. How could you talk back to their points? Be sure you have something to say back to their most powerful reasons and evidence. Be ready to tell them why they are wrong!"

I didn't allow too much time here, even though, of course, it could take an enormous amount of time! The point is that the children had to go back again to their notes and see them in a new light—this time in the service of refuting the opposite side. I moved quickly from club to club, prompting for students to remember to plan to use evidence in their rebuttal, not just present reasons they disagree.

"We don't have time right now to actually present the rebuttal debates—even though I would love to, as I've heard you planning such strong counterattacks! But here's how you will get to continue this work."

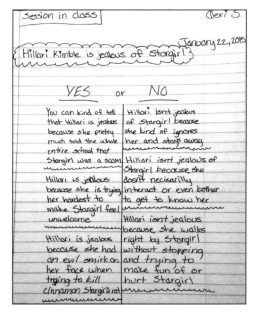

FIG. 13–2   Alexi and his club debate *Stargirl*.

SESSION 13 HOMEWORK

TRANSFERRING DEBATE WORK INTO TONIGHT'S READING

Readers, tonight, as you're continuing to read, keep thinking about the debate you started today. Think about your opponent's points, and read to gather new evidence to counter those points. When you have finished tonight's reading, spend five minutes writing to talk back to the other side.

Be sure to use evidence to back up your thinking, and to talk back to the evidence your opponent used. Is there another way you could read those parts that the other side mentioned?

Session 14

Reflecting on Ourselves as Book Clubs

THIS SESSION focuses on the quality of conversation in book clubs. The kids may be surprised that you are focusing on their talk as opposed to their writing or reading. One of the curious things about school is that talk is often devalued. If your principal, says, "I walked past your room today and looked in—everyone was talking," you won't tend to respond, "Thanks! I'm so proud of them." Yet the funny thing is that when we human beings want to grow, what do we do? We talk. We attend advanced seminars, we talk things over with a friend, we go to counseling, we form a study group with our colleagues. No matter which way we choose, what are we doing? Talking.

It is important that you attend to your students' ability to talk in their clubs. You'll be teaching them to be stronger, more thoughtful readers. You'll tell students that people who rank the skills that will be most needed by upcoming generations all place a great premium on the ability to work in small groups. That is one of the reasons for today's focus.

But the reasons are wider and deeper. There is a very thin line between comprehension and talk. When talking with a club, the reader does the exact sort of thing that he ideally does in his own mind during reading. Perhaps in the club, the reader says, "Did you notice the way . . . ?" Then others add on. "Yes, I think that's because . . ." "Or maybe, it is because . . ." "This reminds me of that other text which also . . ." Learning to pursue a conversation has a lot to do with learning to follow a trail of thought. And the important thing is that the conversations people have in the air with others become conversations that they have in their own minds as they read.

To teach clubs to raise the level of their talk, you will once again return to the video of students discussing *My Name Is María Isabel*. This time, however, you'll focus their attention not on the ways in which the club develops ideas, but rather on the behaviors and routines that allow them to have such high-level discussion. You'll ask students in each book club to divide up, each focusing on a different aspect of the club's work and reporting back to the team as a whole. Your goal is for students to not only learn from the students in this other club, but to feel inspired to lift the level of their own club conversation.

IN THIS SESSION, you'll guide students through an inquiry to explore how an effective book club elevates the level of its reading, thinking, and conversations about books.

GETTING READY

✔ Before today's session, read aloud "Last Day," "Summer," "More Bad News," "Sleep Story," pages 184–200 in *Home of the Brave*.

✔ Prepare a video clip for students to study. We recommend using the book club conversation about *My Name Is María Isabel* or *Bud, Not Buddy*. Links to these video clips are available on the online resources (see Connection, Teaching and Active Engagement).

✔ Prepare a chart titled "What Makes Book Club Conversations the Best They Can Be?" with four columns (see Teaching and Active Engagement and Homework).

✔ Provide students with copies of Reading Literature Progression, grades 3, 4, and 5 (see Share).

Reflecting on Ourselves as Book Clubs

CONNECTION

Set readers up for the work of the day: inquiry, self-reflection, and goal-setting.

"You already know that goal-setting and self-assessment are important. Anyone who aspires to become dramatically better at anything sets goals and then uses tools—stopwatches, scales, statistics—to check on progress toward those goals. You've been doing that as well—setting goals for your reading and writing growth and using checklists, learning progressions, feedback from partners and clubs, to help you keep track of your progress.

"Today, I want to think with you about goal-setting not in relation to the volume of reading you are doing, or to the qualities of writing about your books that you are doing—although both are important. Instead, I want to spotlight something equally important: your participation in your book club.

"You might be surprised. You might be thinking, 'Really, you are going to assess my participation in the book club?' But here's something you may not know. There is a lot of research about the skills that kids are going to especially need in the years ahead, like when you guys are grown up and starting in jobs, and all of the research says that an ability to work really productively in small groups is one of the most valuable skills that a person could have. When you are grown up and it is your job to coordinate New York City's subway system, or to protect California from devastating drought, or to rebuild a bridge, or to develop a cure for a new disease . . . you won't do any of those projects alone. You'll work shoulder to shoulder with others, and your ability to do that matters.

"We've studied student writing that is especially effective and you've used that work to help you aspire to do better at writing about reading. So today—as we finish our second bend in this unit and prepare to start our last, a final stretch of time working in clubs—I thought it might be helpful to study a club that many of us think is especially effective so that perhaps you can use that club to help you aspire to do better within your own."

Explain that studying another book club can help students identify goals worth working toward.

"You've seen this video earlier in this unit, when you were studying ways to grow ideas through talk. It won't surprise you that we are revisiting it—in the writing workshop you revisit 'Eleven' and other mentor texts repeatedly. This time when you watch this club talking about *My Name Is María Isabel*, I hope you watch with the goal of noticing something these kids are doing that you might try to do, too."

You are setting students up for an inquiry. It is important that, just as they reflect on their reading and writing about reading, they have the opportunity to assess their book club conversations (and then set goals to raise the level of the work they are doing). We've found that showing students another club's work is far more effective than simply telling them what they should be doing. Then, too, watching a proficient club gives students the opportunity to create their own student-facing rubrics, which means they will better understand the goals and have increased investment in meeting them.

If you would prefer to show students another book club, the video of a group discussing Bud, Not Buddy *is an especially potent example of strong interpretation work. The relationships among the club members are not as notable, but the way in which the club stays with and develops an interpretation by staying on point is impressive. This video is available on our online resources.*

Name the question that will guide the inquiry.

"Today, then, our minilesson will be an inquiry, an investigation, exploring an important question: 'What do book club members do in an effective book club that lifts the level of the club's work?'"

TEACHING AND ACTIVE ENGAGEMENT

Ask each student to take one of the four questions as a lens.

"Let me jot a few subtopics you might watch for," I said, jotting subtopics on a chart. "I'm going to suggest that rather than trying to study *all* of these things on the video, each book club member takes on a different role." I added, "Talk among yourselves, deciding who will take which lens. Once you decide, write your lens—the question you will try to answer—at the top of a sheet in your reading notebook. As you watch the video, jot what you notice so you can share your observations later with the class."

What Makes Book Club Conversations the Best They Can Be?

1. What keeps the conversation about books going?	2. How does writing about reading fuel a book conversation?	3. What happens to the topics that a club member brings up?	4. What kinds of things are talked about?

Then I prepped each group just a bit, quickly. "Group 1, in addition to watching to see how they keep the conversation going, think about whether they use any thought prompts." I gestured to the chart of thought prompts. "If there are new thought prompts you hear, let's chart them. Watch them with eagle eyes, too, studying physical moves and eye contact that might keep the talk going."

Group 2. "Pay attention not only to *what* they have but to *how* they use their writing about reading. Do they refer to it? Read it to each other? Jot what you notice so you can share with the group."

Group 3. "You'll see an idea is brought out. What happens to that idea? How long is it in play? What makes a difference?"

Group 4. "You have a great job—it is one of the most interesting and challenging things to listen for. Here are some tips. Listen for the *kinds* of things the group talks about. You may notice that they don't just retell or predict or make connections. What sort of reading work are they doing? What kinds of things do they talk about?"

We strongly encourage you to show a video (you'll be amazed by the buy-in you get from kids), but if this feels too daunting or is impossible for other reasons, you might, instead, consider a fishbowl. This means you will help a book club prepare a strong conversation that demonstrates the elements you want other students to notice (see our finished chart below for ideas) and then have the group repeat the conversation in front of the class. The class will gather around the students and peer in on their conversation, which is where the term fishbowl *comes from.*

I give each group one lens and tips about what to look for, knowing that this will allow them to focus keenly on one element of the conversation. Later, each club will have a chance to share what they noticed about their category.

Show the video, stopping intermittently to give students a chance to share observations with their group. Coach in as they watch, helping them to spot major moves made by the book club.

I began the video, ready to stop it once or twice to highlight key points and to nudge group members to watch with alertness and to record.

Stop the video as needed, channeling students to notice the moves the book club is making.

After the first boy in gray spoke, I paused the video. "Be sure you are jotting right from the start. Group 2, did you notice that he returned to a part he had Post-it'ed? Group 3, did you notice that he started the conversation with an idea and text support? Group 4, what reading skill is he demonstrating? Group 1, how are the other group members showing that they are listening? Also notice how the next person *builds on* what this student says. What language does he use? I'll replay that part in case you missed something and then we'll go forward."

When working with kids, you'll find that a little extra help at the start (you'll notice we're even suggesting you give away a bit of what students should have noticed) goes a long way in supporting them as they do this work with more independence going forward.

I replayed the beginning of the scene and students immediately began jotting as the first boy in the club shared his thinking. After watching the rest of the video, I channeled students to talk among themselves. I carried my clipboard, jotting a few of their ideas on the class chart, writing these as things people can do to make a club conversation better (rather than simply as records of their observations).

This is really a time-management move. I didn't want to keep kids on the rug much longer, and charting anything and everything each group noticed takes a long time. By charting a few things beforehand, then letting each group add one or two more items, I'm expediting the process.

Call the students back together, share the chart you've begun to fill in with overheard observations, and ask them to add to the chart by sharing more ideas.

"I jotted some of what I heard you say on this chart," I said. "Look it over and think about these things—did I capture the main things you noticed or should we add onto the chart?"

What Makes Book Club Conversations the Best They Can Be?

1. What keeps the conversation about books going?	2. How does writing about reading fuel a book conversation?	3. What happens to the topics that a club member brings up?	4. What kinds of things are talked about?
• Try prompts like: "It is is not only that, but also . . ." "And also, . . ." • Look interested. • Make eye contact. • Speak nicely, even when you disagree.	• Do some writing about reading and use Post-its in your notebook before meeting with your club. • Bring your reading notebook to the conversation.	• Ideas are repeated. • Return to important examples in the book and study them together. • Talk about one person's ideas, trying to say something new about the idea.	• Retell a part of the book with a lot of feeling • Think about why things happen. • "Maybe it is because . . ."

The children named things that should get added to the chart, saying things like, "They give a lot of evidence from the text," Peter said, "but they don't just say it, they open up the book and read it." Anna added, "And they point to it."

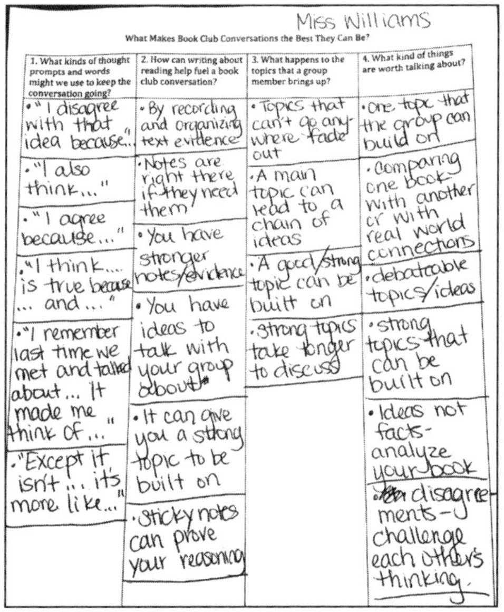
Miss Williams

What Makes Book Club Conversations the Best They Can Be?

1. What kinds of thought prompts and words might we use to keep the conversation going?	2. How can writing about reading help fuel a book club conversation?	3. What happens to the topics that a group member brings up?	4. What kind of things are worth talking about?
• "I disagree with that idea because..." • "I also think..." • "I agree because..." • "I think.... is true because ... and..." • "I remember last time we met and talked about... It made me think of..." • "Except it isn't ... it's more like..."	• By recording and organizing text evidence • Notes are right there if they need them • You have stronger notes/evidence • You have ideas to talk with your group about • It can give you a strong topic to be built on • Sticky notes can prove your reasoning	• Topics that can't go anywhere fade out • A main topic can lead to a chain of ideas • A good/strong topic can be built on • Strong topics take longer to discuss	• One topic that the group can build on • Comparing one book with another or with real world connections • Debatable topics/ideas • Strong topics that can be built on • Ideas not facts-analyze your book • disagreements-challenge each other's thinking.

FIG. 14–1 A teacher compiles her own chart based on what students shared.

"They also repeat what each other said. When the girl in the pink shirt was talking, she repeated what the person said before, but she added a bit more." Anna looked at her notes. "She said that the character was vulnerable *and* nervous. And also sometimes they disagreed." As they talked, I added to the chart.

LINK

Prepare students to use what they noticed to lift the level of their own book club conversations.

Then I said, "We've made a long list of observations, but here is my question. So what? Are you going to be different as a club member because of what you noticed? I want to go back to what I said earlier about the importance of learning to work well within small groups. It is the truth that any list of twenty-first-century skills that all kids really, really need includes that you need to know how to work well in small groups.

"The key is the word *work*. The goal is not just warm, fuzzy, feel-good groups. The goal is learning to work well in small groups—and that means that not only you work well, but others in the group work well because you are there.

"We've thought a lot about what is involved in really effective book clubs. There could be a lot of things we haven't yet listed. My point is that this matters.

"So that this new thinking doesn't get too far away from you, I'm going to suggest that your clubs talk first and then read later today. But rather than going straight to your clubs, take a few minutes to prepare. Remember that some of what made the María Isabel book club talk successful was that each member came to the conversation prepared. They had Post-it'ed, they had written about ideas in their notebooks. Do the same for the next five minutes. You might also mark a few scenes in your book that are worth rereading and studying with your club. I'll let you know when it is time to transition into book clubs."

You can either write on a large chart, for all to see, or jot responses (and perhaps some of what you hoped kids would notice!) on a sheet of paper that you later distribute to students.

When teaching a lesson on talk, it is best to have students go off and talk first, while the learning is fresh in their minds.

Methods for Teaching into Book Clubs

WHILE THERE IS PERHAPS nothing quite as powerful as the one-to-one conference, small-group instruction allows teachers to efficiently meet the needs of multiple students, all the while coaching them independently to meet individual needs. Book clubs offer unique opportunities for small-group work. First, the students are already grouped with other readers at the same (or similar) reading level. These readers often benefit from help with similar strategies, as well. Because the students are all reading the same book, in-book work becomes increasingly easy for the teacher to manage. Also, students can rely on each other. If a book is a notch too hard or has a tricky part, they can work through it together.

You'll want to seize the opportunities provided by this unit, especially the "ready-made groups." Use small-group instruction to lift the level of skill work *and* help students tackle more challenging texts. As discussed in an earlier Conferring and Small-Group Work section, one method of instruction that will be particularly potent for moving readers is guided reading. Aside from your standard strategy group, when teaching books clubs, there are a few additional methods we've found especially effective.

Proficient Book Club Member

Rather than stopping a book club conversation to teach something, simply join it! After noting the particular needs of a club through quiet observation, you'll want to join in on the conversation, prepared to help them tackle the difficulty they are having. Let's say a book club is doing a superb job of listening and talking, but is not returning to their text to gather evidence or reread. You might pull up to this club and ask, "Can I join in on the conversation?" Then, as students discuss their ideas, you'll want to interject with a few, carefully calculated comments. "Is there evidence for that in the text?" you might ask one student after he or she shares a thought. "Let's all look back and see if we can find a scene to reread." After a few minutes of being a proficient club member, nudging students to look back at the text and reference specific examples, call "time out" and return to the role of teacher. Explain the situation to students. "I joined your book club because I was noticing that, while you were having wonderful

ideas, you weren't citing evidence or returning to your book to reread. Do you see the way that I asked Jared for evidence to prove his idea? Later I suggested that we all go back and reread a key scene in your book. These are things you can do, without me, to raise the level of your book club conversation."

Your participation in the club allowed students to experience what it feels like to have a more text-based conversation, and you named your teaching point at the end so that they can continue to do the same work on their own.

MID-WORKSHOP TEACHING **Ask Clubs to Set Goals for Strengthening Their Talk before Sending Them Off to Read Independently**

"Wow, today's conversations sounded fantastic! So many of you were applying what you learned from the María Isabel group—to the ideas you bring to your club, your body language, your writing about reading, your talk prompts—to strengthen your club conversations. I think you talked longer and more powerfully than you ever have before!"

I continued, "We want to make sure your book clubs continue to get stronger. To do that, will you take a moment for self-reflection work? Use the chart from today's inquiry to consider what your club did well today and what could still be improved upon. Decide on a few goals, jot them on a Post-it, and put them in your club folders. This will help you remember what you are working on the next time you meet.

"Let's spend the rest of our time reading today!"

Whisperer

We often use the "whisper" method when we want to empower students to raise the level of their own conversation. Rather than joining the conversation and modeling high-level work, you'll act as a quiet coach, whispering into the ears of students and suggesting they try one talk move or another. For instance, you might pull up next to a student who is dominating the conversation and suggest she ask quieter members of the group to join in. Coach her a bit on how to include others in the conversation.

You might then move to a quieter student and help him or her gather some thoughts. "Let me help you get started," you might whisper. "Sometimes it helps to repeat the words of the club mate who spoke before you, before you try to add on. Let's try it. I'll stay here and help you along."

If you choose this method of teaching, imagine yourself as a quiet little elf, sprinkling a bit of teaching here and there and then leaving the group as quietly as you came.

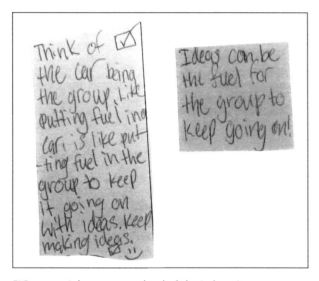

FIG. 14–2   Jake compares book clubs to keeping a car running.

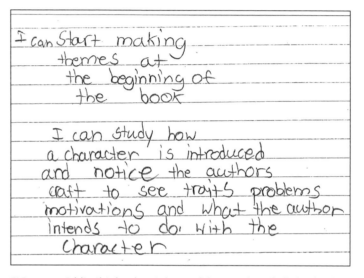

FIG. 14–3   Eddie thinks about the work he can do to help his book club have stronger conversations.

Using a Learning Progression to Assess and Set Goals for Determining Themes

Keep students in club formation to add another layer to the self-assessment work of the day.

"Fifth-graders, your reading time flew by! I could tell that your reading was influenced by the goals you set for your clubs. I noticed many of you using Post-its in a more focused way than I've seen before. Others were stopping to jot questions and notes. I think that being in a club and planning for your talk is helping you take your reading more seriously.

"I think that this can work the other way around as well. If you really work on reading and rereading to track themes well, your club conversations are going to be so much stronger. For our share time today, I want you to use a different kind of tool to assess your club work—and this time, it's about the level of your reading and thinking.

"Do you remember the learning progressions you used on Day 3 of our unit, to lift the level of your responses to your preassessments? Just the way you go to the doctor every year to make sure you are growing up strong, it's important to check in on yourself as a reader now and again, too. Let's focus on theme for today, since that is what we've been working on during this bend of our unit. Use the learning progression to assess yourselves. Take a look at it, and talk to each other about where you think your conversations and thinking have been so far. Have you only been thinking about theme as something to read for at the end, as in the third-grade level? Or have you been having conversations about what your book is really about—check out the fourth-grade column. Or have you been tracking many possible themes—this is the work you want to be doing as fifth-graders. Be honest with yourself so that you can set goals that will allow you to grow into a stronger and wiser reader. Once you've identified a few things that can be goals for you, the next step is to record these goals. And for the rest of the unit, let's make sure to use these progressions to check on ourselves and raise the level of our thinking and reading."

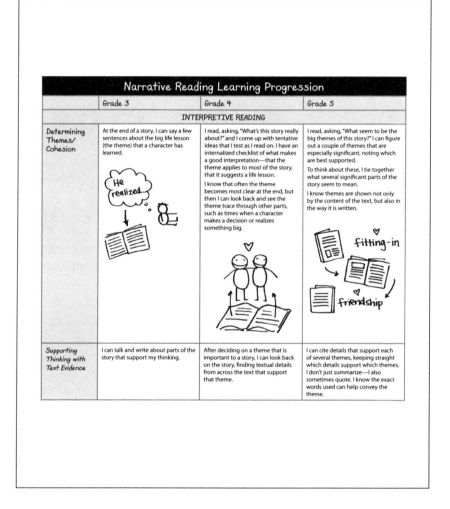

I gave students a few minutes to self-assess their reading work and set goals, before asking them to tuck their checklists safely into their reading folders.

"Keep these goals in mind as you continue reading tonight to meet your reading volume goals."

 ## SETTING YOUR OWN GOALS AS A READING CLUB CONTRIBUTOR

Readers, after you read to meet your reading goals for tonight, think back to today's work. Think about the video you watched and your discussion of how to improve your book club conversations. Then reflect on your own individual contributions to club conversations. Study the chart from today's lesson again.

What are some things you do well in the club as an individual? What are some things you might do better? How could you contribute more effectively to club conversations? Jot down specific things you might have said or done differently today, and write your own club goals. Keep those goals in mind as you prepare for future club conversations.

(See the table of ideas and suggestions on the next page.)

What Makes Book Club Conversations the Best They Can Be?

1. What keeps the conversation about books going?	2. How does writing about reading fuel a book conversation?	3. What happens to the topics that a club member brings up?	4. What kinds of things are talked about?
• Try prompts like: "It is is not only that, but also . . ." "And also, . . ." • Look interested. • Make eye contact. • "Except it isn't just because . . ." • "Like ___ said, (then add on)	• Do some writing about reading, marking in your notebook with Post-its before meeting with your club. • Bring your reading notebook to the conversation. • Use your writing about reading to come up with ideas to talk about.	• Ideas are repeated. • Return to important examples in the book and study them together. • Talk about one person's ideas, trying to say something new about the idea.	• Retell a part of the book with a lot of feeling. • Think about why things happen. • "Maybe it is because . . ." • Talk about ideas, not facts. • Add onto each other's ideas to make them more complex. • Give evidence to support ideas. • Return to important parts of the book and study them together. • Talk more about one person's idea, trying to say new, interesting things about it. • Challenge someone's idea if you disagree with it.

BEND III

Thematic Text Sets: Turning Texts Inside Out

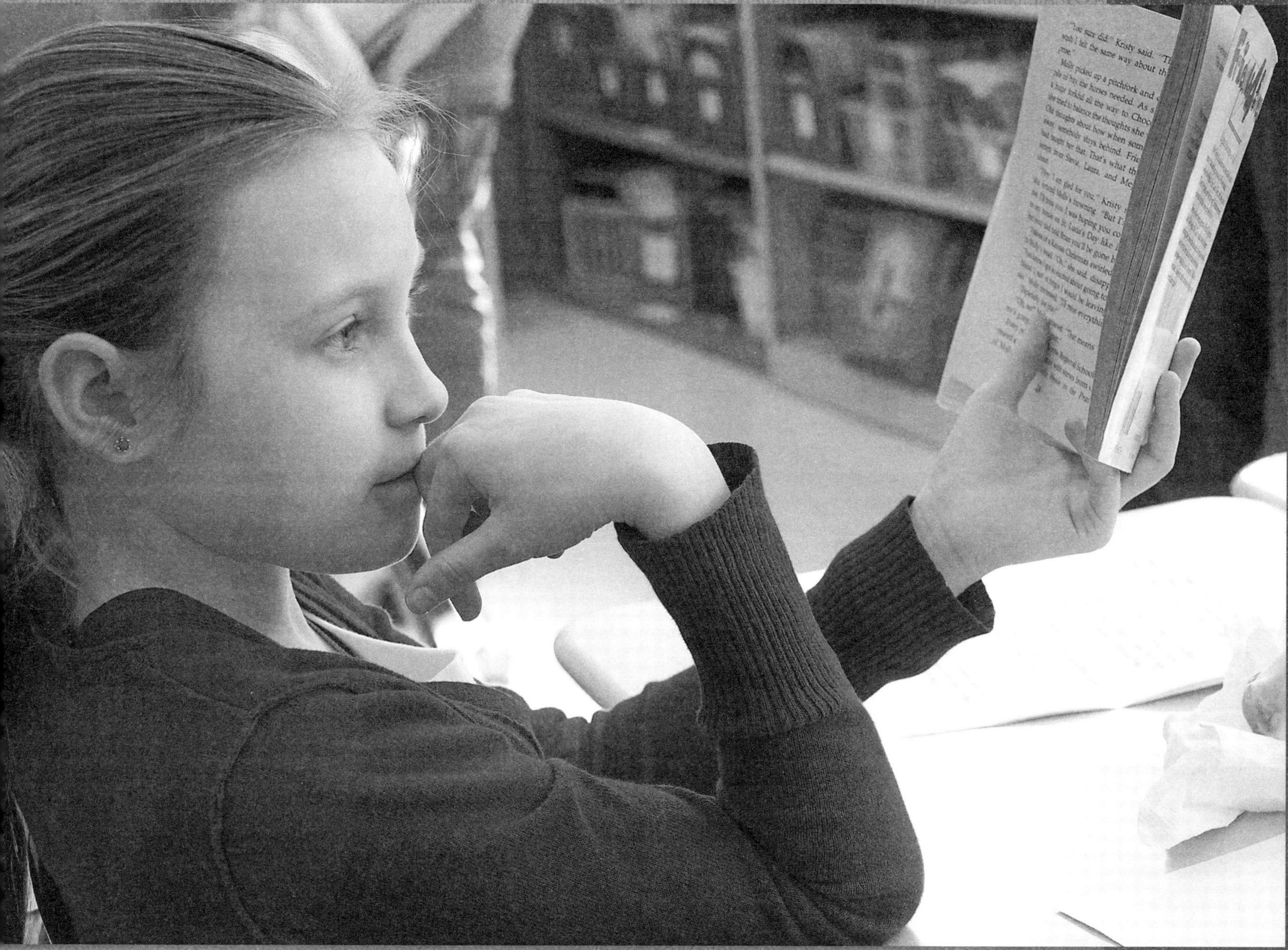

Two Texts, One Theme
A Comparison Study

IN THIS SESSION, you'll teach students that sophisticated readers consider universal themes as they read, comparing and contrasting those themes across different texts.

GETTING READY

✔ To prepare for today's session, make up "starter" text sets for students to compare themes. You may want to refer to lists of stories, poems, and other texts provided on Online Resources (see Link, Conferring and Small-Group Work, Mid-Workshop Teaching and Share).

✔ Before today's session, read aloud *Fly Away Home* (or a comparable text that you choose) to familiarize students with this text. Be prepared to read aloud excerpts to students during the minilesson (see Teaching).

✔ Provide sentence strips and markers for each club to write selected book themes (see Connection).

✔ Have a white board (or chart paper) on hand so you can jot students' ideas for themes (see Teaching).

✔ Display chart, "Prompts to Explore Similarities and Differences in Texts" (see Share and Homework).

✔ Introduce Bend III anchor chart, "To Deepen Interpretation, Readers Can . . ." (see Share).

IF YOU'VE EVER BEEN IN A BOOK CLUB FOR ADULTS, you'll remember those moments when, as you're talking about a book, someone says, "You know, this same idea came up in . . ." Then you're off and running, comparing how two authors develop a similar theme. You'll also find that when club members choose books, they may be drawn to books that might cultivate similar themes. Often one proactive member will say, "We should read *this* next, because it may deal with this idea as well . . ." The truth is, it's incredibly satisfying to find that an idea you committed to comes up again in other books. It's more than satisfying, though. So much of what makes stories meaningful is how the lessons and themes that authors suggest appear transferable. It's the act of applying themes to other texts that suggests the possibility of these themes being at work in many lives, including our own.

Today, you play somewhat the role of the proactive club member, to all your kids' clubs—that is, you offer suggestions for texts that will be interesting to lay alongside the novels kids have been reading. Be sure to invite your students to make suggestions, as well. If the teacher is in charge of "finding texts with a certain theme," you take on too much of the intellectual work. Also, make your suggestions somewhat tentative. Saying "I'm not sure, but I'm thinking it might be interesting to lay this text alongside the one you just read . . . see what you think, and let me know . . ." creates an intellectual invitation. The kids will feel as if you are wondering if these texts might go together, not that you've decided for them. Your tentativeness will increase students' agency.

You'll begin by inviting each club to list some of the themes they've investigated in their novel(s), then to choose a theme they want to explore in other texts. As you hear kids' themes, you'll make comments such as, "Oh, I can imagine some other stories and poems already!" You may point out how it's fascinating how different authors develop similar themes, and remind students of earlier work they've done comparing themes before in stories, songs, and poems.

Then you'll bring up a recent conversation with someone about Eve Bunting's book, *Fly Away Home* (or a similar text), describing how that person made a connection between the character Andrew, in *Fly Away Home*, and Kek in *Home of the Brave*. You will want to explore that idea with your students, starting with the differences between those characters, and digging deeper to uncover the life lessons about hope that they seem to share. This will then lead to a discussion of the thematic similarities and differences between the two texts.

"Applying themes to other texts suggests the possibility of these themes being at work in many lives, including our own."

At this point, you will rally reading clubs to delve into this exciting thematic work on their own. To get this started, provide each club with a bin of multiple copies of two or three short texts, asking kids to read texts together and find one that may develop the same theme as their club novel.

To help with the efficiency of your planning, we've made some suggestions, which we have compiled as short lists of poems, short stories, and other texts that address many themes. These can be found on the online resource that accompanies this series.

Two Texts, One Theme

A Comparison Study

CONNECTION

Have each club pick a theme that applies to the book they are currently reading and about which they feel passionate.

"Readers, before we start today's minilesson, I'm going to ask you and your fellow club members to think back across the book you've been reading and name two or three themes you've been exploring. Then I want you to choose one of these themes that you might be interested in exploring more, in *other* texts, and write that theme on a sentence strip." I gestured toward the sentence strips at my feet.

I gave club members a few minutes to settle on their theme, listening in and coaching as needed. Soon each club had recorded a theme onto a sentence strip (writing the book title under that theme), and all the themes were posted on a chart like this:

As kids are working on naming themes, you'll quickly coach into these decisions, so that they name a theme that will appear in other texts. Often kids need a little help in keeping the theme more universal—you might even think of an overarching theme as a motif, such as "the significance of hope."

Themes and Messages We Are Finding in Our Books

- Hope can help you survive hard times and go on. *Home of the Brave*

- **You need courage to be who you really are. *Becoming Naomi Leon***

- *Friends can help us face things we couldn't face alone. Bridge to Terabithia*

- You can be brave and still be scared. Being brave doesn't mean you are strong all of the time. *Shooting the Moon*

- Writing can help you remember good times and move on from sadness. *Locomotion*

- Don't be afraid to start over. Just keep going! *Esperanza Rising*

These are some of the themes developed by students in our pilot groups, but of course yours will be different.

Explain that themes are universal and can be found in many places.

"Readers, I suggested you choose a theme that you might be interested in exploring in *other* texts, because it's fascinating how different authors develop similar themes. I know you've done this before—you've discovered a theme in one story, or maybe in a song or poem, and then found it in another. Those are often called 'universal themes.' Today I want to teach you how to do even more sophisticated work—to explore *how* different authors develop similar themes."

❖ **Name the teaching point.**

"Today I want to teach that when you're exploring universal themes, what's really interesting is how authors will develop those themes somewhat differently. Sophisticated readers, therefore, ask: what's the same and what's different in how this theme plays out in different texts?"

TEACHING

Recall that when reading a book recently, someone said it seemed similar to the class read-aloud. Suggest that though the specifics are different, two texts could advance the same theme. Ask kids to explore this idea.

"I got the idea for this minilesson because yesterday, when we were talking about Eve Bunting's picture book, *Fly Away Home*, someone suddenly said, 'Hey, Andrew is like Kek!'

"At first that seemed preposterous. I mean, is Kek living in an airport? Has Andrew just come to this country from the Sudan? Does he live in Minnesota?

"But last night, I thought about a life lesson that Kek learns—*hope can help you to survive*. I wondered if this theme was developed in both stories . . . Do you think both texts support the idea that hope can help people survive? Talk with your club and compare your thinking."

The room erupted into conversation. Then I said, "Hmm, . . . it sounds like we're all thinking this theme might be true in both texts. That means there are two things we should do next as readers. First, we should test our theory by seeing if the theme really does play out in *Fly Away Home*. And then, we should see if this theme is exactly the same in both stories, or a little bit different. Okay . . . let's test it!"

Remind students to use an idea as a lens through which to read a text, especially when considering a theme.

"Do you remember how earlier, you learned to take someone else's idea—say, a club member's idea—and read on with that idea almost like a pair of glasses, seeing the upcoming text through the lens of that idea? Are you game to try that now—to read key parts of *Fly Away Home*, seeing if the theme of *Home of the Brave* seems applicable to this text as well?

Session 16 of the fourth-grade Historical Fiction Clubs *unit has kids finding themes across texts, and naming those as universal—so we build on that, and do not introduce it as if it's a new concept.*

By keeping your language tentative—as if you are wondering about the validity of this idea, you keep your students engaged in inquiry. You might also invite students to come up with a few themes that run across both stories, then choose one to test out.

"Sometimes it helps to ask if there are specific parts of the text that seem to especially carry that theme. Where, in *Fly Away Home*, do we especially see the idea that hope helps people survive?"

Soon I read aloud this passage, asking kids to see if the theme of "hope helps people survive" is applicable to this story.

> *Once a little brown bird got into the main terminal and couldn't get out. It fluttered in the high hollow spaces. It threw itself at the glass, fell panting to the floor, flew to a tall, metal girder, and perched there, exhausted.*
>
> *"Don't stop trying," I told it silently. "Don't! You can get out!"*
>
> *For days the bird flew around, dragging one wing. And then it found an instant when a sliding door was open and slipped through. I watched it rise. Its wing seemed OK.*
>
> *"Fly, bird," I whispered. "Fly away home!"*
>
> *Though I couldn't hear it, I knew it was singing. Nothing made me as happy as that bird.*

"The big question is: how does this relate to the idea that 'Hope can help people survive'?"

Encourage students to explore and share different ideas.

"What do you think? Now remember that you all can have different ideas on this. There's no one right answer."

Children called out ideas. "The bird has hope. That's why it keeps banging on the window." "That shows the bird has hard times, not hope." "But this has gotta be about people." "Andrew keeps telling the bird to fly, he has hope for the bird." "Andrew has hope for himself too. He thinks he will find a home."

As students shared their ideas, I jotted them quickly on the white board so we could reference them later. I reread the lines that showed Andrew's response when the bird finally found his way out of the airport:

> *Though I couldn't hear it, I knew it was singing. Nothing made me as happy as that bird.*

"So we began today saying that *Home of the Brave* advances the theme that hope helps people survive in hard times. Now, I think I hear you saying you aren't totally sure, but you think you could write another title under this theme, that *Home of the Brave* and *Fly Away Home* both advance the same theme."

Debrief in a way that is transferable to other texts, other days.

"Do you see how we first came to an 'aha' insight, 'We think these books might be similar in this important way'? Then we tested that idea by rereading parts of the second book, testing to see if the theme seems important across that book. We did the same work across *two* books that we did earlier across *one* book."

You'll embed a tucked tip: readers can ask themselves if specific parts of a text relate to a theme or message. While this isn't the main teaching point, it is a tiny tip that will help students succeed with today's strategy.

Jotting as students talk helps to capture each student's ideas (as well as draw attention to them) so you can reference them as the lesson proceeds. When students go off to work independently, you are apt to see many of them looking back at the board as they try to transfer this complex work to their own books.

ACTIVE ENGAGEMENT

Turn over the reins to students as you read a few more scenes from _Fly Away Home_—and shift their thinking toward comparing and contrasting.

"There's more to do, readers! It's not enough to identify this theme—we need to begin to compare it in both stories. So let's read on, thinking more about this idea of hope in _Fly Away Home_. How is it similar to _Home of the Brave_? How is it different?" I reviewed the ideas I'd jotted so far on the white board and then began to read again from the last few pages of _Fly Away Home_.

> _When Dad comes home from work, he buys hamburgers for us and the Medinas. That's to pay them for watching out for me. If Denny and I have a good day, we treat for pie. But I've stopped doing that. I save my money in my shoe._
>
> _"Will we ever have our own apartment again?" I ask Dad. I'd like it to be the way it was, before Mom died._
>
> _"Maybe we will," he says. "If I can find more work. If we can save money." He rubs my head. "It's nice here, though, isn't it, Andrew? It's warm. It's safe. And the price is right."_
>
> _But I know he's trying all the time to find us a place._
>
> _[. . .]_
>
> _Sometimes I get mad, and I want to run at them and push them and shout, "Why do you have homes when we don't? What makes you so special?" That would get us noticed, all right._
>
> _Sometimes I just want to cry. I think Dad and I will be here forever._
>
> _Then I remember the bird. It took a while, but a door opened. And when the bird left, when it flew free, I know it was singing._

"Talk with your clubs. What ideas are you having about how our theme, 'Hope can help people survive,' applies to this story now? How is _Fly Away Home_ similar to or different from _Home of the Brave_?" After a few minutes I called the students back together.

Share students' thoughts about how the theme applies similarly and differently to the two texts.

"Readers, I heard you come to a few fascinating insights. Some insights are about characters—you're talking about how Kek and Andrew both try to hold onto hope, and how they sometimes get angry, or discouraged, in different ways. But you're also doing something else that's important—you're talking about how hope matters in slightly different ways to these boys. For Kek, his whole life has changed, he's lost everything, he's alone, and hope helps him survive these enormous changes. For Andrew, he has to hold onto hope even though nothing changes. He _wants_ his life to be different, and he has to hold onto hope as a way of holding onto that dream.

I have prechosen parts of Fly Away Home _where I know students will be able to think about hope. In this way, I am setting them up for success and allowing them to focus their attention on the work of discerning the similarities and differences between the theme in these two texts._

"You might have said something slightly different—what really matters is that you looked at how the theme of "hope helps you survive" plays out similarly, but also slightly differently in these stories."

LINK

Recap today's teaching, emphasizing the implications it has for each club's reading work.

"As you just saw, thinking about a theme across *two* texts opens up all sorts of new thinking and possibilities. I'm going to give each club a bin with multiple copies of a couple texts. They are short—a poem, a picture book, a short text. Right now, read over those texts together and decide on one or two that you're going to start with. Find a text that you at least think possibly advances the same theme as the novel you have been reading. If the ones in the bin don't work for you, find one that does. Any text in this room is yours for the taking!

"After you've chosen a text, spread out to work alone for half an hour or so, rereading the text and preparing for a conversation. The texts are short, so you'll spend more time thinking, writing, and preparing for conversation than reading."

As mentioned earlier, you will have followed each book club's conversations enough to know the general ideas they will focus on. Then too, you'll want to rely on your own instincts to pick a text that you know will be well matched to their novel. You can also rely on the lists (mentioned in the Getting Ready section of this session) that we have pre-prepared to help you pick rich texts that are chock-full of various themes, messages, and lessons.

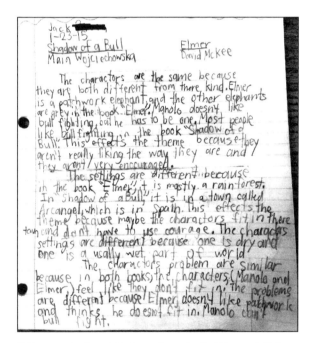 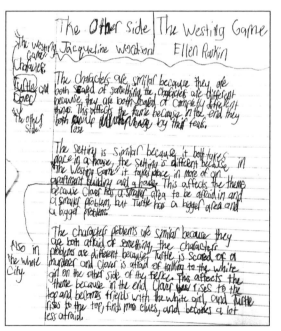

FIG. 15–1   Jack and Cody explore similarities and differences between their book club book and short text.

Supporting Clubs as They Think Across Two Texts

AS STUDENTS THINK ACROSS TWO TEXTS, you may need to revisit some of the larger points made in this unit, and in years past. One predictable issue is balancing small details with larger, interpretive work. You want students to think big, to develop abstract ideas that are large enough to act as umbrellas for more than one book, but you also want those ideas to be grounded in concrete details from the texts. Helping students to find a balance between the large and small, abstract and concrete, will go a long way toward helping them to refine and strengthen their overall thinking.

Help students move between large ideas and small details, ultimately balancing the two.

No doubt you have some typical reader profiles in your class. You may have readers who love big ideas, but they don't back them up with details from the text. Often these thinkers slip into cliché. "Don't put your eggs in one basket," they'll say. Then there are the kids who put Post-its on every page, crammed with detailed notes. They observe everything but construct little from these observations. Interestingly, in both cases, it is helpful to teach and reteach into the relationship between details and big ideas. In this conference, you'll see some moves you can make to help very literal readers begin to make more meaning around details that they notice are repeated in more than one book.

When you approach a club, start by watching how they work with their two texts and listening as they articulate their thinking. "What are the similarities between these texts?" you might ask. Or, "What have you been thinking as you try to apply your theme to both texts?" Listen for whether they are making large, sweeping generalizations or focusing on small details. Many students will resort to focusing on plot—naming out ways in which their club book and their second text have concrete similarities (both characters are poor, for example). You'll want to help them make something bigger of these facts.

"May I teach you one thing to help you take your next step?" you might start. With their assent, you'll go on, "You've walked me through the similarities between the books. Now, see if you can make something bigger and more interpretive of these similarities. One way is by writing out what each similarity stands for. Take the fact that both characters live in poverty. Interpretive readers take that fact and ask: 'What does this mean to the character? What lessons does the character learn about living in poverty?' Let's try this with your first text."

As a group, you might guide students to think about the meaning of poverty in their first text. Perhaps they realize that it leads the character to feel powerless, to hate home, to look for other places where he can belong, or, alternately, to be strong and resilient. Then, you'll coach them to ask, "What about the other text? What does poverty mean to the character in the other text?"

(continues)

MID-WORKSHOP TEACHING   **Rereading Key Scenes to Uncover New Details and Build Stronger Interpretations**

"Readers, I'm impressed to see you not only rereading the new text, but also sections of your original text. You are right that to think between these two texts means thinking about each of them in new ways. You may find, even, that you want to change the way you talk and think about the theme that binds the two texts together.

"Rereading, rethinking: they go together. Will you also be sure that you try to think really closely and clearly about ways the texts are similar and ways they are different? I'm pretty sure that to do that, you will need to do some writing about these texts."

Help the club to articulate the larger meaning of this detail in the second text before asking them to consider whether poverty means the same in each text or something different.

Bring students back to the text, helping them to gather evidence to support their ideas.

Once students have moved beyond the text and developed ideas that are larger and more interpretive, channel them back to the text in search of evidence to support their ideas. "So what you are saying," you might begin, "is that in your first book, poverty is a source of loneliness for the main character. He feels like he doesn't belong because he doesn't have what the other children have. But in the second text, poverty empowers the main character. He works hard and is persistent—constantly looking for ways to make things better for himself and his family. These are big, beautiful observations about the effects of poverty on a person. Let's think about where you see evidence of this in the text."

You might help students develop a T-chart, with one side for the similarities across the texts and the other side for differences. Then, ask students to go back to each text and find specific page numbers to prove the points they are trying to make. If they believe that a character is lonely and isolated because he is poor, what part of the text *shows* this? See if students can go back into the story and find one, two, even three scenes to support this big idea.

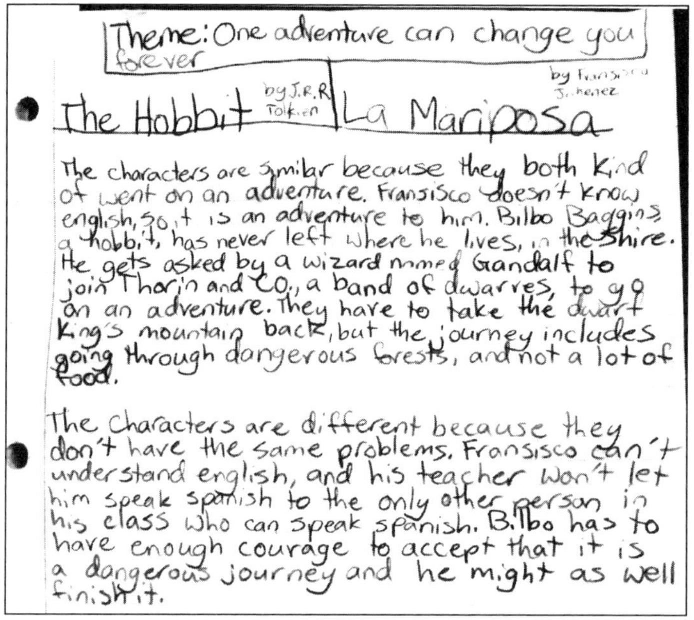
Theme: One adventure can change you forever

The Hobbit by J.R.R Tolkien | La Mariposa by Fransisco Jimenez

The characters are similar because they both kind of went on an adventure. Fransisco doesn't know english, so it is an adventure to him. Bilbo Baggins a hobbit, has never left where he lives, in the Shire. He gets asked by a wizard named Gandalf to join Tharin and Co., a band of dwarves, to go on an adventure. They have to take the dwarf King's mountain back, but the journey includes going through dangerous forests, and not a lot of food.

The characters are different because they don't have the same problems. Fransisco can't understand english, and his teacher won't let him speak spanish to the only other person in his class who can speak spanish. Bilbo has to have enough courage to accept that it is a dangerous journey and he might as well finish it.

FIG. 15–2 The teacher works with Natalia to think about how the similarities and differences she notices about characters affect the theme of the texts.

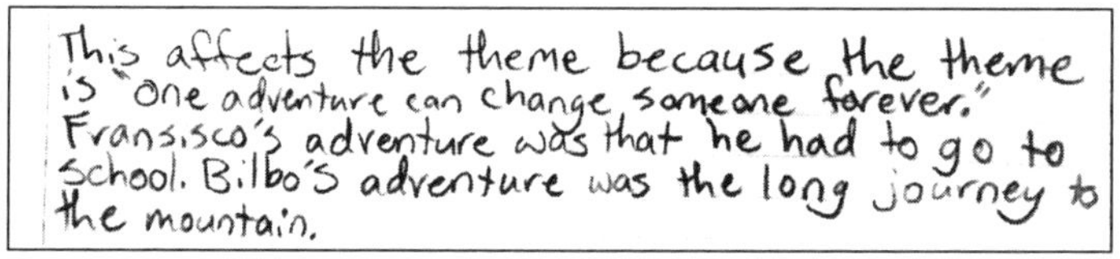
This affects the theme because the theme is "One adventure can change someone forever." Fransisco's adventure was that he had to go to school. Bilbo's adventure was the long journey to the mountain.

FIG. 15–3 Natalia adds on thoughts about the theme.

Using Thought Prompts to Help Express the Similarities and Differences We See Across Texts

Remind students that rehearsing for book club conversations helps to improve the quality of discussion.

"Readers, I can see that you are like shaken soda bottles—bursting to talk about what you have seen as you look between these texts. Remember that you've found conversations go best if you rehearse for them, just as you rehearse for performing in a play or a concert.

"Will you take a few minutes to review your insights and decide on something fascinating to bring to your club? Be sure you not only have an idea, but that you also have some citations from the text. I've been working with Natalia and other students, and feel confident that you will have *great* things to discuss.

"To get started, you may want to use some of these thought prompts to trigger ideas on similarities and differences in texts."

Prompts to Explore Similarities and Differences in Texts

<u>In each text, you might consider</u>:

- The characters are similar because . . . The characters are different because . . . This affects the theme because . . .
- The setting is similar because . . . The setting is different because . . . This affects the theme because . . .
- The characters' problems are similar because . . . The characters' problems are different because . . . This affects the theme because . . .
- The characters' relationships are similar because . . . The characters' relationships are different because . . . This affects the theme because . . .

I gave children a few minutes to prepare. "When your club meets, will one person present first? Whoever that is, I want you to think about this. Take time to lay out your ideas—and not in just a few sentences. You need to make a claim, share your reasons for believing it, and offer examples from the text that support your point. Think of it this way—you will be 'talking in essay structure.'

"The rest of you, your role will be to listen intently to your club mates' ideas, and to look closely at the text to find grounding for those ideas. I'll expect a lot of back-and-forth conversation. Get started!"

Prompts to Explore Similarities and Differences in Texts

Same? ☑   Different? ☑

- The <u>characters</u> are similar because... The characters are different because... This affects the theme because...

- The <u>setting</u> is similar because... The setting is different because... This affects the theme because...

- The <u>characters' problems</u> are similar because... The characters' problems are different because... This affects the theme because... *Nobody understands me... I wish...*

- The <u>characters' relationships</u> are similar because...The characters' relationships are different because... This affects the theme because... *friends misunderstood rivals protective enemies*

Once students had finished meeting in their clubs, I introduced our Bend III anchor chart with today's teaching already added.

ANCHOR CHART

To Deepen Interpretation,
Readers Can . . .

- Compare and contrast the way a theme develops in two different texts.
- Study settings, characters, and key scenes to develop new, stronger thinking about themes in two texts.

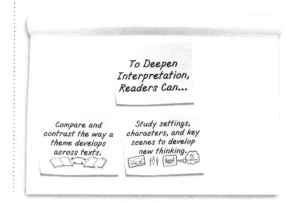

To Deepen Interpretation, Readers Can...

Compare and contrast the way a theme develops across texts.

Study settings, characters, and key scenes to develop new thinking.

SESSION 15 HOMEWORK

WRITING TO EXPLORE THE SIMILARITIES AND DIFFERENCES IN THEMES ACROSS TEXTS

Readers, tonight, continue the work you began in class today. Where do you see your chosen theme appearing in a second text? How is your chosen theme similar in your two texts? How is it different? Use the thought prompts you used in class today to help push your thinking. Write a bit about the similarities and differences you notice.

Prompts to Explore Similarities and Differences in Texts

In each text, you might consider:

- The characters are similar because . . . The characters are different because . . . This affects the theme because . . .
- The setting is similar because . . . The setting is different because . . . This affects the theme because . . .
- The characters' problems are similar because . . . The characters' problems are different because . . . This affects the theme because . . .
- The characters' relationships are similar because . . . The characters' relationships are different because . . . This affects the theme because . . .

Rethinking Themes to Allow
for More Complexity

ear Teachers,

In the previous session you invited your readers to read with the lens of universal themes, and to begin to compare how those themes play out in different stories. This is the heart of reading work that your kids will do in middle school, high school, college, and beyond! Today, you lead your children to be more specific in contrasting how a theme plays out in different stories—which ultimately sets kids up to learn important life lessons from books. For a child to learn from the characters in their books, to learn life lessons from Kek and others' stories, is a big deal.

In the previous session you gave your students somewhat of a free pass, letting it slide a bit if they were more excited about their first thinking than about revising their thinking. Today, though, you'll push your students to revise the wording of their theme statements to allow for more complexity.

Prior to this session, you will want to read aloud "Confession," "Running Away," "Bus," and "Treed," pages 201–12, from *Home of the Brave.*

MINILESSON

Your connection could simply point back to your observations from the previous day's class. You might let students know that you were reading over their shoulders as they wrote about the similarities and differences they noticed in the texts. You could compliment them on the analytical work they have taken on, even mentioning a couple of notable examples as evidence. Then let them know that this work feels so important that you think it's worth spending more time with it today. You might say, "Today I want to teach you that when readers see similarities between texts, thinking 'These texts seem to support the same theme!' they often look again, and may find the texts actually convey slightly different messages."

In your teaching, you could do a brief demonstration, continuing to compare *Home of the Brave* with *Fly Away Home.* You might say to your readers that as you've thought more about it, you've realized that although *Home of the Brave* and *Fly Away Home* both offer important messages about hope, it doesn't feel completely accurate to say that they say the same thing about hope. You might demonstrate how you go from a general unease ("The messages about hope that these two texts convey aren't exactly the same") to rereading, rethinking, and reaching for precision. You'll want to show yourself muddling along, demonstrating that new ideas don't just snap into place like magic.

In the end, you might mention that in *Fly Away Home*, while it's true that hope helps Andrew get through hard times, it's also true that hope doesn't actually change his situation. A theme for Andrew might be "Hope can change your attitude, but it won't necessarily change your situation." Then too, the ways in which Andrew actively tries to change his situation are just as potent as the moments where he simply hopes. Might this lead us to think, "Hope means little if you don't also work to change your situation!?"

For an active engagement, ask students to once again think between the theme of their club's book and of the short text they studied, this time reaching for more depth in what they notice. Similar to your demonstration, encourage them to reread and rethink their texts, and reach for more precision about themes, their similarities, and their differences. Point out that while they may arrive at more precise, nuanced ideas supported by the text, there is no one right or wrong answer in this kind of interpretation work.

Finally, in your link, make clear to your students that this is a process, not something that will happen right away. In fact, they will spend the next 10+ years of their academic lives working to master it! Invite them to spend their reading time today rereading texts or reading new short texts, reconsidering the themes and messages conveyed.

ANCHOR CHART

To Deepen Interpretation,
Readers Can . . .

- Compare and contrast the way a theme develops in two different texts.
- Study settings, characters, and key scenes to develop new, stronger thinking about themes in two texts.
- **Revise interpretations to make them more nuanced and precise.**

Revise interpretations to make them more nuanced & precise.

CONFERRING AND SMALL-GROUP WORK

Some students may need more support with thinking comparatively across texts. Direct prompts can be a way into this work. Some examples that you may try: "What does this book say about [friendship]?" "What *else* does it say about _____?" Another support for these students could be having them flag pages that connect to the topic, then do shared reading of those passages, stopping periodically to consider, "What is this scene saying about this theme?" Doing this across a couple of scenes can help students build the muscles to see patterns across parts of the text.

As an extension of this work, for students who are already thinking well across texts, you might decide to pull a group to create more nuanced, complex theme statements that incorporate both texts. This might involve teaching a more sophisticated sentence framework, such as: "Although it's true that _____, it's also true that _____." For example, a theme about hope that encompasses both class texts could be phrased this way: "Although it's true that hope can help people through hard times, it's also true that hope is not enough to solve real problems."

You might also teach students to sum up their thinking about a text using sentence frames that reflect a change in thought. For instance, the following sentence starters can help students lay out what is nuanced in the differences in a theme across two texts.

At first I thought _____, but then I realized _____.

Although it's true that _____, it's also true that _____.

Mid-Workshop Teaching

Perhaps during the mid-workshop, you'll want kids to think about their evidence supporting an interpretation. You could remind them that in fourth grade, they learned about the importance of revising interpretations based on their understanding of what constitutes an effective interpretation of a text. For example, one characteristic of an effective interpretation is that it pertains to the whole text. Often kids generate interpretations that relate to the ending of a text, but not to the entire text. If the story tells of two children fighting and in the end they make peace, some children are apt to say the story represents the idea that "it is important to make peace with each other." But such an interpretation ignores three quarters of that text. A better interpretation might be, "Although every day there are a million little things that can divide people up, it is best to find ways to make peace."

SHARE

Your share can echo the share from the preceding day, using the prompts below and giving students an opportunity to master using them. Give students time to prepare to share, and today ask a different reader to lay his or her ideas out for the group in some detail, talking in essays. This time, you might remind listeners of ways to grow ideas through talk, giving them thought prompts such as:

Prompts to Explore Similarities and Differences in Texts

<u>In each text, you might consider</u>:

- The characters are similar because . . . The characters are different because . . . This affects the theme because . . .
- The setting is similar because . . . The setting is different because . . . This affects the theme because . . .
- The characters' problems are similar because . . . The characters' problems are different because . . . This affects the theme because . . .
- The characters' relationships are similar because . . . The characters' relationships are different because . . . This affects the theme because . . .

Homework

For homework tonight, you will want your students to again be thinking across texts. You may want to ask children to continue reading what they read in class, but give them the option to find their own short texts or novel that they can lay alongside the other texts. They might even find a picture that somehow represents the theme you see forwarded in the texts.

Remind children to keep in mind that reading volume matters, and they will want to get a lot of reading done, especially on days when they spend more time talking or writing about texts in class. Point out that if a student hasn't already done so, that child and his or her club should be getting ready to start a new book club book, thinking about their theme across a second novel. Encourage kids to make sure their reading goals are ambitious each night and that they are getting lots and lots of reading done.

Yours,
Lucy and Ali

Prompts to Explore Similarities and Differences in Texts

Same ? ☑   Different ? ☑

- The <u>characters</u> are similar because... The characters are different because... This affects the theme because...
- The <u>setting</u> is similar because... The setting is different because... This affects the theme because...
- The <u>characters' problems</u> are similar because... The characters' problems are different because... This affects the theme because... Nobody understands me... I wish...
- The <u>characters' relationships</u> are similar because...The characters' relationships are different because... This affects the theme because... friends misunderstood rivals protective enemies

Session 17

Comparing Characters' Connections to a Theme

ONE REASON your students have been able to launch right into interpretation in this unit of study is that they've worked in character study and book club units before. So instead of leading into interpretation by developing ideas about characters, they jumped right into a study of theme. We see, however, that there is a richness in studying characters more deeply as the novels kids are reading become more complex, and the characters become more numerous and complicated. Today, therefore, you'll bring character and theme together, by teaching your readers to study how characters manifest a theme—and when they actually work against a theme.

When we talk about characters this way, it sounds as if they are real agents, rather than authors' creations. Kids often think this way as well, and it's part of the joy of reading, conceiving of characters as real entities. When you ask an eleven-year-old why Professor Snape is so malevolent in *Harry Potter*, he wants to talk about Snape's childhood and his suffering under Voldemort. The young reader doesn't want to bring J. K. Rowling into it. One of the arts of your teaching, therefore, is to make high-level literary analysis seem a natural and fascinating part of book club conversations. In this case, today, you'll let kids in on a secret—that while a lot of people talk about how certain characters represent or develop a theme, it's also true that some characters, often the more evil or flawed ones, actively represent an opposite theme! So where Harry illustrates that you can overcome a childhood of loneliness and suffering, Snape demonstrates that it's almost impossible not to be shaped by these conditions, despite his ultimate redemption. If you bring those perspectives together, a more nuanced theme emerges, that it's possible to rise above childhood conditions, but it's really hard not to be shaped to some extent by them, as evidenced by both Harry and Snape in different ways. That's the kind of path toward complexity you'll lead your readers toward today.

In this session, you'll ask students to compare how different characters, first in the same text, then across texts, relate to the theme they are studying. This analytic work of comparison is high-level cognitive thinking, and will compel conversations such as: "Who represents this theme the most clearly?" "Who is on the fence?" "Who seems against this

IN THIS SESSION, you'll teach students that one way readers think about a theme in more complex ways is to consider how different characters connect to and represent that theme, and also how some characters may work against a theme.

GETTING READY

✔ Before this session, read aloud "Ganwar," "Talk," and "Changes," pages 213–24, in *Home of the Brave*.

✔ Prepare chart titled with the theme, "Hope can help people survive hard times and go on," and a grid with three categories (characters closely connected to theme, somewhat connected, far away from theme). You may wish to provide students with blank charts and character names (cut up) to complete this chart (see Teaching and Active Engagement).

✔ Display and add to the Bend III anchor chart, "To Deepen Interpretation, Readers Can . . ." (see Link and Share). ✋

✔ Display chart titled "How to think about characters who seem to go against the main theme" (see Mid-Workshop Teaching). ✋

theme?" This also raises important questions about complex fiction, such as why an author includes characters who seem to go against the main idea of the novel (see Mid-Workshop Teaching).

This work connects to other kinds of perspective work, which you may get a chance to support during conferring and small-group work today. If you notice that students reading novels in the third person are having a hard time determining which characters' perspectives are clearer, this would be a good time to work on that. The connection to theme is just one way into the perspective work, and it may be necessary to teach other ways to consider perspective, such as thinking about how the author allows readers to listen in to some characters' inner thinking, but does not allow such access to other characters.

> *"There is a richness in studying characters more deeply as the novels kids are reading become more complex."*

In the share, students will have an opportunity to decide if their theme statement needs revising to become more nuanced, based on thinking through different characters' connections as well as the layering of additional texts. This work is strongly connected to the work of research-based argument, in which students also craft claims and ultimately revise them to be more precisely worded.

Comparing Characters' Connections to a Theme

CONNECTION

Set up a parallel, analytical, nonreading activity to let students try this skill in a more playful setting.

"Readers, last night, I was playing a game with friends called Apples-to-Apples. Some of you may know this game. We're going to play it now because it might help us with our thinking about themes.

I deliberately chose two examples that could be considered "entertaining" in different ways, to set up students to later see how characters may be connected to themes in different ways.

"In Apples-to-Apples, there are two kinds of cards—cards with a person, place, or event, and cards with an adjective, a descriptive word. The goal is to convince a judge that the card you pick best connects to the description. For example, when I was playing, the description we had to think about was 'entertaining/fun.' We had to argue that one of our cards was the most entertaining thing—more entertaining or fun than other people's cards. I drew the card 'pigs.' The other two cards were 'construction paper' and 'eggs.' I think I made a good argument about how pigs can be super entertaining. What do you think I said? Tell your partner." I let partners talk for a minute and watched as they playfully made oinking sounds and scrunched their noses up into snouts.

"Yes, I said some of that too! I said that pigs make funny noises, and that they can be great pets. I also said they make great movie animals! But then my friend made really good points about how construction paper, too, can be entertaining. What do you think my friend said?" I allowed kids to share ideas for a moment.

"In the end, which do you think better matches with the idea of something entertaining? Pigs or construction paper? Quickly tell your partner and say why."

A connection like this allows students to have some fun. Don't underestimate the power an interactive connection can have in getting students' minds running!

After a couple of minutes, I said, "I was thinking that we can do this same interesting thinking as a way to analyze how different characters connect to a theme we are studying."

❖ Name the teaching point.

"Today I want to teach you that one way readers think about a theme in more complex ways is to think how different characters connect to that theme. Readers think about which characters best represent a particular theme through their thoughts, actions, and dialogue, and which characters work against the theme."

TEACHING AND ACTIVE ENGAGEMENT

Channel students to figure out how different characters connect to a theme.

"Let's try this together using a theme we've been considering in both *Home of the Brave* and *Fly Away Home*." I uncovered the theme statement "Hope can help people survive hard times" at the top of a piece of chart paper.

"We're going to think about how different characters connect to this theme. We can ask, 'Which characters show this theme the most clearly, and how?' Let's consider the characters in *Home of the Brave*. We have Kek, of course, but also Ganwar, Dave, Kek's aunt, and Hannah. Quickly, let's sort these characters into three categories: which characters seem to strongly support this theme (meaning they show us or seem to believe that "hope can help people survive hard times"), which seem less strongly connected, and which seem like they wouldn't support our theme statement."

Under the theme, I revealed a list of the characters, followed by a chart with headings:

Hope can help people survive hard times and go on.

Kek

Dave

Ganwar

Kek's aunt

Hannah

Closely connected to the theme	Somewhat connected to the theme	Far away from or against the theme

"With your partner, sort the characters. Which ones seem closely connected to the idea that hope can help people survive? You might think about which character you can picture saying this and believing it. Recall what these characters have said, what they've done, what they've thought (if you know). Which characters, based on the same evidence, seem a little less sure about this—like they themselves can't decide if they believe it? And finally, which characters seem far away from this idea—even against it?"

This lesson is a guided practice lesson—the teaching and the active engagement will alternate as a way to engage the students during most of the lesson. Be on the lookout while listening in to students' partner talk for those who are having trouble articulating how characters connect to this theme. You will want to figure out if it is because they are not understanding it in this context, or if the work of connecting characters to theme is problematic in their own reading as well.

For some students who may have trouble visualizing how so many character names would go into different categories, you may decide to pass out a bag of cut-up character names and a blank chart as printed above. Coach them to treat this as a sort, physically putting the characters into the slots that best show their relationship to the theme. This is also something you could decide to do for all students, asking them to sit in clubs and handing out a sort for each club. Sometimes making the abstract more tactile can be incredibly supportive for learners.

Remind students to use evidence to support their ideas.

I listened in as students talked, moving from one partnership to another and giving lean prompts. I reminded the whole group, "Remember to always use evidence to support your ideas. Tell your partner what the character has said or done to show how they feel about hope."

Marcus said, "Well, Kek for sure is close. It's kind of his theme. And Dave sort of helps him get there, so I think Dave is close, too." Denise replied, "I agree those two are close, but Ganwar, we've already talked about how he's not the same as Kek with hope. He doesn't think it's worth hoping because you just get disappointed again. So I would put him far away."

Coach students to also think about minor characters and how they relate to the theme.

Since the students seemed ready to stop there, I coached them to continue thinking about the more minor characters. "What about Hannah and Kek's aunt? What have they have said or done that helps us understand how they feel about hope?"

Both students were quiet for a minute, thinking. "Well," said Marcus, "Hannah does eventually write to her mom, but only because Kek makes her. But it seems like there is part of her that wants to hope. So I'd put her in the middle. She wants to believe this but she can't yet."

I brought the group back together.

Complete the chart based on what you heard from students and discuss ideas that one can draw from the chart.

"Fifth-graders, I heard a lot of conversations about these characters and their connections to the theme we're talking about today. Based on several of your talks, here is what I heard."

I quickly filled in the chart:

Closely connected to the theme	Somewhat connected to the theme	Far away from or against the theme
Kek	Hannah	Ganwar
Dave	Kek's aunt	

"Now, these are not the only 'right' answers. Depending on where we are in the book, this could change! I know some were saying Kek's aunt seems *closely* connected to the theme, except that she is so worried about Ganwar and how he can't seem to find hope, but some might put her in the close column. Which partners thought she might be in the close column?" A few hands shot up.

As students tackle this challenging work, you want them to be aware that characters provide readers with a variety of connections to the themes of a text. Even a central theme, one that runs through most of the text, connects to different characters in different ways, in varying degrees. Often the main character is the one who learns the lesson of the theme (if it is a kind of lesson) by the end of the story. But other characters may conflict with this theme, or may offer examples of how this theme is not always true, or is only true in certain circumstances, or is hard to live by. These are different lenses you can offer students during the Minilesson and in your Conferring and Small-Group Work afterward.

It's important to remind students that when you prompt for guided practice in a lesson, you are not asking something with black-and-white answers. Otherwise, they will learn to wait until you come back and give "the answers" rather than engaging in the process.

I went on to discuss how this work lets us track different characters and how they help us to see the theme in different ways. I encouraged students to continue to track characters and how they relate to the theme as they read on. Readers could also think about characters from other texts, perhaps considering Andrew from *Fly Away Home*, asking if he's closer or farther away from this theme than Kek. Readers might conclude that he is younger, and his experiences are different, so those factors will affect how he feels about hope.

LINK

Channel students to plan their book club work to read and reread texts and use all they have learned about analyzing themes.

"As you continue to read on in your books, keep today's teaching in mind. We have many different ways that we have practiced thinking about themes, and now you know that you can think about the ways that different characters connect to a common theme."

I pointed to the anchor chart, with today's teaching point added in:

ANCHOR CHART

To Deepen Interpretation,
Readers Can . . .

- Compare and contrast the way a theme develops in two different texts.
- Study settings, characters, and key scenes to develop new, stronger thinking about themes in two texts.
- Revise interpretations to make them more nuanced and precise.
- **Compare how different characters connect to a common theme—in the same and in different texts.**

Compare how different characters connect to a common theme.

HOPE

In a recent talk at Teachers College, Grant Wiggins, coauthor of Understanding by Design, *reminded us that transfer is always the goal of teaching. It's what kids do when we're not there that shows if they have learned what we've been teaching. To work toward this, Wiggins insists that students get opportunities to use judgment every day. Giving choices about work time is one way to embed this opportunity into your workshop.*

"Talk in your club to plan the reading work each of you will do today. Of course you will read on, but perhaps you will also decide to reread parts of your book to think through your author's decisions. Or you may decide to read a new poem or story to see how a different author presents this theme. In your notebook, write down what you will read and what you plan to think about."

Theme and Perspective in Assessment-Based Teaching

TODAY, many book clubs will spend their time reading to think about the author's presentation of the theme in their books or short texts. Given that clubs are not meeting until the share at the end of class, you'll be able to meet with students in other configurations today, which is important because there are individuals and groups who need support that may not be in sync with the needs of club mates. Use what you just heard from students in the lesson, along with observations in their Post-its and reading notebooks, to determine who needs support in talking/thinking through their club's theme with supporting evidence from the text, and also who would benefit from extra teaching around the importance of perspective.

There may be individual students or small groups who you pull for more work on talking about theme—using lots of words to dig into the different angles of this universal idea, and pulling from multiple places in the text as support. Teach them to think about topics or issues that are hiding inside the bigger idea, as a way to have more ideas and more to say. For example, in the idea "Hope can help people survive hard times," we can think about "hope" and "hard times," and then think about which parts of the story go with these different topics. This might help to generate more evidence and some new ways to approach the theme.

(continues)

MID-WORKSHOP TEACHING   **Considering Characters Who Don't Support the Theme**

"Readers, I'd like to stop you for a moment. I've been wondering about characters like Ganwar since our lesson earlier and want to ask you about this. If Katherine Applegate wanted to get across the theme that 'Hope can help people survive hard times,' why put Ganwar in at all? Why include characters who don't connect to the theme or have very different perspectives on the theme? Wouldn't it be easier to just create characters who clearly show us the theme?

"There are a few different ways we might think about these characters. If you have characters like this in your books—characters who seem far away from or against the main theme or the theme the main character is closest to—think about *why*. Here are a few possibilities."

How to think about characters who seem to go against the main theme.

1. *This character is an example of how <u>not</u> to be. The author has included him/her to show readers a foolish or immoral way of being.*

2. *This character interacts with the main character mostly through conflict—and these conflicts help the main character figure out what he/she believes.*

3. *This character shows how complicated life really is. It may be necessary to revise thinking about the theme to include this character's point of view because the author takes this character very seriously.*

"So what do you think about Ganwar? Why did the author write him into this book in this way? Is it because of reason 1, 2, or 3? Talk to your partner and decide. It could be more than one of these reasons, so there is no one right answer." Students talked for a bit and I sent them back to consider the same in their own text sets.

Today, you may also want to teach students to think more critically about perspective, one of the most complex literary elements, and one that is highlighted in most systems of world-class standards. For more information on teaching into perspective and point of view, you might also look at the "Establishing Point of View" thread in the Narrative Reading Learning Progression as well as the "Analyzing Author's Craft" strand. This will help you see the trajectory students are expected to travel (for instance, understanding that by the fifth grade students needs to be able to not only identify the point of view but understand how it influences the telling of the story).

If possible, you could group students from different clubs who are reading books written from a similar perspective (the main character, for instance, or an unnamed narrator). Let them know you've gathered them so they can learn a new way to think about theme, and that they will now be ambassadors to their clubs, charged with the job of teaching their club members what they learned today. In some ways, this teaching will be similar to today's minilesson. Since the concepts are complex, this will give you and your students another try at this complex thinking.

Point out that even books with a third-person narrator have a main character, and in more complex books, maybe two or three main characters. You could say, "Right now, think about which character is the main character in your book. It shouldn't be hard to figure out!" The teaching point for this small group will be this: readers think about whose point of view is strongest in their book, and ask themselves how that is affecting how the theme comes through. Some ways that point of view might affect the theme are: (1) The main character's choices are the ones we understand the most. (2) The main character says things and thinks things that are close to our theme idea. (3) At the end of the story, the main character's final emotions and thoughts connect strongly to the theme. It also will be important to readers to understand that authors may not necessarily give them much access to another character's thinking, and to imagine how the story might be different if they had.

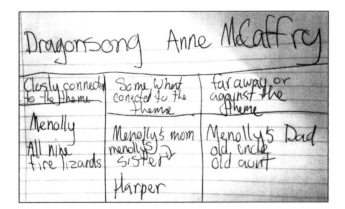
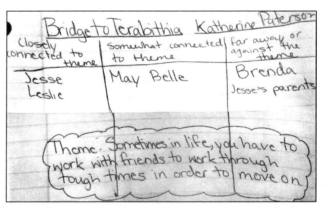

FIG. 17–1   Students think about which characters are and are not connected to one of their themes.

Revising Theme Statements to Incorporate More Characters' Perspectives

Call students to the meeting area and explain that readers often revise their theme statements to include the perspective of multiple characters.

"Readers, let's come back together for a share. Be sure to sit with your club." The students moved back to their meeting area spots, sitting in clusters.

"You've all done some more reading and thinking today, keeping on your theme glasses and thinking more about the theme you're studying. Earlier today, we talked about how different characters can connect to the theme in different ways—some characters may even seem to go against the theme. This can be fine—not everyone has to agree, and there are many themes in a book. But sometimes, it's helpful to ask: is there a way to revise the theme a little so that it includes more characters' points of view?

"Let's take our theme, for example: 'Hope can help people survive hard times.' How might I change this a little to include more of Ganwar's point of view? Earlier I heard Tyler say that Ganwar thinks that hope is silly, because you'll just get disappointed by it.

"Hmm. Is there a way to make it clear that hope doesn't mean everything will turn out just fine? Turn and talk with your clubs. Try out a few revisions to our theme and see what you can come up with."

I listened in as students tried to reconcile Ganwar's and Kek's perspectives on hope before calling them back together. "What I hear many of you discussing is the idea that hope can be a good thing (something that helps us get through hard times, something to hold onto), but that it doesn't fix things. Yoon and Dominic were talking with their club about how hope might stop you from moving on. Anna, Deena, and their group thought that hope can even trick you into thinking that something is true (like if Kek's mom ends up being dead).

"What if we tried this: 'Hope can help people survive hard times, even if it doesn't change how hard it feels to get through them.' Or, 'Hope can help people survive hard times, but it can also hold them back from moving on.' Do you hear how that adds in some of Ganwar's thinking and feeling?

"In your club, decide on a character who seems far away from your theme. How might you add in some of their thinking to make a new theme that is more complicated? When you decide on something, jot it at the top of a fresh sheet of paper in your reading notebook so that you have a new lens to read through. I'll come around and help you out with this new work."

After working with each club for a bit, I added a new bullet to our anchor chart:

ANCHOR CHART

To Deepen Interpretation,
Readers Can . . .

- Compare and contrast the way a theme develops in two different texts.
- Study settings, characters, and key scenes to develop new, stronger thinking about themes in two texts.
- Revise interpretations to make them more nuanced and precise.
- Compare how different characters connect to a common theme—in the same and in different texts.
- **Revise your theme statement to include all characters' perspectives.**

Revise your theme statement to include all perspectives.

REVISIT AND REVISE YOUR NEW THEMATIC STATEMENT

Readers, tonight for homework read on in your book to achieve your daily reading goal.

Then, turn back to the reading notebook page you created today. Look at your revised theme statement. Does it encompass that character's beliefs, ideas, and feelings? If not, try to rewrite it again.

Now test out your new, improved theme with a few other characters in your book. How do those characters relate to this revised theme? Does your theme statement incorporate those characters' perspectives? If not, try writing another theme statement that includes their perspectives. All of this work will make for great conversation with your club tomorrow!

Session 18

Studying the Choices an Author *Did Not* Make to Better Understand the Ones They *Did*

C HILDREN, like many of us, find themselves talking about books and movies as if they were real. "Jesse never should have left Leslie alone that day," we overheard one club saying during a conversation. "He basically lied to her about what he was doing, and that's why she died." The students were *really* mad at Jesse, because of his flaws. Yet it's Jesse's flaws that make him such an interesting character, and *Bridge to Terabithia* such an intriguing and illuminating story. One of your challenges, then, is to lead your students into richer discussions of authors' choices, while holding onto the utter magic of surrendering to storytelling. You'll know it's working when your kids have more to say, and are *more* excited about what they see in the stories they're reading.

It might be a good idea for you to ask yourself: why do this work, so that you sound convincing when you suggest it will be rewarding for kids? They will be asked to analyze authors' craft in middle and high school, and on exams. That's *not* a valid reason, though, to push them onto an analytical path. For us, the valid reason for teaching kids to consider authors' craft is that the kids you are teaching are not only readers, they are also writers. They too write narratives. They write fiction, personal narrative, and memoir. If you are in our units of study, they are writing narrative right now. Reminding them to remember to read with an eye toward writerly decisions will surely enrich their writing life, and it will give them another, particular, expert perspective as readers.

Just as your students do in writing workshop, authors consider every detail, character, setting description, and message. As readers, you will teach students that they can study the choices authors make. Why did the author choose this particular word or image? Structure? Point of view? Why does this object show up again and again? Studying these decisions can help readers strengthen their ideas about stories and develop new interpretations.

To launch this work, you will help students consider the choices an author did *not* make, to better understand the choices they *did make*. Take *Home of the Brave*, for example. It begins with Kek in a plane, gazing out the window, wondering what all of the white is (snow) and where all the world has gone. While students spent some time thinking

IN THIS SESSION, you'll teach students that readers think about the choices that authors make (and the ones they don't), as a way to come to new insights about texts.

GETTING READY

✔ Before today's session, read aloud "Herding," "Traffic Jam," pages 225–32, in *Home of the Brave*.

✔ Provide students with copies of "Snow," the opening scene of *Home of the Brave*, page 3, or be ready to display the text (see Teaching).

✔ Prepare to display and add to Bend III anchor chart, "To Deepen Interpretation, Readers Can . . ." (see Link).

✔ Prepare an enlarged copy of the "Determining Themes" strand of the Narrative Reading Learning Progression, Grades 4 to 6 (see Conferring and Small-Group Work).

✔ As students to bring their copies of the "Determining Themes" and "Analyzing Author's Craft" strands of the Narrative Reading Learning Progression to the meeting area (see Share).

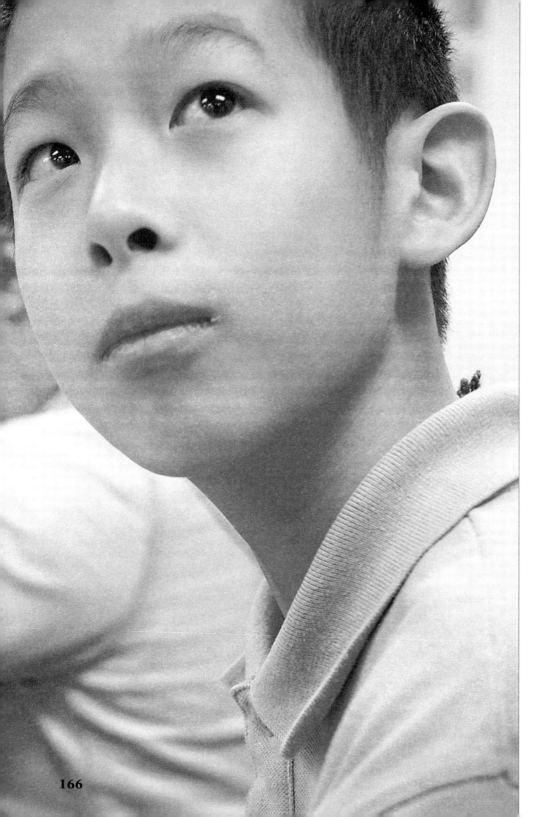

about this opening passage and its complexity, it is doubtful they stopped to ask why, exactly, Katherine Applegate chose to begin the book in this way. After all, the book could have taken place in Arizona, in a climate that is similar to the one Kek is familiar with. Then too, she could have begun with him exulting over this strange new thing called "snow," perhaps making snow angels or a snowman with Dave. Instead, he is in a strange "flying boat" that one assumes is an airplane, unable to see the world because of the swirling white snow.

"One of your challenges is to lead your students into richer discussions of authors' choices, while holding on to the utter magic of surrendering to storytelling."

By helping students to study the choices Applegate made for the opening of her book, as well as others, you will help them begin to understand that these choices have a significant influence on us as readers.

Studying the Choices an Author *Did Not* Make to Better Understand the Ones They *Did*

CONNECTION

Play a quick game of Twenty Questions with students.

"Have any of you played the game Twenty Questions? My family and I used to play this on long car rides to pass the time. Let's play a quick round. I'll choose the category—animals—and quickly think of an animal." I turned away, making a show of my thinking. "Okay, I've got one."

I looked out at the students. "Now, each of you has to guess the animal that I am thinking of. You can ask me questions to help you guess, but you only get twenty, and I have to be able to answer them with 'yes' or 'no,' so choose them carefully." Immediately hands went up, and I began calling on students.

"Does it live in the jungle?" asked Chris.

"It does!" I said, surprised that he had already asked such a great question.

Then Dominic asked if it was green, and I said "no." Next, to answer Erin's question, I told her she was right, the animal was furry. This went on for a bit of time and soon the students had deduced that the animal was a gorilla.

Explain that sometimes the best way to understand what something *is* is to understand what it is *not*.

"In the game we just played, you were able to figure out that I was thinking of (a gorilla) by narrowing your choices and figuring out what animals it could *not* be. Knowing what it wasn't or couldn't be helped you to think of what it *could be*. For instance, when Dominic asked if the animal was green, I bet he was thinking of some sort of reptile or bug. My answer 'no' sent him on a new line of thinking.

"Two days ago, you began thinking about theme across texts. Most of you realized that while authors might be writing about the same thing—loss, hope, belonging, change—they often do so in different ways. Today I want to teach you a new way to think about theme in your texts—by considering the choices an author makes. It's fascinating to think about things like why Kek is going to a snowy place and not a sunny one. Or, why the book is called *Home of the Brave*, and not *Kek Goes to America* or *Kek's Escape*.

Don't let this game take up too much time— even if you end up having to tell students the answer. Your primary goal is to show them that by considering what something is *not, we can deduce what* it is.

"As readers, it is important to remember that everything that is written in a story is there because the author wanted it to be. By thinking about the words an author chooses, the objects or symbols they describe, the characters they create, we can better understand what a text is trying to teach us.

"Sometimes, when you are getting started thinking about an author's purpose or intent, it can help to think about the choices an author might have made but didn't."

❖ **Name the teaching point.**

"Today I want to teach you that it can be helpful to think about the choices authors make (and the ones they don't), as a way to come to new insights as readers."

TEACHING

Model how you do this work in *Home of the Brave*, asking students to think along with you.

"Let's try this together by returning to the opening scene of *Home of the Brave*." I read the passage below.

> ***Snow***
>
> *When the flying boat*
>
> *returns to earth at last,*
>
> *I open my eyes*
>
> *and gaze out the round window.*
>
> *What is all the white? I whisper.*
>
> *Where is all the world?*

"Let's start by thinking about the title, 'Snow.' This chapter could have been called 'Kek Arrives' or 'Going to America.' But instead, the author decided to call it 'Snow.' Kek is staring out the window, looking at all the snow and wondering where the world has gone, so obviously it is an important part of his trip to America. The author could have made it a bright, sunny day. But no, it is cold and snowy."

I leaned closer to the children as if to impart a secret: "Do you see the way I keep imagining *alternatives*—what Katherine Applegate *could* have done? She could have created a different title. She could have had Kek arrive in America on a beautiful, sunny day . . ." I looked back at the poem, noticing that students were beginning to raise their hands and clamor for a chance to share their thinking.

"I wonder," I said, turning back to the text, "if the snow helps to create a mood—if it helps us to understand what Kek is feeling. He isn't feeling warm and sunny. He is confused, alone. Because of the snow he can't see anything and

Because you are asking students to think along with you, it will be helpful if you give them copies of this text or put it on an overhead projector. This will allow them to study the passage more closely than if you read it aloud.

In your modeling, be sure to continually return to the teaching of the day. Specifically, note what the author could have done before noticing what they did do.

wonders 'Where is all the world?' He's never seen snow before, which makes this whole ordeal even more confusing for him. Perhaps Katherine Applegate wants us to feel what Kek feels in this opening scene: cold, alone, and utterly confused."

Debrief.

"Do you see what I did there? By thinking about the alternatives, I came to some new thinking about why this part of the story is important—and why this actual language matters."

ACTIVE ENGAGEMENT

Ask students to revisit the beginning of their books, asking what an author could have done but chose not to.

"Will you turn to the beginning of your book club novel? Read the first lines with your club, the way I did with *Home of the Brave*. Your goal is to figure out *why* the author started the book the way he or she did. Try imagining other ways the story could have begun, other choices the author could have made, to understand the choice he or she *did* make. Ready?" The students nodded and I gestured for them to circle up in their clubs and begin reading.

By time I made it to their club, Caleb, Lily, Peter, and Denise had finished rereading the opening to *Shooting the Moon*—their first book club book—and were talking.

"I think it means that Jamie is really nervous and that she shows it by playing cards fast," said Peter.

I interjected, calling for the whole class's attention: "Readers, don't forget to try out today's strategy step-by-step. I promise it will pay off! You'll want to start by thinking of the different ways the author *could have* started the book. What are some possibilities?" I held up one finger and then a second. "Next, you'll want to ask, 'So why did he or she start it *this* way? The beginning the author chose might create a mood, reveal something about the characters, the setting, the plot, or more."

Lily began, looking back at the opening passage: "Well, in the first paragraph it says that Jamie and Private Hollister played thirty-seven games of gin rummy. She says she was 'fired up hotter than a volcano.' Instead, Frances O'Roark Dowell could have . . ." She paused and looked back at the text.

Caleb interjected. "She could have played very slow. Maybe if she was so upset about her brother going to war she could have been crying or something."

"Or she could have said that she didn't feel like playing," added Denise. "'Cause she was too sad. Like she was depressed."

"Yah," Lily began again. "So maybe this is how she shows that she is sad. She doesn't get the crying kind of sad. She gets like a volcano."

I could have asked students to try this strategy with another part of Home of the Brave. *But because I know that transference to independent reading, especially with a strategy like this, is the hardest part for most students, I decided to get them started thinking about their book club novels in the meeting area, with my help.*

If you find that students are off base when you listen in, don't be afraid to interject. If they don't practice the strategy you taught in this highly scaffolded experience, they will have a much harder time trying it on their own, back at their desks. Use this opportunity to give students in-the-moment feedback about the work they are doing well and the work they can be doing differently.

"Almost like she's angry," added Caleb. "Volcanoes are angry, you know?"

After a bit of talk, I called the students back together and shared out the work the *Shooting the Moon* club had done.

LINK

Recap the work students just did and send them off to consider today's strategy as they look between their two texts.

"I've added today's strategy to our chart." I revealed our Bend III anchor chart with today's teaching point included:

> **ANCHOR CHART**
>
> To Deepen Interpretation,
> Readers Can . . .
>
> - Compare and contrast the way a theme develops in two different texts.
> - Study settings, characters, and key scenes to develop new, stronger thinking about themes in two texts.
> - Revise interpretations to make them more nuanced and precise.
> - Compare how different characters connect to a common theme—in the same and in different texts.
> - Revise your theme statement to include all characters' perspectives.
> - **Consider the choices the author *could have made* to better understand the ones they *did* make.**

Consider the choices authors could have made and the ones they did make.

"There are many ways to make interpretations across texts, to study the ways that an author moves a theme forward. Today you practiced yet another. Whenever you are trying to understand a text more deeply, you can think about the choices an author has made. To do this, many of you will find it helpful to first think about the choices an author could have made (but didn't), and then think about why they chose something different instead. I hope this work will help you and your clubs to develop even deeper interpretations as you think across your text sets."

Supporting Students as They Balance Ambitious Reading Goals with Rich Interpretation

Continue to support volume.

Throughout this bend, you will want to anticipate predictable problems and plan to tackle them in conferences and small groups. As students embark on increasingly sophisticated work, one issue will be the balance between *reading time* and *thinking/writing/talk time*. You will want to give students ample time to do the required heady work, but you will also want to (and encourage students to) track reading volume. There are several ways you might do this. Your students will likely fall into two camps—those that spend a majority of their reading time analyzing, Post-it'ing, and writing about their reading, and those who breeze through their texts without stopping.

Support students whose volume is dropping.

You'll want to praise students who are stopping often to think and write about their reading. After all, they are tackling the work of the unit head-on and working to become more interpretive readers. That said, you'll want to raise a red flag if their writing about reading is getting in the way of their reading volume and help them to develop a plan for balancing the two.

"Many strong readers," you might begin, "find themselves in a position like yours. They are so thoughtful about their reading, so attentive, that they find they are stopping so often that they simply aren't reading enough each day." Ask students to look back at their logs to see if this is a problem (though because you have pulled them in a small group, you already know the answer will be "yes!"). "The key," you might continue, "is to make a plan that will allow you to continue to think and analyze deeply, and yet allow you to get lots of reading done each day."

It is often best to offer students some choice regarding their plan. One size does not fit all, and this is no different when it comes to one's reading life. Suggest that they try a couple of different systems and see what works best. For instance, they might use Post-its to quickly jot a word or two when they get to a part of a text where they want to stop and do some thinking. These Post-its can act as reminders for places worth revisiting. Then, for the last five to seven minutes of their daily reading time, they can return to these Post-its and decide on one or two to explore further. Alternately, students might allow themselves one or two breaks during their reading time, stopping at key parts as they come upon them and stopping to write long for just a couple of minutes. Then, back to reading. You might even encourage students to develop their own systems and be ready to share them with the group in a follow-up meeting. The key is to help children be aware of their volume and rally them to be partners in a solution that values both reading and writing about reading.

Support your speedy readers in pausing to think.

Other students, who we lovingly call "plot junkies," will be breezing through texts, reading for what happens next with little attention to detail. Helping these student to

(continues)

MID-WORKSHOP TEACHING **Studying Texts Side by Side**

"Readers, I've loved watching you work today. Your books are full of Post-its where you've noticed the choices authors made, and you developed theories about why they did that. Well done!

"Here's a quick tip. As you study the choices authors make, it can be helpful to put two parts of two texts side by side. For instance, if you are studying the beginning of text, you might put the lead of one story side by side with the lead of your second story (or poem or song) and study those next to each other. If you are studying a scene where a character's problem is revealed or where he or she has to make an important decision, see if there is a similar kind of place in your second text and put those side by side. By doing this, you can study the *different* choices that authors made in similar parts of a text."

stop and think can be a bit more challenging since it will require a bit of detective work on your part. Some students simply don't like to stop. "I just get so into my reading I don't want to stop," they might say. "I have a lot of ideas but I like to keep them in my head." Oftentimes these words come from some of your strongest readers. From conferences and discussions you know that it is not that they don't know what to write, it's simply that they don't want to. For these students, you might use some of the same tactics you tried above. You'll want to explain to them why writing about reading is important: namely, that it makes them stronger readers and allows you to have insight into their thought processes so you can teach them. Consider offering several systems for stopping and jotting, allowing them to choose what works best for them.

For other students, the problem will be more complex. Their resistance to writing about reading is less about the interruption, and instead, because they aren't sure what, exactly, is worth paying attention to in a text. You'll want to work with these students closely, studying what they do and don't understand about interpretation. Some students might need concrete strategies for finding places to stop and think, or ways to explore the deeper meaning in a text.

Studying a piece of the learning progression, like the one you see here, can help inform the next instructional steps for these readers. Given that this is the beginning of the year, it's unlikely that students are consistently and independently working at the end-of-fifth-grade level as described. This was introduced in Bend I, but it may be a good time to revisit it with certain groups.

Ask your small group members working on theme, comparing and contrasting, or analysis of author's craft to bring their copies of these learning progressions to the meeting area. "Readers, we've been working hard to think about all of the skills. And I admit that it's not the easiest work. I know we've looked at these progressions before, but I want to look carefully at them now, to be honest about where we think our work is and to set goals for making it even better."

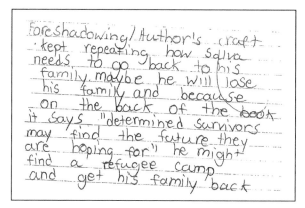

FIG. 18–1   One student mulls over an author's use of repetition.

think the theme of the story is to be different to make decisions on your own. Every author writes a book for a reason and thats why I think Jerry Spinelli wrote this book. Stargirl was different until Leo told her that no one liked her. She listened to him I think that she is just doing it to see how he reacts then out of the blue she going to go back to Stargirl and not be Susan. Jerry Spinelli is a good writer so he used good details to support the theme so that is why I think the theme is that it's okay to be different. Stargirl is a good person just no one will dare to be different. In the book I wish Hillari would see that Stargirl is a good person not only Hillari but everyone who is ignoring her. My prediction is that Stargirl will find her place in the school and everyone will appreciate her again like they did when she won the talent contest. I hope my perdiction is right because it is okay to be different.

FIG. 18–2   Pilar thinks about Jerry Spinelli's use of details in *Stargirl*.

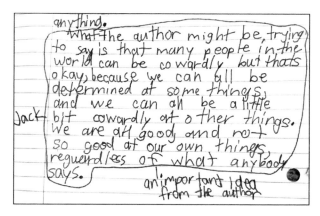

FIG. 18–3   Jack rereads his thinking, synthesizing it into a possible message the author is conveying.

Self-Assessing to Set New Goals

Explain to students that as their reading becomes more ambitious, it is important to keep their goals in mind and to self-assess their reading work.

"Readers, we have been focusing intently on raising the level of our interpretations. As part of this work, we have started to think about how themes apply *across* multiple texts and we have been studying author's craft. As we continue to do each of these things, it is important for us to know what, exactly, we are aiming to do and to ask, 'How am I approaching these goals? Can I get stronger?' In other words, we need to take stock."

Ask students to take out the "Inferring About Characters" and "Analyzing Author's Craft" strands of the Narrative Reading Learning Progression from Day 3 of the unit.

"A few of us were using these progressions to assess our work during a small group and we thought it would be helpful for everyone to have the same opportunity. Right now, will you spread your reading materials in front of you? Put out anything that will help you get a sense of what you've been doing well and what some next steps might be. You might gather some of your strongest Post-its, your most recent notebook entries, work you've created as a book club, anything. Then, we'll each take some time to really analyze the thinking and writing work we've been doing as readers, just the way we've done with the "Determining Themes" strand and on Day 3."

Coach students as they work, helping them to both assess and set goals. Voice over to the class as needed.

After working with Deena, I interrupted: "As always, you'll want to remember that if you *aren't* doing something, this can become a goal for you. If your method of goal-setting hasn't been working for you, try another. Deena decided that she didn't like having a list of goals in her notebook because she keeps forgetting to look at them. Instead, she has decided to draw big circles and stars around the goals she has right on the progression. She'll keep this in her folder where it will be easier for her to see each day. There are markers and colored pencils in the writing center if you'd like to do the same."

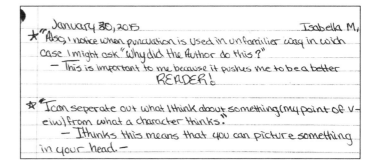

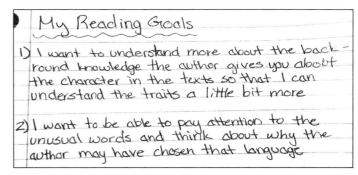

FIG. 18–4   Isabella and Alexi set goals for studying author's craft.

Later, I interrupted again. "D. J. noticed that he is doing *part* of what Level 5 readers do but not *all* of it. Many of you may notice the same thing about your own work. If this is the case, find a way to check off the description of the work you are already doing and circle or star or highlight the parts that you aren't."

Make sure that students understand that doing something *once* does not equate to mastery.

I pulled up next to Dominic and saw him looking back and forth between a Post-it he had written and the progression. "I think I have already done this," he said. "So I guess I can just check it off."

"You seem unsure, Dominic. Why do you think that is?" I asked.

"I'm not sure. I guess it's because I kind of did this," he pointed to the part of the fifth-grade progression about "details reflecting the whole." "But," he added, "I don't really know."

"Tell me if I'm wrong, but it seems to me that you might be a little hesitant because you have started to realize that details in a text can relate to the larger interpretation you have, but it isn't something you are doing all the time. Is that true? Are there other places where you have done this same work?"

Dominic shook his head. "No, this is it." He held up his Post-it.

"This is *so important*, Dominic, that I think we should share it with the whole class." I called for the class's attention. "Readers, Dominic realized something important that I want you to all be thinking about. He has this Post-it," and I held it up for the class, "where he is doing something from the fifth-grade progression. But here's the thing: this is the first time Dominic has ever done this and he's not sure that he should just check it off and say he's mastered it.

"Dominic is smart to think that way. It takes time and practice to become good at something. Just because Dominic did something well on this one Post-it doesn't mean he is an expert! So Dominic will mark this as something that is a goal so that he can continue to work on it, even though he already started doing it. Now you can do the same. If you've just done something once, or you don't feel like you are great at it yet, keep it as a goal. Remember, new learning takes lots of time and practice!"

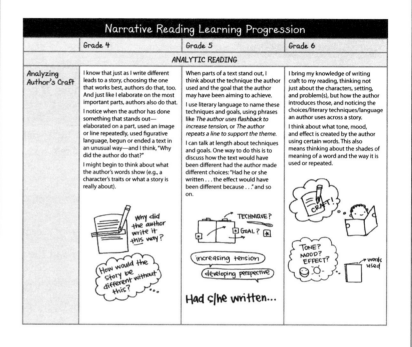

CONTINUE TO SELF-ASSESS YOUR READING

Readers, tonight you'll have a chance to continue assessing your own reading. Continue working with your club books, and spread out your reading materials, such as Post-its, recent notebook entries, and work created with your club.

Refer to the "Inferring About Characters" and "Analyzing Author's Craft" strands of the Narrative Reading Learning Progression that you pasted into your reading notebooks in class. As you reread the progressions, analyze the thinking and writing work you've been doing as a reader.

Delving Deeper into Literary Analysis

Reading as Writers

IN THIS SESSION, you'll teach students that one way readers analyze a literary text is to study the author's goals and how he or she achieves them in specific parts of the text.

GETTING READY

✔ Before today's session, read aloud "Cops," "Zoo," "Homecoming," pages 233–49, and "Reader's Guide," including "Background" and "Historical Context," pages 259–63 in *Home of the Brave*.

✔ Prior to class, you may want to make copies of goal-and-technique cards for students by copying and cutting the charts, "Narrative Writers Use Techniques Such As . . ." and "Narrative Writers Aim Toward Goals Such As . . ."

✔ Make sure students have their writing folders with their narrative drafts (see Connection).

✔ Prepare to read aloud an excerpt from *Home of the Brave*, "More Bad News," page 196 (see Active Engagement).

✔ Display "Writers Use Techniques Such As" and "Writers Aim Toward Goals Such As" on chart paper or on a document camera (see Teaching).

✔ Distribute goal-and-technique cards to students (see Active Engagement).

✔ Display and add a new point to Bend III anchor chart, "To Deepen Interpretation, Readers Can . . ." (see Link).

✔ Have ready to use in conference, box chart showing technique with three examples (see Conferring and Small-Group Work).

✔ Hand out index cards to students so they can make their own goal-and-technique cards (see Mid-Workshop Teaching).

✔ Prepare to display chart, "When Comparing Craft across Texts, Readers Might Say . . ." (see Share and Homework).

I MAGINE that you are looking at the famous painting of Mona Lisa. From the first glance, you would notice an overwhelming feeling of serenity. The demure smile and gently folded hands exude a feeling of peace. Upon closer inspection, you are likely to notice that the dark color scheme also contributes to the quiet mood. You might be thinking, "Da Vinci created a sense of calm in this particular piece through his use of composition and color." Art historians and critics layer this analysis. They add that his painting technique contributes to the sense of calm. He painted in extremely thin layers, making the brush strokes nearly invisible, thus removing the sense of movement or chaos. Da Vinci also used the fine shading technique of sfumato, which created soft transitions, avoiding the harsh edges of lines or borders. To truly interpret a work of art, one must consider the composition and the technique.

The truth is, though, that over the centuries since its creation, the ones who have most closely studied Da Vinci's work have been fellow artists. For a painter, the mysterious woman depicted in his masterpiece is a mentor text, and she's worthy of investigation at the level of brushstroke. Your students are also apprentices. They are apprentice writers, who have mentored themselves to writers, closely studying their techniques. Today, you bring together the work of your writers with the work they are doing as readers. Grant Wiggins, in "What Is Transfer?," reminds us that without explicit cuing systems, kids don't transfer skills from one part of the curriculum to another. So even though you've undoubtedly taught your kids to read like a writer in writing workshop, you'll find it illuminating to remind them to read like a writer in reading workshop!

It helps to hand over academic language to kids—often they can see something happening in the text, but they don't have the words to describe what they see. We've found it incredibly helpful to introduce visual checklists and cues to help kids develop literary language. There's a playfulness to this work that makes it challenging and fun in the best tradition of gaming. We've seen teachers play literary Bingo, and seen kids jumping out of their seats, claiming their author *does* use symbolism, in order to . . . Today you'll build on the previous session's work where you introduced the notion that readers can consider authors' choices and the alternatives. Today you'll suggest that there's a whole technical language for describing authors' techniques, and it's very cool to learn it.

"There's a playfulness to this work that makes it challenging and fun in the best tradition of gaming."

You will see that there are twelve goal-and-technique cards you will use with kids today. You might find yourself wanting to introduce and explain each one, but resist the urge. As children use the tools, and practice analyzing craft across texts, the work will get stronger and their access to language will deepen. If you are sure that kids don't understand some of the goals or techniques, leave them off the chart for now. But expect that kids *can* do this work, can figure it out, and shore up any misunderstandings as they arise!

Delving Deeper into Literary Analysis
Reading as Writers

CONNECTION

Liken the work that authors do to the work that students have done in writing workshop.

"In writing workshop, you have all been working hard to craft narratives that are meaningful. From the beginning of the unit you've asked yourself, 'What is my story really about?' and then wrote to highlight, or convey that meaning to your reader. I asked you all to bring your drafts with you today. Will you take a minute and look over your writing? Think for just a minute about what your story is really about and *how* you have been trying to convey that to your reader. You might take a quick peek at your narrative checklist to help guide you." I gave the students a minute to think and then said, "Right now turn and talk to your clubs. What is your story really about and *how* have you, or will you, make that clear to the reader?"

After students shared briefly, I gathered the class together. "I overheard many of you saying that you blended dialogue, description, and action. Others mentioned that you made the less important parts smaller, while stretching out the more meaningful parts of your story. A few of you even created symbols that stand for something that really matters in your story.

"Like you, the authors of the texts you have been reading think, 'What is this story really about and *how* can I show that to my reader?' They make decisions about what to include in their writing and *how* they can write their stories to make that meaning clear to the reader."

✤ **Name the teaching point.**

"Today I want to teach you that when you study a text, it can be illuminating to study the author's goals and the techniques he or she uses to achieve them. One way to do this is by focusing in on a part where the author seems to be trying to achieve something and asking how."

◆ COACHING

This assumes that you are using the Writing Units of Study. If you aren't, of course you will want to change this connection.

Instead you might choose to put up a picture of the Mona Lisa and ask students to interpret the work. They might do a quick turn-and-talk about what they notice about the painting. Likely they will notice the color and composition, so you could highlight the art techniques, showing them how you have to study the ways in which the artist creates as well as what they created.

If you have not taught Session 7 from Narrative Craft, *Grade 5 Unit 1 in the* Units of Study in Opinion, Information, and Narrative Writing, *your students might be unfamiliar with this work. We recommend teaching that lesson in writing before teaching students to use the cards in reading, if at all possible.*

TEACHING

Boost students' academic and literary vocabulary by introducing language to talk about techniques and goals.

"Readers, to study *how* an author writes, you need a literary vocabulary or language that you can use to talk about the techniques the author uses." I revealed the chart, "Narrative Writers Use Techniques Such As . . ." "These are a few techniques that authors use. Quickly, turn and talk to your club mates. Which of these are you familiar with? Are any new to you?" The students talked for a couple of minutes, and I listened to their conversations, ensuring that their understanding of each technique was clear.

You will want to create goal-and-technique cards for your students from the two charts below. These cards are not meant for teaching new concepts. That deserves a lesson unto itself. Instead, you'll want to hand out cards that are familiar to students—the techniques they have learned to use in writing workshop or to notice in reading workshop. Leave those that are unfamiliar off of the chart for now.

FIG. 19–1   "Narrative Writers Use Techniques Such As . . ." chart

FIG. 19–2   "Narrative Writers Aim Toward Goals Such As . . ." chart

I put up the "Writers Aim Toward Goals Such As . . ." chart for all to see. "Here's the thing: writers have goals. For instance, we realized that in the opening scene of *Home of the Brave*, Katherine Applegate was most likely trying to show us how scared and confused Kek was. Maybe she even wanted us to empathize with him—to understand and share his feelings."

"But to achieve this goal, she used certain writerly techniques." I pointed to the "Writers Use Techniques Such As . . ." chart. "For instance, we noticed that she described the setting—the swirling snow—to the reader," and I put my finger on "descriptive details." "Kek whispers, 'Where is all the world?'" and I point to the card for "dialogue." "She even uses revealing details—like having Kek keep his eyes shut until the airplane lands on the ground." I looked at the technique sheet, mulling over the other possibilities. "It says here that one technique a writer can use is a 'first-person narrator.' Katherine Applegate does that. She tells the story from Kek's point of view. And by doing that, I think that helps us empathize with him even more because we see the world the way he does."

Debrief.

"Do you see the way I did that? First I identified some of the goals Katherine Applegate seemed to be attempting to achieve. Then, I studied the poem for techniques she used to achieve those goals. To stir empathy in us as readers, Katherine Applegate uses several techniques as a writer."

ACTIVE ENGAGEMENT

Ask students to study another part of *Home of the Brave*, thinking about the goals and techniques the author has used.

I passed out copies of the goal-and-technique cards to students, each on a separate-color paper so as to more easily differentiate the two. "Let's go back to a more recent chapter in *Home of the Brave* and think about *how* Katherine Applegate wrote it and *why*." I read the following excerpt from the section "More Bad News." As I read, I looked at the blue sheet, the Goals sheet, and asked, "What goals might Katherine Applegate have as a writer here? What might she be trying to achieve?" I began to read.

> Listen buddy, Dave says,
> I'm afraid I've got some more news.
> I heard from Diane.
> They tracked down the people who made it
> to the two refugee camps we told you about.
>
> Something grabs my throat
> and tries to steal the air away.

You might choose to put these charts on chart paper or project them using a document camera, if you have the technology to do so. However you display them, you will likely find it helpful to put the two side by side so that students can look between them. Many teachers also find it helpful to put goals on one color of paper and techniques on another so students can differentiate easily between the two.

Because you are asking students to think along with you, it will be helpful if you give them copies of this text or put it on an overhead projector. Some teachers choose to cut the goal-and-technique cards into squares so that students can lay them on the carpet and place them beside the places where they see a goal or technique being used. If you do this, having them color-coded will be especially important so the two categories do not get mixed up!

None of them was your mom, Kek.

I look away.
Nearby a crow flaps his great, black wings
to chase away a sparrow.

"Hmm, . . . that crow with black wings is interesting. Flapping 'his great, black wings . . .'" I let the words sit in the air, hoping to plant a seed for some of my students.

Hannah pats my back.
There's still hope, though,
right? she asks.

I pointed to the goal cards and gestured for the students to do the same. "Let's start by thinking about Katherine Applegate's goals. What might she have been trying to achieve? Turn and talk in your clubs!"

"I think the bird is bad!" said Marcus excitedly. I channeled his thinking a bit by reminding him of the prompt. "I love that you started with the bird, Marcus, and I can see that Spencer has, too. But here's the hard part. Let's think about what Katherine Applegate might be trying to *achieve* by including the bird. Let's take a look at the goal cards and see if they give us any ideas. Is she providing context?" The boys shook their heads. "Introducing the characters?" They shook their heads "no" again, and I gestured for them to keep going. Spencer immediately drew his finger down to the "build a mood" box. "I think she's trying to build a mood. Spooky like on Halloween. That's why the bird has big, black wings." He made a large, flapping gesture with his arms.

"Marcus, what do you think about that? How would that connect with this scene?" I left the two of them to reread the scene and think about whether it makes sense that the author is trying to establish a scary mood.

Meanwhile, I moved over to Emma and listened in as she shared her thinking with her group. "The author's kind of building the mood but she's also kind of setting up the problem. Kek's mom might really be dead, but then Hannah asks if there is still hope and there is, I think. So it's like it makes the problem bad, but not as bad as if they were sure that Kek's mom died. It's more suspense."

Erin added on, "I also think that Katherine Applegate is trying to stir empathy," pointing to the corresponding box. She looked at me, "Can I say how?" I gave her a "one-second signal" and spoke to the class.

"Some of you are getting ready to talk about the *techniques* Katherine Applegate used to create empathy and mood and suspense. Go ahead and do that whenever you are ready!"

Just because this is the active engagement does not mean that you need to be completely hands off. In fact, a little gentle nudging can help students to do work in profoundly stronger ways than they would have alone. In this instance, while I don't expect all of my students to understand the meaning of the crow, I hope to give some of my stronger readers an opportunity to experience deeper, more symbolic thinking about this excerpt.

Erin continued, "I think that when Hannah rubs Kek's back it makes us feel bad for him because we know that he is sad." I whispered to Erin, encouraging her to use the technical vocabulary on the cards. "It's . . ." Erin searched the cards, "a 'revealing action'!" I gave her a thumbs up and moved on.

"Readers, let's all gather again." I shared out some of the students' thoughts to help those who had more trouble with the work.

LINK

Restate today's teaching point and add it to the anchor chart while reminding students of all they have learned.

"Studying *how* a writer writes is an important part of being a close, interpretive reader. Writers use techniques to highlight what really matters. To deepen our interpretations, we can study a section of text and think about the goals an author has and the techniques he or she uses to achieve them. I've added this strategy to our chart." I revealed our anchor chart with today's teaching point added.

ANCHOR CHART

To Deepen Interpretation,
Readers Can . . .

- Compare and contrast the way a theme develops in two different texts.
- Study settings, characters, and key scenes to develop new, stronger thinking about themes in two texts.
- Revise interpretations to make them more nuanced and precise.
- Compare how different characters connect to a common theme—in the same and in different texts.
- Revise your theme statement to include all characters' perspectives.
- Consider the choices the author <u>could have made</u> to better understand the ones they <u>did</u> make
- **Study an author's goals and techniques.**

Study an author's goals and techniques.

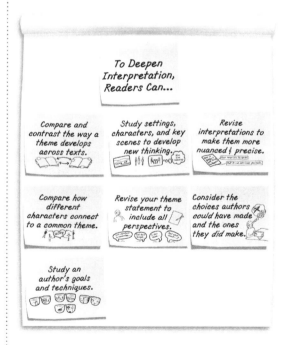

"Before you go off, take a minute to make a reading plan with your club. This might include rereading parts of your text or just forging ahead. As you read, remember that studying an author's craft is a powerful way to develop new ideas."

Digging Deeper
Attending to the Text and Looking for Patterns

AS STUDENTS TAKE OFF OUT OF THE GATE, they will be eager to use their new tools and newly acquired literary language. In some classes we've heard them whispering to each other even before their club talks, "I see metaphors," or "Look at the way that the author uses the first-person narrative." You want kids to feel this level of excitement, confident they can approach this rigorous work with independence and engagement.

In their excitement to use the new, sophisticated, academic lingo, you might find students calling out or jotting about just about every technique on the chart. It is true that authors use multiple techniques and have multiple goals when writing, so there will be much to see. But you will want to ensure that what the students are naming actually matches what the writer has done. So as you pull alongside students, when they name the author's techniques you might say, "Would you turn to the page where you saw that and read the lines aloud to me?" Or you might ask them to put their finger on the relevant section of text and say more about it.

As mentioned earlier, many students have enjoyed being able to manipulate their tools. So you could take the chart and then cut it up into small playing cards, color-coding to differentiate techniques and goals. This will help students to keep them straight as they physically lay the technique cards onto the text where they see it in action. This lets them attend to the text and not just call out the techniques.

If you find that the students are inaccurately matching techniques or goals to the work of the text, use this opportunity to teach into literary terms, techniques, or concepts. Name the techniques or goals being used, and then clarify the other term so students will understand the work going forward. If, for example, a student says the author is using flashbacks, when instead the author is using multiple plotlines you might say, "This is actually an example of multiple plotlines. There are several stories inside of the text and they will intersect at points. There is Jack's story, Sarah's story, Blake's story, and these stories are all happening at the same time. Flashbacks are when the author jumps back in time to explain what happened in the past." It may be helpful to have a read-aloud text at your fingertips so that you could show a quick example of the term that the student was using but confusing. If it is a longer text, try putting Post-its on the pages where you see techniques in action so you can flip quickly to that point. If all else fails, do a little storytelling of your own, embedding a flashback in the midst of the story.

Perhaps many students excel at identifying the techniques, but are forgetting to correlate them to goals. For these students, a sentence frame is often helpful. You might

(continues)

MID-WORKSHOP TEACHING
Adding New Techniques and Goals to Our Sheets

"Readers, Yoon just shared some work that could be helpful for all of you. As Yoon was studying her short story, 'A Pet,' she realized that Cynthia Rylant includes things like dialogue and internal thinking, revealing actions and descriptive details. But one of the most powerful things that Yoon found Cynthia Rylant doing was using strong words! Guess what, that isn't a card! So Yoon took an index card and made her own technique card—with 'Word Choice' on the top and a little picture of words. Will each of you now see if the author you are studying uses word choice as a writing technique?"

Within moments, most of the class had their hands raised and were shaking their heads affirmatively that Yoon had uncovered a new technique. I said, "When you become the kind of close reader that studies an author's craft, you are apt to notice lots and lots of little things—even more than the twelve items on this sheet I gave you. If you find yourself in a position like Yoon, make a new card to add to your collection. Be sure to tell me, too, so that I can share your discovery with the rest of the class."

set them up to say, "I notice the author used ____________ to ____________." Or, "The author's goal was ____________ and he or she did this by ____________." Or you might find yourself doing some lean prompting, simply coaching them to find a technique and then identify goals and saying, "That's the technique. Find the goal!"

For those students who are ready for a nudge, you might remind them that this work does not follow a clean, direct, one-to-one correlation. That is, the author might in one section of texts use several techniques to forward the goal. Or, vice versa, there might be one technique that achieves several goals. Push them to explore all the options by saying, "Authors often use many techniques in one spot. Can you find another? How does that support the goal?"

Writers often use techniques over and over again. Another way to push students, or clubs, is to have them track the techniques that an author uses across a text. You might say, "Writers generally use techniques repeatedly throughout a text. Sometimes they do this to highlight one particular goal—or one technique helps them achieve several goals. As you read the text, look for a pattern, noticing when a technique is used more than once and then stopping to consider if it supports the initial goal or another." To track this work, kids might put Post-its on the pages where they see the author use the technique, or start charts in their notebooks, noting the technique and charting different examples they find across the text.

Technique	Example 1	Example 2	Example 3

After following the technique through the text, the students might look over the chart and then write long about the pattern that has emerged. You might share a few sentence starters like, "I notice the author ________ when ___________," or, "One technique that kept repeating is ________. In each instance the author did this because ________," or, "One technique that kept repeating is ________. In one instance the author used it to ________. In another the author used it to ___________."

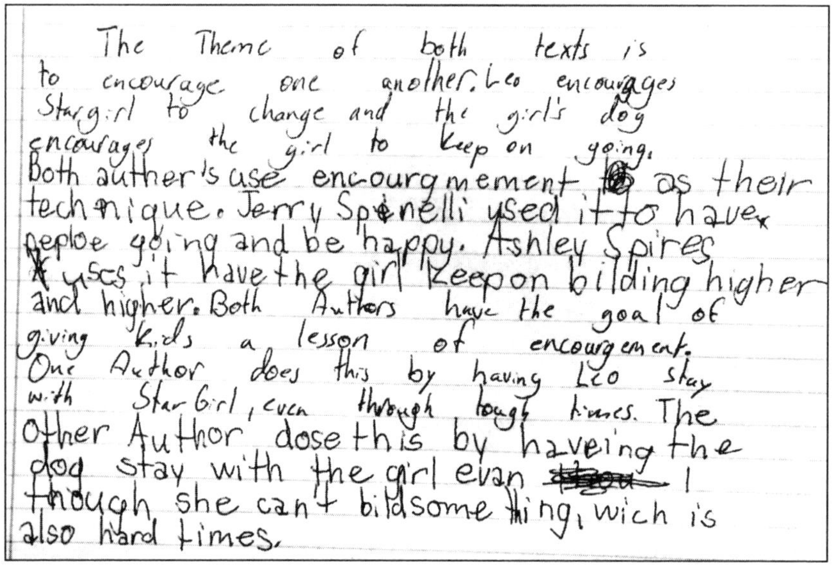
The Theme of both texts is to encourage one another. Leo encourages Stargirl to change and the girl's dog encourages the girl to keep on going. Both auther's use encourgmement as their technique. Jerry Spinelli used it to have peploe going and be happy. Ashley Spires uses it have the girl keep on bilding higher and higher. Both Authors have the goal of giving kids a lesson of encourgement. One Author does this by having Leo stay with Star Girl, even through tough times. The other Author dose this by haveing the dog stay with the girl evan though she can't bild some thing, wich is also hard times.

FIG. 19–3 Alexi works to identify techniques and goals across *Stargirl* and her short text.

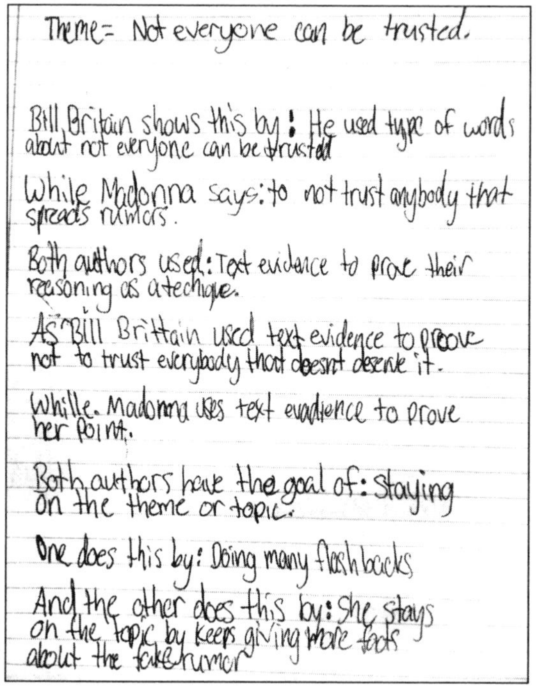
Theme= Not everyone can be trusted.

Bill Britain shows this by: He used type of words about not everyone can be trusted

While Madonna says: to not trust anybody that spreads rumors.

Both authors used: Text evidence to prove their reasoning as a techique.

As Bill Brittain used text evidence to proove not to trust everybody that doesn't deserve it.

While. Madonna uses text evadence to prove her point.

Both authors have the goal of: Staying on the theme or topic.

One does this by: Doing many flashbacks

And the other does this by: She stays on the topic by keeps giving more facts about the fake rumor

FIG. 19–4 A student studies goals and techniques across his two texts.

Comparing and Contrasting Authors' Craft

Guide students to look across their texts to compare *how* authors wrote them.

"Readers, in just a few moments, your clubs will meet and talk about your texts. Often clubs can lift their level of conversation by looking across the texts in their set and comparing *how* the authors wrote their texts. You know they forward similar themes. Now you might look for similarities and differences in style—you might examine their techniques and think about why each author chose the ones they did.

"This is hard work, so I have some sentence starters that might help you." I revealed the chart.

> ### When Comparing Craft across Texts, Readers Might Say . . .
> - The theme of both texts is _____. _____ (author A) shows this by _____ while _____ (author B) uses _____.
> - Both authors use _____ as a technique. _____ (author A) uses it to _____ while _____ (author B) uses it to _____.
> - Both authors have the goal of _____. One does this by _____. The other does this by _____.

"As you talk, remember that the best book talks are rooted in specifics. So, whether you talk about *what* the authors have written or *how* the authors write their texts, you'll want to back it up with examples. Open your books, point to the page, reread parts. Really get in there! Let's go off to our book clubs and give this a try now!"

WRITE TO COMPARE AND CONTRAST *HOW* EACH AUTHOR WROTE TEXTS

Readers, tonight think about your club's conversation today. Then write an entry comparing and contrasting *how* each author wrote his or her texts. Be sure to explain how those techniques helped them to forward the theme and other goals.

Use the prompts from today's share to help you.

When Comparing Craft across Texts, Readers Might Say . . .

- The theme of both texts is _____. _____ (author A) shows this by _____ while _____ (author B) uses _____.
- Both authors use _____ as a technique. _____ (author A) uses it to _____ while _____ (author B) uses it to _____.
- Both authors have the goal of _____. One does this by _____. The other does this by _____.

Celebrating with a Literary Salon

ear Teachers,

Today, you will celebrate the end of the unit with a mix-and-mingle of sorts. You will give students the opportunity to participate in a literary salon where they can give mini-book talks and show off their literary thinking.

Today's session will not follow the traditional minilesson model, so feel free to play with it and have fun. Use this letter to help develop your own minilesson. Your main goal is to help students feel a sense of achievement for all they have accomplished and to leave them with the sense that they can (and do!) have a lot to say about literature.

MINILESSON

You may want to begin your minilesson with an experience that helps children see how thinking thematically opens up a whole new world of connections—and that those connections are fun to talk about.

For the connection, you might begin by saying, "Last night, I was rummaging through some papers and came upon this poem by Langston Hughes. I thought it was amazing and wanted to share it with you today."

Dreams

by Langston Hughes

Hold fast to dreams
For if dreams die
Life is a broken-winged bird
That cannot fly.

Hold fast to dreams
For when dreams go
Life is a barren field
Frozen with snow.

Consider reading the poem to students and asking them to think about any connection they see between "Dreams," *Fly Away Home*, and *Home of the Brave*. In our experience, students immediately see a connection between the bird in *Fly Away Home* and the bird in this poem. You'll want to give students some time to talk in their clubs and then as a class to explore the symbol of the bird. "What does a 'broken-winged bird' stand for?" you might ask. If students are able, you might also explore the image of snow and its connection to a life without dreams. You might ask questions, such as, "How does Langston Hughes's description of snow connect to Kek's experience with snow? Is it similar? Different?"

Then you'll want to invite students to participate in today's events. "Today, I want to invite you to participate in a literary salon as a fun way to show off your new, sophisticated thoughts about literature."

In the teaching portion of your minilesson, explain to students that just as you were anxious to share this poem with them, readers often feel compelled to share passages, thoughts, ideas, and more with fellow readers. Perhaps you could say, "Readers talk about books all the time. They love to talk about literary craft, technique, and style in book reviews and blogs. People write about books in newspapers like *The New York Times* and magazines like *The New Yorker*, and on websites like Amazon.com and Goodreads. I exchange book lists with my grandma and then we discuss the books when I go to visit her. Readers love discussing books with each other almost anywhere, anytime. One of the most famous ways to discuss literature is in a literary salon. This is a kind of party where writers and intellectuals discuss books and other literary topics."

Then you might share with students that literary salons began back in the seventeenth century and still happen today. Tell students that salons are often made up of a group of authors that get together to talk about the ideas and craft moves in their books. "Today," you might say, "I thought it'd be fun to celebrate the end of our unit by taking part in our own literary salons."

To get the salon started, you may want to break up each book club and create new groups, with six or seven students in each. And of course, to add to the sense of celebration, we recommend bringing some apple cider or hot chocolate for students to sip on as they chat!

CONFERRING AND SMALL-GROUP WORK

The amount of support and structure you give students will depend on their needs, and what you are comfortable with. You might ask children to pretend they are the author of one of the books they read recently, or of a favorite book, and mingle with the author friends in their literary salon to talk about the amazing ideas in their books. For students in need of a bit more support, you might give them a few ideas for topics worth discussing. "When giving a mini-book talk," you might explain, "it often pays to talk about what you (what the author of your book, really!) tried to accomplish in terms of character, plot, or theme. Giving specific examples from your book is always helpful, as is discussing the techniques you used to achieve your goals." Consider having students carry their narrative goal-and-technique cards around with them, to guide their conversations as they chat.

SHARE

While the literary salon helps students become more adept at talking about books, your primary goal is to have some fun and celebrate the hard work they put into this unit. You might end the celebration with each book club making its way back together to reflect on their own work. Perhaps each member of the club decides on a compliment for another member. Alternately, one or several members could construct a small apple-cider toast to end their work together.

Regardless, you'll want to congratulate each of them on the collaboration and dedicated work that went into their clubs and into their rich, interpretive work.

Yours,
Lucy and Ali